RISKING THE CHURCH

Risking The Church

THE CHALLENGES OF CATHOLIC FAITH

RICHARD LENNAN

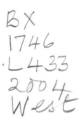

BX
1746
·L433
2004
West

OXFORD
UNIVERSITY PRESS

OXFORD

UNIVERSITY PRESS

Great Clarendon Street, Oxford OX2 6DP

Oxford University Press is a department of the University of Oxford.
It furthers the University's objective of excellence in research, scholarship,
and education by publishing worldwide in

Oxford New York

Auckland Bangkok Buenos Aires Cape Town Chennai
Dar es Salaam Delhi Hong Kong Istanbul Karachi Kolkata
Kuala Lumpur Madrid Melbourne Mexico City Mumbai Nairobi
São Paulo Shanghai Taipei Tokyo Toronto

Oxford is a registered trade mark of Oxford University Press
in the UK and in certain other countries

Published in the United States
by Oxford University Press Inc., New York

© Richard Lennan 2004

The moral rights of the author have been asserted
Database right Oxford University Press (maker)

First published 2004

All rights reserved. No part of this publication may be reproduced,
stored in a retrieval system, or transmitted, in any form or by any means,
without the prior permission in writing of Oxford University Press,
or as expressly permitted by law, or under terms agreed with the appropriate
reprographics rights organization. Enquiries concerning reproduction
outside the scope of the above should be sent to the Rights Department,
Oxford University Press, at the address above

You must not circulate this book in any other binding or cover
and you must impose this same condition on any acquirer

British Library Cataloguing in Publication Data
Data available

Library of Congress Cataloging in Publication Data
Data available

ISBN 0–19–927146–1

1 3 5 7 9 10 8 6 4 2

Typeset by Kolam Information Services Pvt. Ltd, Pondicherry, India
Printed in Great Britain on acid-free paper by
Biddles Ltd., King's Lynn, Norfolk

In Memory of

EDWARD YARNOLD (1926–2002)

who welcomed, encouraged, and counselled
caution in the use of adjectives

CONTENTS

Love is hard to believe, ask any lover. Life is hard to believe, ask any scientist. God is hard to believe, ask any believer. What is your problem with hard to believe?

Yann Martel, *Life of Pi*

Introduction

The appeal of the church is puzzling. Indeed, were the existence of the church to depend on the outcome of a cost–benefit analysis, it is unlikely that there would be a church. After all, are not the disincentives obvious? What about the focus on Jesus Christ, which gives the church an aura of sectarianism in an age suspicious of divisive religion? What about the doctrines, which appear to be narrow and arbitrary, even incomprehensible? What about the structures, which seem remote from the priorities of the Gospel, disconnected from the members of the church, and beyond the possibility of reform? Those factors, to say nothing of historical or present-day scandals involving various aspects of the church, underscore the fact that ecclesial faith will always be a challenge; indeed, a risk.

Nonetheless, the Roman Catholic tradition stresses that Christian faith is not simply faith lived *within* the church; it includes faith *in* the church as a component of God's self-revelation. As if it were not sufficiently challenging that Christian faith is inseparable from the notion of Jesus Christ as fully human and fully divine, the emphasis on the church can make that faith seem doubly burdensome. Worse still, the ecclesial dimension of Christian faith is not even conditional on the church being attractive or being a body that never impinges on individual freedom. All the more remarkable, therefore, that people commit themselves to such a faith even though the imperfections of the church, present not simply past, are no secret.

While the source of the church's appeal might be its claims to offer hope that embraces the present and the future, the value of such claims are far from obvious. After all, what does 'salvation' mean? Even a satisfactory answer to that question cannot disguise the fact that the connection between the church and salvation comes with encumbrances: 'membership in the ecclesial community saves people only of it is shouldered as a new and more profound responsibility.'[1] There is, then, much about the linkage between Christian faith and the church that demands explanation: Is there any foundation for the claim that the church is an irreducible element of faith in the God of Jesus Christ? Does faith *in* the church mean anything more than submission to the authorities of the church? How could faith in an imperfect church, a church unable even to ensure the safety and well-being of those in its care, be anything other than an irrational, perhaps even self-destructive, act? If the church is always less than perfect, is it futile to desire reform in the church?

In order to address such questions, as well as many others that orbit around 'the church', it will be necessary to explore the meaning of 'faith'. Since faith, in any form, involves self-surrender, an element of risk will always be part of it, since 'risk' implies what is beyond our control, implies the need for choices whose outcomes we cannot determine. While risks are usually daunting, the willingness to accept them, to embrace the self-surrender expressive of faith, is less likely to be the product of blind courage or foolhardiness than the recognition that the surrender of faith can be the means to human well-being. Although highlighting the connection between faith and well-being does not necessarily blunt the radical edge of faith, it at least suggests that faith need not involve either irrationality or disregard for human welfare, our own or that of others.

The connection between faith, human flourishing, and the church is at the heart of this book, since its primary interest lays in what might draw people to embrace the risk that is inseparable from being part of the church.

If membership of the church expresses something other than psychological dysfunction on a grand scale—an explanation that not everyone would necessarily discount—there must be something about the church that draws people to it. That 'something' must be substantial enough to triumph over the

---

[1] Juan Luis Segundo, *The Community Called Church*, tr. J. Drury (Maryknoll, NY: Orbis, 1973), 82–3. The responsibility to which Segundo refers is that of authentic discipleship, which manifests the church as 'an undreamed of possibility for love', a concept that is the focus of Chapter 1 of this book.

challenges, even disincentives, of any involvement with the church. That 'something' must also be compelling, since apparently clear-eyed people continue to risk involvement with the church, the revelations of its failings notwithstanding; indeed, notions such as 'gift', 'joy', and 'love' are by no means alien to the vocabulary that members employ in their discussion of the church. Nor are such sentiments simply the manifestation of naïve idealism or what results after ecclesial faith has leeched the critical faculties from believers. In fact, paradoxically perhaps, it seems even to be the case, in the present no less than the past, that the most powerful critiques of the church's priorities and practices not only spring from within the church, but also claim to be an expression of love for the church.[2]

Since 'the church' is a complex reality, one with a plethora of manifestations, it is important to specify immediately that this book will focus on the Roman Catholic church. Even more particularly, the 'world' from which this book emerges, and which it seeks to address, is that of the Roman Catholic church in contemporary Western culture. There are, of course, numerous differences in history and outlook between the Roman Catholic church in, for example, various parts of Europe when compared to North America or Australia, but it is also true that Catholics in all of those nations have sufficient commonalities, and challenges, to justify regarding them as an identifiable cross-section of the church.

The book's focus, however, does not imply a lack of commitment to the unity of the Christian church, a disregard for the Catholic story in other parts of the world, or a denial of the interconnection of the whole human experience. Indeed, those factors will all influence various discussions in the book. On the other hand, the positive implication of the book's concern with the life of the Roman Catholic church in particular areas is that it respects the fact that 'the church' is other than an abstraction:

---

[2] For an example of a contemporary critique of the church that is both incisive and committed to the value of the church, see Heinrich Fries, *Suffering from the Church: Renewal or Restoration?*, tr. A. A. Swidler and L. Swidler (Collegeville, Minn.: Liturgical Press, 1995).

If we believe that we can honor and know the church apart from or beyond the particularity of the church's humanity in historical and social contexts, then we are utterly mistaken. To attempt to construct a theology of 'The Church' that is not fundamentally informed by (and shaped by) churches in particularity is to construct a Platonic fiction.[3]

Implicit in that principle, and also in the notion of membership of the church as a risk, is the conviction that the church is inseparable from normal human dynamics. A central feature of those dynamics is the fact that human existence is historical and social. Members of the church, therefore, do not live in a vacuum, but are always subject to the impact of history and the influence of the wider world. Consequently, it is vital that a historical consciousness inform our understanding of the church.

In fact, it would be meaningless to speak of 'risk' in the context of a church that was timeless, a church that transcended history and culture. Nothing could affect such a church, either to damage it or to improve it. Since there could be no unknown factors about such a church, people who committed themselves to it could be certain that no surprises or challenges would ever confront them. Such a commitment, however, like such a church, would be pointless, as it would bear no relationship to the reality of human existence. On the other hand, a church that has a history, a church that cannot inoculate itself again the vicissitudes of human actions and culture, will be less predictable. As a result, involvement with such a church is unlikely to be risk-free.

In order to honour the fact that membership of the church is inseparable from living at a particular time and place, the first task for this book is to detail the shape of the church's present. Since the church's present is itself the product of a past, it is also important to explore the history of the present. Accordingly, Chapter 1 will seek to identify not only the shape of contemporary Catholic life, especially in Western societies, but also how it came to have that shape.

---

[3] Michael Jinkins, *The Church Faces Death: Ecclesiology in a Post-Modern Context* (New York: Oxford University Press, 1999), 100–1.

What will emerge from Chapter 1 is a church that itself appears to be at risk. It might seem, then, that the greatest element of risk about membership of the Catholic church today is that it involves associating oneself not only with a group that looks to be both disunited and powerless to affect its situation, but also with an institution whose flaws and limitations would be difficult to disguise. The present state of the church, therefore, might lead an observer to conclude that being part of the church is a risk primarily because the church's social structure is less than appealing.

That conclusion, however, would mask other, even more significant, aspects of 'risk' associated with the church: those inseparable from the implications of faith in the God of Jesus Christ, from a communal life in the Holy Spirit, and from the challenge to live in the world as a disciple of Jesus Christ. These are the elements of risk that Chapters 2 and 3 will highlight.

Since the challenges of Christian faith and discipleship are so comprehensive, it might seem that issues that concern the church as a structured community, one with traditions, doctrines, and various institutional elements, ought never to be more than incidental matters, which believers could generally pass over in order to concentrate on more fundamental issues. Such a conclusion, however, fails to take into account that, as a consequence of both our social and historical existence, even the word 'God', to say nothing of understanding the implications of faith in Jesus Christ, is something that we receive from others. Christian faith, then, depends on what comes from the past and, therefore, on mechanisms for preserving, explaining, and passing on that inheritance; hence the role of doctrines and structures.

Indeed, Christian faith declares that such mechanisms are not merely necessary as aspects of the way that human beings organize their common life, but that they can be vehicles for the Holy Spirit. Chapter 4, then, will explore the connection between the Spirit and the role that 'tradition' and structures play in the life of the church. The goal here will be to show that the structured reality of the church, as complex and frustrating as it can be, is inseparable from a fully human response to the God of Jesus Christ.

What I will attempt to develop in this book is an approach to the church that respects not only what we know of the dynamics of human existence, but also what we understand of the dynamics at work in the relationship between God and humanity. That approach will not produce a church that we can accept without risk. It might, however, depict a church that can invite us to embrace such a risk. One measure of the authenticity of such a church would be that those who form it would be unafraid of the questions and challenges that the wider culture presents to the church. Under that caption, however, the situation of today's Catholic church looks particularly parlous.

Indeed, it might seem to many within the Catholic church, no less than those outside of it, that not only are the prospects of the church bleak, largely as a result of the circumstances that Chapter 1 will describe, but also that the church at large has few ideas on how it might address the gap between contemporary culture and itself. So often do its contemporary critics herald the demise of the church that any theology of the church that fails to address this issue would appear naïve and unrealistic; such a failure would reinforce the perception that the church and the contemporary world travel in unrelated orbits.

In order to illustrate that membership of the church ought not to be a folly or an excuse to opt out of the demands of contemporary society, Chapter 5 will focus on the questions and challenges that contemporary culture addresses to the church. It will explore also whether there are resources in the community of faith to respond to them. In so doing, the chapter will seek also to specify the present-day implications of authentic ecclesial faith.

In the light of all of the above, Chapter 6 will explore how the church might present itself to the world in ways that are faithful to its tradition while also being sensitive to the concerns of contemporary society. Inevitably, that presentation will include proposals for change in the church.

As we shall see, 'change' is always a vexed issue in the church, the more so as it can suggest that people of the past were either less intelligent or faithful than ourselves. Less polemically, however, proposals for change can reflect the recognition that aspects of what we have received from the past might speak more of a former moment in history and culture than of God's life-giving presence in the contemporary context.

While the church could not exist without what it has received from the past, we need also to respect the present, in which the primary influences are circumstances, knowledge, and attitudes that are different from those that prevailed in the past.

We could debate, of course, whether 'different' suggests 'better' or 'worse'. Such a debate, however, would not alter the fact that those who live in the present have no option but to respond to the present. As a result, it would be inaccurate to characterize an intransigent resistance to the present as noble opposition to circumstances more vulgar than those of an allegedly glorious past. In fact, such resistance might be tantamount to setting our face against the possibility of an encounter with God in the present. On the other hand, a response to the present does not require the abandonment of our patrimony. Nonetheless, we can do justice to the present only when we accept that it is impossible to repeat the past.

A Gatsby-like fixation on repeating the past not only denies that anything in the past might have been less than perfect, it also denies goodness to the present. In addition, it implies that there is little hope for the future, which will grow out of the present. Thus, the willingness both to accept that the future of the church must be different from its past, and its present, and to explore possibilities for the future is another aspect of the risk involved in acceding to the church.

Nor is the concern with change and the future merely a quest for the fashionable. As we shall see, the Christian tradition, while grounded in God's self-communication in history, does not apotheosize the past. Indeed, the tradition proclaims the fullness of God's reign over all creation as a future reality. Furthermore, to add to the complexity, the emphasis on the future does not reduce the present to irrelevance: the church relies on the resources received from the past to inform appropriate responses to God in the present, responses that can provide an orientation to the future. In short, the Christian tradition values the past, the present, and the future. While it is no small task to achieve a healthy ordering in the relationship between those three foci, authentic Christian theology is not free to ignore any of them. Accordingly, a failure to consider the future or an unwillingness to countenance the possibility of any change, would not only impoverish the life of faith in the present, but also suggest that what came from the past lacked dynamism and the capacity to stimulate change.

An authentic theology of the church, then, must promote the journey ahead, not simply describe where we are or canonize where we have been. Such a conviction can challenge the stolidity that appears often to afflict the church, making it an object of bemusement for many outside it and of frustration for many inside it. While the need to work creatively with the legitimate demands of the past, present, and future subverts an obdurate rejection of change, it is no less subversive of the notion that the church could begin again in every age, as if the past were disposable. One-dimensional approaches to the church, therefore, cannot do justice to its complex nature. This too compounds the risk of involvement, particularly if we want such involvement to be undemanding.

Although it is possible to do justice to the full implications of ecclesial faith only if we take the future into account, talking about the future is itself a risky business. Membership of the church does not bring with it a formula for secure knowledge of the future. In the church, as in the wider society, those who make predictions about the future often live long enough to see those predictions fail to become reality. Fortunately for its author, the final chapter of the book is less a compendium of such predictions than an attempt to identify the factors that underscore the symbiosis between the mission of the church and its need to remain open, to address new questions, and consider movement as a valid expression of its identity. More than anything else, the chapter will stress that authentic ecclesial faith must promote the risk of making decisions about the possible shape of Christian discipleship in changing circumstances.

In addition to failed predictions, another danger in talking about the future is that popular culture, at least in the West, is awash with dark forebodings about that future—a disposition likely to intensify in the wake of '9/11'. Thus, in the classic literary portrayals in H. G. Wells' *The Time Machine* and John Wyndham's *The Day of the Triffids*, as well as in the films that comprise *The Matrix* or the *Terminator* series, the future appears in apocalyptic hues, a physical wasteland peopled by a ghostly remnant. In that context, life is indeed 'solitary, poore, nasty, brutish, and short', the qualities chosen, in the seventeenth century, by the philosopher Thomas Hobbes to describe those living in a state of anarchy.[4]

Beyond the general societal sense of angst about the future, specific issues about the church's future seem equally to offer dark prospects. Clouds have gathered over the church's future not only because of the fading appeal of Christianity in Western societies at large, but also because of the damage done in North America, England, Ireland, Australia, and other countries by clerical sexual abuse, including the flawed responses to it by some authorities in the church. While the immediate impact of that scandal has been evident in dramatic events such as the resignation of the archbishop of Boston and an avalanche of lawsuits, it is impossible to predict the long-term effects. What is clear, however, is that there must be an acknowledgement of the darkness if any consideration of the church's future is to be authentic.

In fact, members of the church ought not to be afraid of acknowledging the darkness since they claim hope as a fundamental dimension of their faith. Hope is not naïve optimism, still less wishful thinking, but manifests the conviction that present experience does not exhaust the sum total of possibilities. It does so, however, without denying the reality of darkness:

hope is not simply the attitude of one who is weak and at the same time hungering for a fulfilment that has yet to be achieved, but rather the courage to commit oneself in thought and deed to the incomprehensible and the uncontrollable which permeates our existence, and, as the future to which it is open, sustains it.[5]

In short, hope generates a sense of possibility, possibility that has its source in God. Most significantly, it does so without needing to douse reality in saccharin. Identifying the basis for such hope in the church is a project for the whole of this book.

The book, then, is an attempt to highlight the possibilities for a more effective presence of the church in the future that will

---

[4] Thomas Hobbes, *Leviathan* (Harmondsworth: Penguin, 1982), 186. The book was published originally in 1651.

[5] Karl Rahner, 'On the Theology of Hope', *Theological Investigations*, 10, tr. D. Bourke (New York: Seabury, 1977), 259.

result from our particular present. The book proposes that the church is always a project, one that is the product of God's initiative and constant care, but one that is also fully dependent on human responses and decisions. As a project, the church is never finished. It will always be in need of review and reform to ensure that all of its manifestations are indeed about God.

Clearly, a book that discusses ideas for a positive future for the church, even one that promotes the need for change in the church, is itself an endorsement of the risk of faith in the church. This book, then, is not simply a catalogue of what is wrong with the church or what no longer works about it, but an attempt to identify what is possible for the church. Furthermore, the book seeks to base those possibilities on the resources provided by the church's own tradition.

Nonetheless, given the vexed history of proposals for change in the church, it would be naïve to think that all readers will agree with everything in this text. Not everyone will accept the book's analysis and assessment of the church's present situation, its theology of the church, or its suggestions for what might be a better response to the present situation. Still, the hope that underpins this work is that it might stimulate further reflection both on the current state of the church and on the overall project of the church. If it does so, then even those who disagree with what they read here will be prompted to think again about how the church responds to the contemporary world. The effectiveness of the church's mission in the world, the health of its communal life, and the possibility of a positive embrace of the risk of ecclesial faith must surely benefit from such a rethinking.

1

A Church in Peril

In August 1996, Cardinal Joseph Bernardin, who was then the Archbishop of Chicago, launched a document entitled *Called to be Catholic: Church in a Time of Peril*. The primary purpose of the document, which was the work of 'The Catholic Common Ground Project', a group representing a broad cross-section of the Roman Catholic church in America, was to promote among American Catholics a renewed, and shared, sense of the identity and purpose of the church. The authors of the document hoped that such a shared vision would help to overcome the toxic climate of division and recrimination that they believed had become endemic within the Catholic community.

Previous generations of Catholics would have assumed that any 'peril' facing their church could result only from the machinations of Protestants or Communists. Cardinal Bernardin and his associates, however, argued that the source of the contemporary peril lay in the loss of a clear sense of identity and purpose among Catholics themselves.

As evidence of the haemorrhaging within the church, 'The Catholic Common Ground Project' highlighted a broad range of experiences: the leaders of the church feeling 'under siege' and 'increasingly polarized'; many members of the church, especially the young, feeling 'disenfranchised, confused about their beliefs, and increasingly adrift'; and many of the church's institutions feeling uncertain of their identity and 'increasingly fearful about their future'.[1] The overall effect of such circumstances was that 'many Catholics are reaching adulthood with barely a rudimentary knowledge of their faith, with an attenuated sense of sacramentality, and with a highly individualistic view of the church'.[2] Hence: 'the peril'.

---

[1] Joseph Bernardin and Oscar Lipscomb, *Catholic Common Ground Initiative: Foundational Documents* (New York: Crossroad Herder, 1997), 34.

[2] Ibid. 38.

The *Called to be Catholic* document portrays a church at risk of disintegration. It seems obvious that devising creative responses to that risk would require the concerted energy of all in the church. Achieving such a concert, however, presents no less a challenge than overcoming the peril itself. In part, this is because of a factor not yet mentioned: that the Christian church as a whole seems peripheral to the priorities and interests of the emerging world of the twenty-first century. Indeed, concern about the likelihood of a future for the Christian church in contemporary society can be as paralysing as the divisions within the Catholic church:

Unable, for the moment, to undertake its own passage, the church hovers timidly on the threshold of the post-modern age, enduring so to speak constant enemy attacks—the end of politico-religious supremacy, the reconfiguration of spiritual customs, the discovery of other traditions made accessible in this time of advanced globalisation. The church is standing still while the world is moving at top speed—inaudible, while the world communicates intensively. The church has not been able to find ways to think about the issues of the moment which, though difficult, are also inspiring—that is, etymologically speaking, capable of firing us with divine inspiration.[3]

In addition, because Catholics do not agree on the causes of the disintegration facing them all, they struggle to work together to meet that threat. While all Catholics might acknowledge that the present state of their church is far from the ideal, or even what is desirable, this does not mean that they would all accept the analysis of 'The Catholic Common Ground Project' or its description of the challenges facing Catholics.[4] As a result, Catholics are even divided about the cause and extent of the divisions between them.

On the one hand, there are those who ascribe the church's situation to what they regard as the loss of, even rejection of,

---

[3] Isabelle Graesslé, 'From Impasse to Passage: Reflections on the Church', *Ecumenical Review*, 53 (2001), 27.

[4] It is a sad irony of contemporary Catholic life that even the search for 'common ground', which underpins the *Called to be Catholic* document, can engender divisions: thus, a number of prominent American bishops responded dismissively, even angrily, to the methodology and conclusions of Cardinal Bernadin's group; see, for example, *Origins*, 26 (29 Aug. 1996), 170–1 and *Origins*, 26 (12 Sept. 1996), 197–9, 202–3.

both the distinctiveness of the church and the challenge of such distinctiveness. More than anything else, they regret that the contemporary church:

functions as a warm matrix within which and from out of which individuals have unlimited freedom of action, without the danger that membership in the church will make inconvenient demands on them.[5]

On the other hand, there are those who, while no less distressed at the lack of challenge that seems to be a hallmark of the present-day church, attribute the church's situation not to an excess or abuse of freedom, but to what they perceive as the absence of genuine freedom. More disturbingly, they characterize the contemporary church as being devoid of passion:

the dominant perception of Catholicism among young people today is an institution in decline and growing old, its members controlled by an addictive guilt and deep patterns of codependency and without much genuine interest in either 'the profound' or service to those in need.[6]

There is, therefore, a danger that all discussion about the church might degenerate into a clash of ideologies, each with its representative heroes and villains. Nonetheless, it is impossible to understand contemporary Catholic life without an attempt to account not only for the divisions within the church, but also for the divisions about the divisions. Undertaking such an exploration is the task of this chapter. In so doing, the goal will be to explain rather than blame, to identify the complex elements, and the complex relationships between those elements, that shape today's Catholic church.

What will become clear from this chapter is that the Second Vatican Council (1962–5) is pivotal to every discussion about the contemporary Roman Catholic church. That fact alone has determined the structure of this chapter, which will review Catholic life as it was in the hundred years before the opening of Vatican II, sketch both the methodology and primary

[5] James Hitchcock, *Catholicism and Modernity: Confrontation or Capitulation?* (New York: Seabury, 1979), 35.

[6] Robert Ludwig, *Reconstructing Catholicism for a New Generation* (New York: Crossroad, 1995), 31.

teachings of the Council, and detail the impact of the Council on the life of the church. The chapter has a threefold aim: to identify in the period before Vatican II the roots for much of the tension and division evident in today's Catholic church; to provide a context in which to understand Vatican II and its effect on the church; and to account for the emergence of 'the peril' in the decades since the Council.

As a point of entry to understanding the context of Vatican II, the following sections will examine two key areas of limitation within the pre-Vatican II Catholic church: the lack of an historical consciousness, which bred both a defensiveness and a tendency to canonize a particular form of Catholic life as the eternal form, thereby engendering suspicion of 'the new'; the style of relationships both between the church and the wider world and within the church. These areas are worthy of attention because they provide windows into the worldview and processes of previous generations of Catholic life, including the ways in which Catholics viewed the world beyond the church. In addition, the insight into the past that the two foci offer will not only facilitate the effort to understand the contribution of the Second Vatican Council, it will also help to indicate why reception of Vatican II has proved to be so disruptive.

Although the following sections will focus on limitations, these suggest only that the Catholic church before the Second Vatican Council was less than perfect, not that it was without any redeeming features. Nonetheless, if the need for historical balance and the demands of justice make it necessary to avoid any suggestion that the Catholic church before Vatican II was merely a gulag, it is those same requirements that promote resistance to any temptation to romanticize the earlier period as a golden age, an approach that would suggest that Vatican II lacked rhyme or reason for its programme.

To anyone with either an historical consciousness or an appreciation of the eschatological orientation of Christian faith, it might seem obvious that the church, in every epoch, will realize only imperfectly all that it seeks to be. The following sections, however, will show why the ecclesiology that prevailed among Catholics before Vatican II made such an acknowledgement far from obvious.

GUARDIAN OF A PURE—AND FINAL—TRUTH

At first glance, it might seem absurd to suggest that the Catholic church prior to the Second Vatican Council was anything other than a harmonious, settled, and thriving universe, one in which 'limitation' was in short supply:

A kind of 'sacred canopy' covered the Catholic experience and galvanized the Catholic identity. Few, if any, would have called it a 'Catholic ghetto' because it seemed so right. It touched people at a vital chord. It illuminated the radical questions that plagued the riddle of their existence. It gave them a zone of truth, a place to belong, a challenging vision.[7]

That canopy, in matters as diverse as sacramental theology and practice, the training of students for the ordained priesthood, and the forms of piety practised by most Catholics, owed its emergence and dimensions, either directly or indirectly, to the Council of Trent (1545–63), which formulated the Catholic response to the Reformation. Although not the only influence on Catholic life from the seventeenth to the twentieth century, Trent 'had a direct and long-term impact on modern Catholicism that in its pervasiveness transcended the immediate influence of any single person or any other happening in the period'.[8]

In response to the trauma of the Reformation, Trent sought to reaffirm truths of the Christian faith against what they perceived as their dilution or distortion at the hands of the Reformers:

it is the chief concern, responsibility and intention of this holy council that, when the darkness of heresies (which for so many years have covered the earth) has been dispelled, the light of catholic truth (by favour of Jesus Christ who is true light) may shine forth again in its

---

[7] Edward Braxton, *The Wisdom Community* (New York: Paulist, 1980), 27–8. For a similarly warm portrayal of Catholic life in Australia during the same period, see Edmund Campion, *Australian Catholics* (Ringwood, Vic.: Penguin Books, 1988), 93–156.

[8] John W. O'Malley, *Trent and All That: Renaming Catholicism in the Early Modern Era* (Cambridge, Mass.: Harvard University Press, 2000), 135. O'Malley points to the central role of the papacy in Catholic life as an example of something that developed after Trent, but not because of Trent.

brightness and purity, and matters which require reform may be duly amended.[9]

The Council of Trent was itself a reforming assembly, but its primary concern was to emphasize the church's role in preserving, safeguarding, and teaching divine truth. In order to achieve that goal, Trent accentuated the apostolic identity of the Catholic church:

No council had ever insisted so explicitly, so repeatedly, and so forcefully on the continuity of the present with the apostolic past as did Trent. This defensive rhetoric signalled a recognition that the break Trent's own reforms instituted would somehow have to build on the old ways or at least live side-by-side with them.[10]

Trent's efforts to highlight the continuity between apostolic faith and the contemporary Catholic church sought to delineate the differences between Catholics and Protestants in the sixteenth century. In the following centuries, Trent's teaching, expounded not just in papal documents but also in catechisms that were accessible to all, reinforced the conviction of Catholics that their church alone was both faithful to the apostolic tradition and the carrier of institutions that were the product of God's direct initiative. A corollary of that conviction was that 'change' did not feature prominently in the Catholic vocabulary. Accordingly, even under the 'sacred canopy' that sheltered Catholic parochial life in America in the 1950s, it was scarcely conceivable that Catholic life had been—or could be— different from the way it appeared at that moment:

Two important qualities of a vital organism that were not prominent in the American scene were a sense of history and a dynamic openness to change. Because of the times, perhaps, and through no fault of their own, many laypeople, priests, theologians, sisters, and bishops were not sufficiently aware of the fact that the Church had had a long dynamic history marked by many and sometimes bold and turbulent changes.... In such a stable context one was not likely to think about

---

[9] Council of Trent, 'On the Manner of Living and Other Points to be Observed at the Council' (Session Two, 7 Jan. 1546) in Norman Tanner (ed.), *Decrees of the Ecumenical Councils* (London/Washington: Sheed & Ward/ Georgetown University Press, 1990), ii. 661.

[10] O'Malley, *Trent and All That*, 122–3.

the fact that things had not always been the way they were and, therefore, might well not remain the same.[11]

Within the confines of their church, then, Catholics could be sure that the truth that came from Jesus Christ was safe, that it was protected by the care of strong and diligent pastors. Catholics could also be confident that if they remained obedient to those pastors, above all to the Supreme Pastor in Rome, they would hear the truth, which would not only challenge them to faithfulness in the present, but also open the way to the fullness of life. This emphasis on the bishops and Pope resulted not just from the Tridentine settlement—although, as a later section of this chapter will illustrate, it was certainly prominent in post-Tridentine ecclesiology—but also from developments in the reign of Pius IX (1846–78), most particularly the definition of papal infallibility by the First Vatican Council (1869–70).

As already noted, life under the canopy that covered Catholics could be rich and varied. It did not, however, help its denizens to recognize that the post-Tridentine form of the church was not its eternal form. Nor did it help them to see that the truth taught by Trent was the product of the church's long history of faith, which embraced a history of questioning and seeking, of struggle and disagreement, and of clarification and refinement. Indeed, it was more likely that Trent's teaching on, for example, the church's sacraments and structures shaped how Catholics read both the words of Jesus in the gospels and the church's history, including the dynamics of the Christian communities portrayed in the New Testament. So dominant was the sense that Trent had clarified the once-for-all faith of the church that there was even a pronounced tendency among Catholics to approach the Bible as if its primary purpose was to provide texts—known as 'proof-texts'—that justified explicitly the post-Reformation form of the church's doctrines or structures.[12]

---

[11] Braxton, *The Wisdom Community*, 28.

[12] For a brief overview of the use of 'proof-texts' as support for the church's doctrine see Raymond Collins, 'Bible and Doctrine', in Richard McBrien (ed.), *The HarperCollins Encyclopedia of Catholicism* (San Francisco: Harper-Collins, 1995), 170–1.

In the wake of the Tridentine settlement, then, it was usual for Catholics to locate the strength of their church in the fact that it did not change, that it was not subject to the same vagaries of history as other churches or civil society. While that conviction might have been comforting, it provided no immunity to the challenges emanating from within a changing world. In addition, a church proud of not changing was unlikely to know how to respond creatively to new questions, especially when those questions concerned the legitimacy of faith or the life of the church itself. The impact of such limitations becomes clear in the light of the effects on the Catholic church of the emergence of 'modernity'.

While 'modernity' is a notoriously slippery term, it is reasonably safe to connect its emergence with the Enlightenment, the social and intellectual upheaval that began in Europe during the late eighteenth century. What provided a common focus for the philosophers of the Enlightenment, who included figures as diverse as Denis Diderot (1713–84) and Immanuel Kant (1724–1804), was their conviction that the key to human flourishing resided in human reason. The primary area for intellectual inquiry during the Enlightenment was the individual human being, 'the subject'. As a result, not only did God cease to be at the centre of all inquiry, but it also became possible to consider human activity, including the dynamics of human society, without reference to religious faith.

The Enlightenment regarded religious faith's focus on the transcendent and the eternal as inimical both to human reason and to concern with the experience of the present. Consequently, much of the new thinking that came to prominence during the Enlightenment sought to remove from the public sphere the influence of religious faith and, more specifically, of the church's institutional elements. As the domain of the State, the public sphere was to be subject neither to God nor the church, but to the public universality of reason. Whatever religious faith remained after reason had liberated people from the thrall of superstition would be nothing more than an inconsequential private matter.

For religious faith, the positive effect of the Enlightenment's turn away from God, which was the outcome of its 'turn to the subject', was a reduction in the State's efforts to control the church—as we shall see in the following section, the struggle between church and State had not only been a major cause of controversy at various times in the late Middle Ages, it had also influenced post-Tridentine theologies of the church. The negative effect, however, was far more noteworthy: the banishment of religious faith from the sphere of public discourse. As a result of this development, there was little opportunity for religious faith to account for itself as a reasonable exercise of human freedom, as other than an irrational superstition.[13]

The emphasis on individual reason and the relegation of faith to the sphere of what was private were also injurious to a communal sense of faith. 'Private' came quickly to imply not only the separation of faith from public discourse, but also that individual conviction was the sole determinative factor for all matters regarding God.[14] Clearly, such a view could not marry easily with an emphasis on tradition and the historical grounding of Christian faith in a 'cultural-linguistic matrix that determines us and to which we remain bound even when we think we ourselves determine what God is and what we believe'.[15]

In addition, the rhetoric of modernity highlighted its superiority over the religious view of the world, which had dominated the previous millennium of Europe's history. Indeed, the advocates of modernity displayed an awareness of the usefulness of slogans—'Middle Ages' or 'Dark Ages'; 'Renaissance'; 'Enlightenment'; and 'Emancipation'—to compare their liberating emphasis on the secular with what they regarded as the narrowness of religious faith.[16] The boast of modernity was that its emphasis on reason, which flowered in the development of 'scientific method', had secured the triumph of knowledge that could be both genuinely universal, unlike the dependence of religious faith on particular 'revelations', and also certain,

---

[13] For discussion of the deficits for religious faith of its removal from public discourse see Ingolf Dalferth, ' "I Determine What God Is!"': Theology in the Age of "Cafeteria Religion" ', *Theology Today*, 57 (2000), 7.

[14] Ibid. 8.

[15] Ibid. 12.

[16] For the notion of the slogans of modernity see John Thornhill, *Modernity: Christianity's Estranged Child Reconstructed* (Grand Rapids, Mich.: Eerdmans, 2000), 7.

since it, unlike religious faith, could be verified empirically.
Scientific knowledge, then, contrasted with religious tradition,
the value of which was difficult to determine with any certainty
because it was historical and particular, not empirical.[17]
The vision of the Enlightenment argued for progress in
human life from unscientific knowledge, a category that defined religion as a form of superstition or uncritical enthusiasm,
to scientific knowledge, which would secure social progress.[18]
This scientific passion flowered in the nineteenth century in
archaeology, history, philology, and numerous other disciplines. Developments in those fields were also significant for
the church since, by casting doubt on the uniqueness of the
texts and history of Christianity, they eroded further any claims
that religious faith could make to a capacity for objective
certainty.

With the onset of modernity, then, the church was dealing,
for the first time in more than fifteen hundred years, with a
challenge from people for whom God, the language of faith,
and the community of faith were not primary. In place of God,
the community, and institution, the advocates of modernity
promoted 'the subject', the rational human being committed
to discovering truth, free of the strictures imposed by any
group or structure. This marked a watershed for the church
since the major internal conflicts of Christian history, including
those that resulted in the split between Western and Eastern
Christians in the eleventh century and between Protestants and
Catholics in the sixteenth century, had been ones in which the
protagonists shared a common faith in the God of Jesus Christ
and, the reality of their differences notwithstanding, common
goals.

Even though this study focuses primarily on the Catholic
church, the Enlightenment posed a challenge to all Christians.
While the gulf between Catholics and Protestants at this time
might suggest that the latter's response to the challenge would

---

[17] Michael Scanlon, 'The Postmodern Debate', in Gregory Baum (ed.),
The Twentieth Century: A Theological Overview (Maryknoll, NY: Orbis,
1999), 228.
[18] Francis Schüssler Fiorenza, 'Fundamental Theology and Its Principal
Concerns Today: Towards a Non-Foundational Foundational Theology',
Irish Theological Quarterly, 62 (1996–7), 122.

have been irrelevant to the former, the Protestant response actually had a profound impact on Catholic life, albeit, as we shall see, one that the authorities within the Catholic church did not welcome. Nonetheless, it is not possible to appreciate the specifics of the Catholic encounter with modernity without an understanding of what occurred when Protestant thought met modernity.

In response to the Enlightenment's challenge to faith, most Protestant theologians proceeded in one of two directions. On the one hand, there was a retreat from rationality in favour of ineffable religious feelings as the basis of knowledge and faith. In its extreme form, this approach developed into 'fideism', which is the assertion of faith without any attempt to account for its inner logic or to relate it to what other sources of knowledge claim to be true.[19] On the other hand, there was an attempt to ensure that faith, doctrine, and the life of the church conformed to what reason alone could affirm. This latter response gave birth to what became known as 'liberal theology', which reduced 'God' to what fitted neatly into the prevailing canons of rationality and 'faith' to rational assent to such a 'God'.[20]

While there was much debate within Protestant theology of the questions raised by the Enlightenment's critique of religious faith, the Catholic response to the challenges of the day came primarily through the church's authoritative channels. Thus, in the encyclical *Quanta Cura,* which Pope Pius IX published in 1864 as the theological underpinning of the 'Syllabus of Errors', there was a sweeping condemnation of modernity's failings in religious, social, and political matters.[21] It was, however, the First Vatican Council that provided the most significant response to modernity.

In its document on revelation, Vatican I reiterated Catholic tradition by asserting that, while our knowledge of

[19] This definition of 'fideism' comes from Roger Haight, *Jesus Symbol of God* (Maryknoll, NY: Orbis, 1999), 29.

[20] For an overview of 'liberal' theology in the Protestant tradition see Bernard Reardon, *Liberal Protestantism* (London: Adam & Charles Black, 1968).

[21] For the text of *Quanta Cura* see C. Carlen (ed.), *The Papal Encyclicals 1740–1878* (Wilmington, NC: McGrath Publishing, 1981), 380–5.

God depended on God's revelation, faith and reason were compatible

Even though faith is above reason, there can never be any real disagreement between faith and reason, since it is the same God who reveals the mysteries and infuses faith, and who has endowed the human mind with the light of reason.[22]

Vatican I, therefore, was unsympathetic not only to the presuppositions of the Enlightenment philosophers, but also to what it regarded as the fideism or rationalism that had become prominent within Protestant theology. While Vatican I was keen to defend the reasonableness of the church's faith, its main form of opposition to contemporary trends invoked the principles of Trent. Thus, it sought to transcend the Enlightenment's critique by highlighting the church's God-given authority to teach the truth, an authority vested particularly in the Bishop of Rome and in the instrument of papal infallibility:

this see of St Peter always remains unblemished by any error, in accordance with the divine promise of our Lord and Saviour to the prince of his disciples ... This gift of truth and never-failing faith was therefore divinely conferred on Peter and his successors in this see so that they might discharge their exalted office for the salvation of all, and so that the whole flock of Christ might be kept away by them from the poisonous food of error and be nourished with the sustenance of heavenly doctrine. Thus the tendency to schism is removed and the whole church is preserved in unity, and, resting on its foundation, can stand firm against the gates of hell.[23]

Just as Trent confirmed Catholic truth against Protestant excesses, so too Vatican I defended the church's truth against the onslaughts of modernity. As a result of Vatican I's doctrine, Catholics could know that their faith was not irrational: God, who was the direct support for the teaching of the church, guaranteed it. The difficulty, however, was that the Council's formulations tended to remove the church from the possibility of dialogue with contemporary ideas, since it was the very notion of an authority not subject to reason that the Enlightenment rejected. Reinforcing the tendency to isolation was the

---

[22] First Vatican Council, *Dei filius* (24 Apr. 1870), in Tanner, *Decrees of the Ecumenical Councils*, ii. 808.

[23] First Vatican Council, *Pastor aeternus* (18 July 1870), ibid. 816.

fact that authorities in the church, in order to protect the social status quo in the face of various revolutionary movements, often allied themselves in the eighteenth and nineteenth centuries with conservative social forces.[24] This point will be developed further in the next section.

If the church's official responses to modernity inclined towards the separation of believers from upheavals in the surrounding culture, Catholic theology was even less open to new ideas. At the time of Vatican I, Catholic theology was generally inward-looking and insular. As a result, it was either largely unaffected by Enlightenment thought and contemporary Protestant theology or ignorant of them. The insularity of Catholic theology reflected not only the consequences of the Tridentine settlement, but also the fact that the principal expression of Catholic theology at this time was neo-scholasticism—'a defensive-traditionalist, non-productive confrontation with the challenges of so-called modernity'.[25]

Catholic theology in its neo-scholastic form was largely derivative, a discussion of the commentators on the theology of St Thomas Aquinas (1225–74) rather than of Thomas' own writings. More than anything else, this type of theology was untouched by the questions and concerns of the contemporary world. Indeed, apart from the efforts of Pope Leo XIII (1878–1903), in the 1890s, to encourage a revival of authentic Thomistic studies, there were few signs of life in Catholic theology as the twentieth century approached.[26] As a result, the Catholic theological world was largely incapable of providing Vatican I with the raw materials necessary to present issues such as divine revelation in ways that addressed the challenges emanating from liberal Protestant theologians.

From the late nineteenth century until the second half of the twentieth century, the theology that was studied in seminaries, which were the primary venue for the church's theological endeavours, was mainly in the form of compendia, called

---

[24] See Thornhill, *Modernity*, 4.

[25] Johann Baptist Metz, *A Passion for God: The Mystical-Political Dimension of Christianity*, tr. J. M. Ashley (Mahwah, NJ: Paulist, 1998), 31.

[26] For a detailed analysis of the contours of Catholic theology in this period see Gerald McCool, *Catholic Theology in the Nineteenth Century: The Quest for a Unitary Method* (New York: Seabury, 1977).

'manuals', of everything that needed to be known on the significant areas of faith.[27] The manuals mined the Bible for proof-texts, portrayed the historical Jesus as the immediate source of the Catholic church's doctrines and order of life, and had as their fundamental focus the articulation of arguments establishing the superiority of the Catholic church over the various manifestations of Protestantism.[28] The methodology of the manuals modelled the ahistorical approach to truth that dominated the post-Tridentine church; the manuals supplied answers that satisfied only if there were no new questions.

Despite the desire for a settled universe, the Catholic church could not remain immune to those forces that had been causing turmoil in Protestantism for more than a century. Nonetheless, the fact that 'the Modernist crisis' is the usual name for what occurred in the first decade of the twentieth century, when new approaches to theology surfaced among Catholics, indicates how thoroughly the development shook the Catholic church.

While there were similarities in the thought of those who were ultimately condemned by the church for their 'Modernist' views, there was no distinct Modernist 'school' or movement. There were, however, numerous theologians who shared a conviction that the doctrines and practices of the Catholic church needed to be open to scrutiny by the criteria of contemporary rationality, historical development, and scientific proof, rather than relying on what they regarded as an indefensible resort to supernatural revelation as the source of truth.[29]

Although it was revelation that was a particular rallying point for the critique of the Modernists, this was not their only concern. George Tyrrell (1861–1909), for example, one of the principal Modernist figures, argued that the faith of all be-

[27] For an overview of the manuals see 'Manualistic Theology', in Réne Latourelle and Rino Fisichella (eds.), *Dictionary of Fundamental Theology* (New York: Herder & Herder, 2000), 1102–5.

[28] A representative example of the theological manuals would be Adolf Tanquerey, *A Manual of Dogmatic Theology*, tr. J. Brynes, (New York: Desclee, 1959), which is a translation of a Latin text published in 1914.

[29] For an in-depth study of the major figures and ideas of the Modernist crisis see, Gabriel Daly, *Transcendence and Immanence: A Study in Catholic Modernism and Integralism* (Oxford: Clarendon Press, 1980).

lievers ought not to be subject to direction by authorities in the church. In advocating freedom from such control, Tyrrell was scathing in his denunciation of papal infallibility and episcopal power—'the nearer one draws to the centre, and the further from the circumference, of the official Church, the tighter and heavier are the fetters imposed on one's mental and moral liberty; and the harder it is to realize one's own personality.'[30] Indeed, so alienated was Tyrrell by what he regarded as an excessive emphasis on doctrine, authority, and the pursuit of earthly power by the church's leaders that he accused the Catholic church of his day of having 'narrowed the borders of her tent and from a world-embracing religion as wide as the heart of Christ has shrivelled herself up to a waspish sect glorifying as none other in her rigidity and exclusiveness'.[31]

The official response to the Modernists was dramatic and uncompromising. On 8 September 1907, Pope Pius X (1903–14) issued the encyclical *Pascendi Dominici Gregis*, a thoroughgoing rejection of all that sprang from the Modernists. In his critique of the philosophy and arguments of the Modernists, Pius X stressed their overstatement of the capacity of human reason to understand and explain the whole of life, an overstatement that the Pope attributed to their excessive confidence in the value of human experience and human history as the sources of all necessary insight. In addition, Pius X saw in the works of the Modernists an approach that left little room not only for the relationship between faith and reason, but also for the presence of God in human history, including the revelation of God in Jesus. In language far removed from that characteristic of today's papal documents, Pius X categorized the theology of the Modernists as an attack on all that was central to the life of the church:

Though they express astonishment themselves, no one can justly be surprised that We number such men among the enemies of the Church, if, leaving out of consideration the internal disposition of the soul, of which God alone is the judge, he is acquainted with their tenets, their manner of speech, their conduct. Nor indeed will

---

[30] George Tyrrell, *Medievalism: A Reply to Cardinal Mercier* (Allen, Tex.: Christian Classics, 1994), 37. The book was originally published in 1908.

[31] Ibid. 166.

he err in accounting them the most pernicious of all the adversaries of the Church.... Moreover, they lay the axe not to the branches and shoots, but to the very root: that is, to the faith and its deepest fibres. And having struck at this root of immortality, they proceed to disseminate poison through the whole tree, so that there is no part of Catholic truth from which they hold their hand, none that they do not strive to corrupt. Further, none is more skilful, none more astute than they, in the employment of a thousand noxious arts...[32]

In the wake of *Pascendi*, several Modernist figures, the most significant of whom were Tyrrell and Alfred Loisy (1857–1940) were excommunicated.

In many ways, the condemnation of the Modernists was the high-water mark of the century-long struggle by Catholic authorities against various trends in intellectual and social life.[33] It was, therefore, an attempt to bring to a halt any possibility that those trends might affect the life of the church. While it might have had its origins in nineteenth-century issues, *Pascendi* also had two major influences on the shape of Catholic life in the first half of the twentieth century.

First, *Pascendi* became a weapon in the hands of those who believed that being a faithful Catholic was synonymous with neo-scholasticism, opposition to all forms of liberalism, and commitment to belief in a God who revealed timeless truth through univocal propositions, which transcended any questions that originated in modern philosophy, history, or philology. In short, the condemnation of the Modernists left little room to believe that anything other than the shoals of atheism awaited those who dallied with modernity. Only with Vatican II did it become possible to recognize how fidelity both to God and the church's tradition of faith could express itself in other than neo-scholastic forms.

Secondly, and more explicitly, the condemnation of the Modernists opened the door to unprecedented levels of invigi-

[32] Pius X, *Pascendi Dominici Gregis*, no. 3, in C. Carlen (ed.), *The Papal Encyclicals 1903–39* (Wilmington: McGrath Publishing, 1981), 71–2.

[33] See, for example, David Schultenover's analysis of the relationship between the condemnation of the Modernists and the ongoing struggle by the church's authorities against social and political liberalism in *A View from Rome: On the Eve of the Modernist Crisis* (New York: Fordham University Press, 1993), 17–34.

lation and control within the church. Since 1557, the church's authorities had been able to proscribe books by adding them to the 'Index of Forbidden Books', the register of texts that constituted a threat to the integrity of the faith and the well-being of members of the church, but the efforts to ensure the extirpation of Modernism went well beyond that measure. The primary agent of the campaign was the 'Anti-Modernist Oath', which remained in effect from 1910 until 1964. The purpose of the Oath was to ensure orthodoxy, especially amongst the clergy who, because they were the primary workers in the church's pastoral and teaching ministries, could do most harm if corrupted by Modernism—'I profess in general that I am completely adverse to the error of the Modernists who say that there is nothing divine in the sacred Tradition.'[34] So intense was the campaign to detect anything that might be at odds with the teaching of *Pascendi* that many Catholic theologians lived in fear or avoided any issues that were likely to be contentious.[35]

In the fifty years that followed the promulgation of *Pascendi*, the forms of Catholic theology that had official sanction showed little vitality. Indeed, in the decade before Vatican II, the theologian Karl Rahner (1904–84), himself a subject of suspicion and censure at that time, claimed that there would be little difference in content between a theological text published in 1750 and one published in 1950.[36] Under Pope Pius XII (1939–58) there was some evidence of a change in the

[34] For the text of the Anti-Modernist Oath see Joseph Neuner and Jacques Dupuis (eds.), *The Christian Faith in the Doctrinal Documents of the Catholic Church* (London: Collins, 1986), 49–51.

[35] As an illustration of the damage wrought by the anti-Modernist fervour, it is worth recording Karl Rahner's observation that Romano Guardini (1885–1968), one of the most creative thinkers in the Catholic Church in the generation prior to Vatican II, had been so 'traumatized' by his experiences as a young theologian that he focused primarily on the philosophy of religion. See, Karl Rahner, *I Remember*, tr. J. Bowden (London: SCM Press, 1984), 74.

[36] Karl Rahner, 'The Prospects for Dogmatic Theology', *Theological Investigations*, 1, tr. C. Ernst, (New York: Crossroad, 1982), 2; the article was originally published in 1954. For the details of Rahner's troubles with the church's authorities see, Herbert Vorgrimler, *Understanding Karl Rahner: An Introduction to his Life and Thought*, tr. J. Bowden (New York: Crossroad, 1986), 87–94.

environment. This came via expressions of openness to the new
methods of biblical interpretation, even though these were
largely the result of pioneering work by Protestant theologians—*Divino afflante spiritu* (1943), and liturgical renewal—
Mediator dei (1947). It remained true, however, that much
of the creative work in Catholic theology was taking place
'underground', through the efforts of those who were officially
suspect.[37]

Although it was primarily in regard to theology that the lack
of a sense of history and the reluctance to embrace anything
other than what had been central to the Tridentine settlement
were most evident, those factors also had an impact in other
areas of the church's life. As we shall see in the next section,
there was a parallel between the church's struggle against the
inroads of modernity into theology and its struggle against
social trends, particularly in European society. Here too, the
church seemed to be chronically at odds with the modern
world. This becomes apparent when we review the church's
response to a raft of social and political changes in Europe
during the late nineteenth and early twentieth centuries.

A PERFECT SOCIETY IN A CHANGING WORLD

Social and political change affected the church in a tangible way
in 1871 with the expropriation of the Papal States, the lands
over which the Pope exercised direct control, by the newly
formed nation of Italy. The dispossession of the Pope was less
an expression of anti-religious fervour than of political prag-
matism, part of the strategy for abolishing the plethora of
independent kingdoms, republics, and other types of state,
that had occasioned Napoleon's remark that 'Italy' was merely
a geographical expression. Although it is likely that the idea of
the Pope as a political ruler would strike today's Catholics as
anomalous—the existence of the Vatican State notwithstanding—the fact that popes had exercised such rule since the early
Middle Ages meant that the expropriation outraged nineteenth-

---

[37] See, for example, a survey of the situation of the creative forces in French
theology in the 1930s in Joseph Komonchak, 'Returning from Exile: Catholic
Theology in the 1930s', in Baum (ed.), *The Twentieth Century* 35–48.

century Catholics. No one, of course, was more outraged than the Pope himself: refusing to recognize the newly unified nation, Pope Pius IX withdrew into the Vatican; this form of protest continued until the achievement of a concordat between the papacy and the government of Italy in 1928.

The image of the Pope's self-imposed isolation in the Vatican captures well the situation of the Catholic church in Europe for much of the modern era. Just as it had sought to 'counter' the Reformation and Enlightenment, the church's response to numerous political developments in the eighteenth and nineteenth centuries displayed the same spirit of rejection.[38]

The papal reaction against the formation of the Italian state shows also that there was a possibility that the sacred canopy might become a ghetto, whose walls were built high and thick to exclude possible contaminants. In a world of change, a world whose sense of itself was being revolutionized by the work of Karl Marx (1818–83), Friedrich Nietzsche (1844–1900), and Sigmund Freud (1856–1939), the members of the Catholic church could feel themselves alone and friendless. In that situation, there was a powerful stimulus to strengthen the bonds between Catholics in order to protect them against an alien or hostile world, and even against Christians who belonged to communions other than the Catholic one. That exigency also accounts for the uncompromising nature of the response to the Modernists.

Such a stance might have helped Catholics to see their church as an oasis of peace and security, but it did little to encourage creative responses to the challenges inseparable from urbanization and industrialization. A consequence of that lack of engagement with the world was that the church, and indeed the Gospel, looked as if their sole concern was private piety, as if the transformation of the world was not part of their brief. Although Pope Leo XIII's encyclical *Rerum novarum* (1891), a response to the impact of Marxism on workers in Europe, was a significant exception to the lack of engagement, even that encyclical couched its vision of the social order in terms that could be read as 'giving support to the traditionalist groups eager to

---

[38] For the notion of the church as a 'counter' movement see Metz, *A Passion for God*, 46.

see the restoration of the *ancien régime*'.[39] If the church of the eighteenth century had lost the intellectuals of the Enlightenment, the church of the nineteenth century lost the working class.[40]

While the separation between the church and the world might have been inadvertent, it would also have been difficult to avoid since Catholic theology in this period did not engage fervently with issues raised by history and 'the world'.[41] The irrelevance of the world for neo-scholastic theology reflected the fact that anthropological issues were not significant for that type of theology. Indeed, even in Christology it was the divinity of Christ that had been the dominant theme for centuries. As a result, theology 'by and large ignored the genuine humanity of Jesus Christ, a matter of scriptural and dogmatic truth'.[42]

The lack of appreciation for the world and humanity as loci for an encounter with God ensured also that there was little affirmation of the enrichment offered by cultural differences within the church. The dominant Catholic emphasis, therefore, was on the uniformity and universality of ecclesiastical culture, even in the mission churches of Africa, Asia, and the Pacific. The use of Latin as the language of the church's liturgy throughout the world facilitated the possibility of that uniformity.[43]

Inevitably, the absence of anthropology and culture as significant themes in theology resulted also in an ambivalent attitude towards the value of human community as an asset in the appropriation of God's presence in history. On the one hand, there were movements, especially in the years after

---

[39] Michael Walsh and Brian Davies (eds.), *Proclaiming Peace and Justice: Papal Documents from Rerum Novarum through Centesimus Annus*, rev. edn. (Mystic, Conn.: Twenty-Third Publications, 1991), 2.

[40] Walter Kasper, 'The Council's Vision for a Renewal of the Church', *Communio*, 17 (1990), 475.

[41] For a survey of the slow movement in Catholic theology towards engagement with the world, see Johann Baptist Metz, *Faith in History and Society: Towards a Practical Fundamental Theology*, tr. D. Smith, (New York: Seabury, 1980), 14–31.

[42] Elizabeth Johnson, *Consider Jesus: Waves of Renewal in Christology* (New York: Crossroad, 1992), 12.

[43] See Daniel Donovan, *Distinctively Catholic: An Exploration of Catholic Identity* (Mahwah, NJ: Paulist, 1997), 140–2.

World War I, which tried to respond to the longing for community and to use it for the benefit of the church.[44] On the other hand, the church's spirituality, sacramental and otherwise, tended to promote the individual's quest for salvation more than the communal dimension of faith. As a result, the strongest source of communal identity for Catholics still remained their separation from Protestants and their suspicion of 'the world'.

Giving strength to the suspicious perception of secular reality was the notion of the church as 'a perfect society'. That notion developed in the aftermath of the Reformation, via the theology of Robert Bellarmine (1542–1621), was intended primarily as a way of emphasizing that the existence of the church was dependent on God, not secular rulers. It was invoked with increasing regularity in the eighteenth and nineteenth centuries to underline the right of the church to be free from attempts by political rulers to impose their will on the church.[45] Thus, for example, Pius IX's 'Syllabus of Errors' denounced the view that the church was not free, complete, or invested by God with rights that were not subject to control by the State.

While the notion of the church as a perfect society was primarily a tool for defending the church from political control, it also affected the interaction between the church and secular society and the understanding of relationships within the church. In those two contexts, its influence tended to be negative.

In regard to the relationship between the church and secular society, there was a danger that the notion of a perfect society could imply not just the right of the church to be independent of the State, but the superiority of the church over all other forms of human association. The spirit of triumphalism engendered

---

[44] On the promotion of communal movements, see Walter Kasper, *Theology and Church*, tr. M. Kohl (London: SCM, 1989), 149.

[45] For a brief overview of Bellarmine's ecclesiology, see Avery Dulles, *Models of the Church* (New York: Image Books, 1978), 20 and Eric Jay, *The Church: Its Changing Image through Twenty Centuries* (London: SPCK, 1977), 202–4. For a history of the application of the concept see Yves Congar, 'Moving Towards a Pilgrim Church', in A. Stacpoole (ed.), *Vatican II Revisited By Those Who Were There* (Minneapolis, Minn.: Winston Press, 1986), 131–5.

by such an attitude is evident in the analysis of the church that Pope Leo XIII promulgated in 1896:

God indeed even made the Church a society far more perfect than any other. For the end for which the Church exists is as much higher than the end of other societies as divine grace is above nature, as immortal blessings are above the transitory things of earth. Therefore the Church is a society *divine* in its origin, *supernatural* in its end and in the means proximately adopted to the attainment of that end; but it is a *human* community inasmuch as it is composed of men. For this reason we find it called in Holy Writ by names indicating a perfect society. It is spoken of as *the house of God*, the *city placed upon a mountain* to which all nations must come.[46]

Despite the religious, indeed eschatological, implications of such statements, there was always a danger that the notion of the church as a perfect society could seduce Catholics into believing that the church—understood expressly as senior clerics—ought to be in charge of secular society. That attitude often promoted anti-clerical sentiments that were not necessarily expressive of a trend towards atheism. Nonetheless, it was difficult for Catholics in the second half of the nineteenth century to hear any rejection, or even criticism, of the church's claims to a monopoly of social and political influence as other than an unholy denial of the truth of the Christian faith and of humanity's need for God. Conversely, the fact that the church saw itself as a perfect society made it difficult for there to be an openness to other—necessarily inferior—forms of society that, unlike the church, were not the product of God's specific providence. As a result, Catholics tended to hold themselves aloof from, or even had disdain for, various social and political developments.

In addition to the difficulties that the notion of a perfect society raised for the church's relationship to secular society, the concept could also have a negative impact on relationships within the church. Indeed, it could determine those relationships according to the social norms of feudalism, where perfection equalled a clear delineation of the social order, a strict

---

[46] Leo XIII, *Satis Cognitum* (1896), nos. 578–9 in C. Carlen (ed.), *The Papal Encyclicals: 1878–1903* (Wilmington, NC: McGrath Publishing, 1981). The emphasis is Leo's.

division between the different grades of society. This not only promoted an increasing centralization of the church, it also ensured that there were few opportunities for the body of baptized members of the church to involve themselves in the processes of the church or to influence its priorities.

By the nineteenth century, it was common to regard the church not only as a perfect society, but also as an unequal one, in which there was a clear separation between those at the top of the pyramid, those who taught, and those at the bottom, those who were to be obedient listeners.[47] While the centrality of the Pope, the unity of the bishops under the Pope, and the required obedience of all the other members of the church maintained the truths of faith across time and cultures, they also generated the perception that immutability and uniformity were the primary pillars of the Catholic tradition.[48] In so doing, they conveyed a sense that all movement in the church was unidirectional: from the top downward.

Although Catholics were united in having common 'enemies', it did not mean that all Catholics were on the one level. Indeed, a German theological dictionary from the last decades of the nineteenth century included the entry: 'Laity—see Clergy'.[49] The vast majority of Catholics, therefore, 'were laity in the secularised sense of non-specialists who know nothing about the subject and so have no say'.[50] Even within the laity, the 'non-specialists' who comprised almost the whole membership of the church, there was usually a difference between the role and place of men and the lesser role and place of women. Such divisions within the church not only intensified the gap between those who taught and those who were to obey, it also put the church at odds with the spirit of democracy gathering momentum in various parts of the world.

---

[47] For a review of the development of the idea that the church was an unequal society, and for the notion of 'hierarchology' that derives from it see Congar, 'Moving Towards a Pilgrim Church', 133–4.

[48] Richard Marzheuser, 'A Revised Theology of Catholicity: Toward Better Communication with Those Who Talk Differently Than We Do about the Church', *New Theology Review*, 8 (1995), 49–50.

[49] Walter Kasper, *An Introduction to Christian Faith*, tr. V. Green, (London/New York: Burns & Oates/Paulist Press, 1980), 141.

[50] Ibid.

As noted earlier in this chapter, the limitations of the church in the period before Vatican II do not mean that the Catholic church at that time was merely a constricted and constricting reality incapable of generating freedom, of expressing authentic faith and hope, or of reflecting the God of boundless love. Nonetheless, the limitations were real. It would be inaccurate, therefore, to regard the Second Vatican Council as if were responsible for wanton vandalism of an idyllic setting. While Vatican II is innocent of such a charge, it is certainly true that the Council had a profound effect on the life of the church as it was until 1962. To illustrate that impact, the next section will survey briefly Vatican II's processes, vision, and major themes— the next three chapters will explore in a more detailed manner particular aspects of the theology of Vatican II.

In the hope of developing a balanced perspective on Vatican II, what follows will suggest that its primary achievement was the recovery—a word that, as we shall see, is indispensable for a proper understanding of the Council—of a broader vision of the church, and its relationship to the world, than the one that dominated Catholic life in the centuries following the Council of Trent. Vatican II not only located itself, unequivocally and deliberately, within the deepest streams of Catholic tradition, it also sought to highlight and apply the capacity of that tradition to be expansive and inclusive. By doing the latter, Vatican II contrasts with many strands of the Catholic experience in the centuries that preceded it. By doing the former, Vatican II challenges today's Catholics to come to a positive appropriation of 'tradition'.

A COUNCIL OF THE OLD AND NEW

Achieving a consensus about Vatican II is difficult. This is so because perceptions about the Council, and about how to interpret its documents, have become embroiled in political divisions within the church.[51] One view, common to those who

---

[51] For an example of divergent interpretations of the substance, style, and impact of Vatican II see James Hitchcock, 'Version One: A Continuum in the Great Tradition', *Commonweal*, 128 (9 Mar. 2001), 16, 18–19 and John O'Malley, 'Version Two: A Break from the Past', *Commonweal*, 128

admire the order and strength of the post-Tridentine church, blames Vatican II for the dawn of a long night of deconstruction, confusion, and mediocrity in the Catholic church. The opposite view, held usually by those who found the former shape of life to be impoverished, regards Vatican II as the great moment of the Catholic church's second millennium, as the end of a defensive church and the birth of hope that there might be a creative interchange with the wider culture—those whose consciousness of the church developed in the decade after the Council often share this view. Yet another perspective, held especially by those who long for the advent of a church committed to a more radical presence in the world, will judge Vatican II to be a step along the way, a small, perhaps even pusillanimous, venture into the waters of authentic discipleship.

Such diverse judgements about the worth of the Council notwithstanding, it is certainly true that, largely as a result of Vatican II, the Catholic church that farewelled the 'Sixties' differed significantly from the one that laid to rest Pope Pius XII in 1958. That fact resonates with the sentiments expressed by Pope John XXIII, the convener of Vatican II, in his opening address in 1962, which stressed that the purpose of the Council was to do more than confirm the existing arrangements within the church:

Illuminated by the light of this Council, the Church—we confidently trust—will become greater in spiritual riches and, gaining the strength of new energies therefrom, she will look to the future without fear. In fact, by bringing herself up-to-date where required, and by the wise organisation of mutual cooperation, the Church will make men, families, and peoples really turn their minds to heavenly things.[52]

John XXIII committed the Council to search for ways in which the church might respond to 'the new conditions and new forms of life introduced into the modern

(9 Mar. 2001), 17, 20–2; see also Avery Dulles, 'Vatican II: The Myth and the Reality', *America*, 188 (24 Feb. 2003), 7–11 and John O'Malley, 'The Style of Vatican II', *America*, 188 (24 Feb. 2003), 12–15. For the impact of divisions in the church on the reception of the Council's documents see, Francis Sullivan, *Creative Fidelity: Weighing and Interpreting Documents of the Magisterium* (Mahwah, NJ: Paulist, 1996), 172–4.

[52] Pope John XXIII's opening speech to the Council, in Walter Abbott (ed.), *The Documents of Vatican II* (London: Geoffrey Chapman, 1967), 712.

world'.[53] That goal—expressed in the Italian word *aggiorna-mento*, which serves often to summarize the purpose and impact of Vatican II—indicated clearly that not only was the era of the 'timeless' church at an end, but also that the differences of the present from the past did not mean that the present was merely a time of 'prevarication and ruin' or that 'at the time of former Councils everything was a full triumph for the Christian idea and life and for proper religious liberty'.[54] Those who held such views, argued John XXIII, were likely to be 'prophets of gloom', people who 'though burning with zeal, are not endowed with too much sense of discretion or measure'.[55]

That the Council was able to engage with the need for reform and renewal both within the church and in the church's relation-ship to its world attests to the impact of the creative theological work done in the 1940s and 1950s by a variety of Catholic thinkers, most of whom, as noted above, had been subject at the time to the forms of ecclesiastical punishment characteristic of the lingering anti-Modernist spirit. The theological re-newal—referred to often as *ressourcement*, 're-sourcing'—had taken three distinct paths, paths that merged in the common search for a theological vision broader than neo-scholasticism. One path followed new approaches to the scriptures; another focused on reclaiming aspects of the church's theological trad-ition, including its liturgical tradition, that stretched back to the early centuries of the church, back beyond the dominance of neo-scholasticism; the third sought to recover the capacity of Christian faith to engage in dialogue with contemporary schools of thought.[56]

The major achievement of the renewal in biblical studies was to refocus Catholics on the Bible as a venue of encounter with God, as something other than a collection of proof-texts. The recovery of neglected aspects of the church's tradition owed much to the French theologians Henri de Lubac (1896–1991)

---

[53] Abbott (ed.), *The Documents of Vatican II*, 714.
[54] Ibid. 712.   [55] Ibid.
[56] For a contemporary overview of the primary influences shaping Catholic theology at the dawn of the Council see Elmer O'Brien (ed.), *Theology in Transition: A Bibliographical Evaluation of the 'Decisive Decade', 1954–1964* (New York: Herder & Herder, 1965); for a summary of the main theologians

and Yves Congar (1904–95). By drawing on 'the Fathers', the name given to the principal theologians in the first few centuries of the church's history, their theologies of revelation, grace, ministry, and the church opened perspectives broader and deeper than those of the immediate past. Similarly, theologians such as Karl Rahner broadened the church's understanding of itself and its place in history by bringing Thomistic theology into dialogue with contemporary ways of thinking. The result was a more dynamic approach to humanity's relationship with God, the recognition that Jesus' humanity was not irrelevant to God's plan to give life to all human beings, and that human history was not irrelevant to encountering the Holy Spirit, the grace of God.

The confluence of the enthusiasm of John XXIII to connect the church to contemporary life, the resources provided by the theological renewal, and the fact that Vatican II was the first gathering of the worldwide episcopate ensured that Vatican II became a watershed in the history of the Catholic church.[57] In order to understand something of the dimensions of its impact, we need to do no more than summarize the effect that the Council had on the dynamics that previously prevailed both within the church and between the church and the world.[58]

The Council reoriented the church's self-understanding in regard to the dynamics of God's self-revelation, the identity of

of the *ressourcement* movement see Paul Lakeland, *The Liberation of the Laity: In Search of an Accountable Church* (New York: Continuum, 2003), 23–44.

[57] There is a vast amount of material on the processes and progress of the Council, but the four volumes, from a projected five, that have appeared as Giuseppe Alberigo and Joseph Komonchak (eds.), *The History of Vatican II* (Maryknoll, NY/Leuven: Orbis/Peeters, 1995–2003) are the most comprehensive. Worth particular mention is Carmel McEnroy's study of the role played by women who were 'auditors' at the Council, *Guests in Their Own House: The Women of Vatican II* (New York: Crossroad, 1996). The most detailed analysis of the Council's texts is in the five volumes of Herbert Vorgrimler (ed.), *Commentary on the Documents of Vatican II* (London/New York: Burns & Oates/Herder, 1967–9).

[58] For a helpful and accessible overview of Vatican II's ecclesiology see Joseph Komonchak, 'The Significance of Vatican II for Ecclesiology', in Peter Phan, *The Gift of the Church: A Textbook on Ecclesiology* (Collegeville, Minn.: Michael Glazier, 2000), 68–92; see also John Markey, *Creating Communion: The Theology of the Constitutions of the Church* (Hyde Park, NY: City Press, 2003).

the church, the nature of its liturgy, and the church's purpose in the world. Perhaps more than anything else, Vatican II stressed God as a 'mystery', the one whom humanity could know, especially because of God's self-communication in Jesus Christ, but the one who exceeded the grasp of every human answer. In that emphasis, Vatican II moved beyond the neo-scholastic focus on answers to stress human life, and the church, as a pilgrimage into the fullness of God.

In its exposition of the church, the Council stressed that it existed, through Jesus Christ, 'the light of the nations', to be 'as a sacrament or instrumental sign of intimate union with God and the unity of all humanity'.[59] Since that task belonged to each baptized person, the church's primary manifestation was as 'the people of God', a biblical metaphor, not as institution or hierarchy.[60] Characteristic of that people of God was the vocation to live a holy life, a vocation that derived from their common baptism and knew no differences based on status or gender. In addition, the people of God existed as a pilgrim people, whose fulfilment lay not in earthly glory, but in communion with the trinitarian God. This not only suggested that dynamism ought to be more a feature of the church, but also that conversion and purification had to be more prominent in the lives of all aspects of the church. In short, the Council left little room for either an ecclesiastical triumphalism, which stressed only the glory of the church, or for a sense that most members of the church were merely passive recipients of what came from those in authority.[61] More than anywhere else, this revised and broadened view both of God's self-communication and of the church's identity and mission found expression in Vatican II's document on the liturgy.[62]

---

[59] 'The Dogmatic Constitution on the Church' (*Lumen gentium*) LG no. 1. All references to the documents of Vatican II are from Tanner (ed.), *Decrees of the Ecumenical Councils*, ii.

[60] 'The People of God' is the title of ch. 2 of 'The Dogmatic Constitution on the Church'.

[61] For an example of one way in which the Council's ecclesiology reshaped relationships within the church see Ormond Rush, 'The Offices of Christ: *Lumen Gentium* and the People's Sense of Faith', *Pacifica* (2003), 137–52.

[62] For an analysis and assessment of what the Council sought to achieve in its approach to liturgy see Joseph Cordeiro, 'The Liturgical Constitution,

In developing a vision for a church that was both dynamic and committed to the participation of all of its members, the Council was neither anarchic nor dismissive of tradition. Thus, in the spirit of *ressourcement*, it drew on ancient forms of envisioning the church, ones that were actually more deeply embedded in the tradition than notions such as the church as a 'perfect society'. Vatican II sought also to be genuinely catholic, to endorse an inclusive 'both . . . and' approach to the church, rather than an exclusive 'either . . . or' approach. Thus, for example, its affirmation of the charisms proper to all baptized members existed alongside its affirmation of the church's hierarchical order as an indispensable aspect of God's guidance of the church. In its understanding of that hierarchical order, however, Vatican II looked beyond Trent and Vatican I to ancient images of the 'apostolic college', in which each bishop made present the character of the 'local church' he led. That college, united with, and under, the Pope also expressed the unity of the whole communion of the church.

While Vatican II's theology of the church revised former emphases, the Council's concern was not simply with internal issues. Thus, Vatican II ensured that Catholics no longer occupied the same space as previously in regard to other Christians. For the first time since the Reformation, there was not only a document promoting reconciliation between Catholics and other Christians, but also one promoting the need for dialogue between the Catholic church and those who were not Christians. When viewed against the history of hostility to Protestantism in the centuries after Trent, and the painful history of violence by Catholics against Jews and Muslims, Vatican II's recognition of past faults and its adoption of the need for dialogue were extraordinary. Similarly, the Council's 'Declaration on Religious Freedom', a declaration that reflected the pioneering work of the American theologian John Courtney Murray (1904–67), was a significant departure from

Sacrosanctum Concilium' in Stacpoole (ed.), *Vatican II Revisited*, 187–94 and Godfrey Diekmann, 'The Constitution on the Sacred Liturgy' in John Miller (ed.), *Vatican II: An Interfaith Appraisal* (Notre Dame, Ind./New York: University of Notre Dame Press/Association Press, 1966), 17–30.

the intolerance that the church had often displayed towards pluralist societies.[63]

Just as the Council's commitment to dialogue initiated a new phase in the church's relationship with other Christians, so its final document inaugurated a new phase in the church's relationship to the rest of the world. That document, 'The Pastoral Constitution on the Church in the Modern World', identified the followers of Christ with the complete gamut of experiences of each member of the human family:

The joys and hopes and the sorrows and anxieties of people today, especially of those who are poor and afflicted, are also the joys and hopes, sorrows and anxieties of the disciples of Christ, and there is nothing truly human which does not also affect them.[64]

'The Pastoral Constitution on the Church in the Modern World' expressed the Council's desire that the church not see itself as an island separated from the rest of humanity, but as called by Christ to enter into the life of humanity in ways that gave light and hope. In so doing, the document inaugurated a new phase in the history of the church, one in which the church was prepared to take responsibility for the shape of the world, rather than juxtaposing itself to the world.[65] In that spirit, the document canvassed a range of contemporary questions: peace and war; economics; marriage and family; belief and unbelief. Significantly, the document acknowledged also that the human sciences could teach the church how to understand better the situations in which the church was to reveal the presence of Christ.

The other aspect of the document that can serve as a metaphor for the achievement of Vatican II is the fact that it

---

[63] The 'Syllabus of Errors' (1864), for example, had condemned the idea that 'it is praiseworthy that in some Catholic regions the law has allowed people immigrating there to exercise publicly their own cult', see Neuner and Dupuis, *The Christian Faith in the Doctrinal Documents of the Catholic Church*, 284.

[64] 'The Pastoral Constitution on the Church in the Modern World' (*Gaudium et spes*), *GS*, no. 1.

[65] Karl Rahner, 'Basic Theological Interpretation of the Second Vatican Council', *Theological Investigations*, 20, tr. E. Quinn (New York: Crossroad, 1986) 77–89.

described itself as a 'Pastoral Constitution'.[66] In other words, it presented the church to the world as a healing and reconciling presence, rather than as a law-maker or enforcer. Vatican II was the first Council in the church's history that neither introduced any new dogmatic definition nor pronounced condemnation against anyone who might disagree with it. All of this was part of the effort to forge a new relationship with the world: to offer the world the riches of the Gospel and to affirm the value of human cultures, even while challenging those cultures to greater generosity and a deeper commitment to justice.

The first half of this chapter examined the ways in which the Council of Trent continued to shape life within the Catholic church long after the sixteenth century. In formal theological terms, that influence expressed the reception of Trent by the church. Reception—'the process through which an ecclesial community incorporates into its own life a particular custom, decision, liturgical practice, or teaching'—is fundamental to the life of the church.[67] Reception highlights both that the church in every age is the beneficiary of a heritage of faith and that the church must search for appropriate ways of living that heritage in each new moment of history in order to pass on that heritage in a living condition.[68] In order, therefore, to appreciate Vatican II fully it is necessary to complement knowledge of the intentions, processes, and decisions of the bishops who signed its documents with an understanding of its ongoing impact on the life of the church.

The following section will survey the stages and factors that have influenced the church's reception of Vatican II. In so doing, it will explore not only the internal life of the church, but also the cultural factors that have affected the reception of Vatican II. The aim of this section is to complete a circle: to bring the chapter to a close by identifying the factors that have

[66] See Karl Rahner, 'On the Theological Problems Entailed in a "Pastoral Constitution"', *Theological Investigations*, 10, tr. D. Bourke (New York: Seabury, 1977), 293–317.

[67] Lucien Richard, 'Reflections on Dissent and Reception', in P. Hegy (ed.), *The Church in the Nineties: Its Legacy, Its Future* (Collegeville, Minn.: Liturgical Press, 1993), 6.

[68] On the task of receiving and passing on a living tradition of faith see Elizabeth Johnson, *Consider Jesus*, 1–3.

produced the 'peril' that characterizes the present-day state of the Catholic church.

RECEIVING VATICAN II: FROM EXUBERANCE TO PERIL

The reception of Vatican II embraces not simply the ways in which the decrees of the Council have shaped 'official' actions in the church in subsequent decades, such as the revision of sacramental rites or the restoration of both the diaconate and the ancient Rite of Christian Initiation of Adults, but how the church as a whole is different as a result of the Council. In this regard, the reception of Vatican II began to have an impact on the church as soon as the final session of the Council concluded.

Indeed, Walter Kasper describes the immediate post-Vatican II period as a 'phase of exuberance'. The primary feature of that phase was an enthusiasm for change 'in the spirit of the Council'.[69] So great was that enthusiasm, argues Kasper, that it tended to reject as 'conciliar scholasticism' any reluctance to accept that the Council had licensed every imaginable change in the church.[70] The most powerful illustration of this phase is the speed with which Latin all but disappeared from the church's liturgical life.

Although the Council's document on the liturgy did indeed endorse the introduction of vernacular languages into the church's liturgical life—'a practice which is really helpful among the people'—it did not intend to end the place of Latin as the normative language of the liturgy.[71] It is likely that the reaffirmation of Latin at Vatican II reflected not only a desire to preserve a venerable tradition, but also some residual suspicion that a substantial change would imply a belated surrender to Martin Luther's campaign in favour of vernacular liturgies. The church at large, however, displayed no such qualms: the vernacular liturgy became so common that Latin quickly ceased to be a significant aspect of liturgical life within most local churches.

---

[69] Kasper, *Theology and Church*, 166–7.   [70] Ibid.
[71] 'Constitution on the Sacred Liturgy' (*Sacrosanctum concilium*), SC, no. 36.

While it would be excessive to portray the style and rate of change in the immediate post-Vatican II years as akin to the rampages of the *jacquerie* uprisings in the fourteenth century, it is true that many of the prominent symbols of the sacred canopy disappeared quickly after the Council. Included among these were a plethora of popular devotions and distinctively Catholic practices, including processions, weekly confessions, and abstinence from meat on Friday. At the same time, there were other changes that reflected a fundamental reordering of Catholic life. The most noteworthy example of that phenomenon was the exodus of ordained priests and religious, and the corresponding decline in the number of new candidates, in the decade after the Council.

Although the immediate post-Vatican II period witnessed intense theological labour, which mined the subtle nuances and hard-won compromises of conciliar documents, the products of that labour were perhaps less influential than the popular perception that the church had 'loosened up', that it had embraced change. Not surprisingly, there is division over whether that perception constitutes authentic reception of the Council or is indicative of 'a superficial adaptation' that hampers genuine reception.[72] What is less debatable, however, is that the widespread enthusiasm for change suggests that aspects of the 'perfect society' and the 'sacred canopy' had not established the church as a community of freedom, hope, and possibility. The passion for change, therefore, could indicate a desire for a church in which the risk of passion was possible.

The most significant illustration of such passion was in the development of what is now known universally as 'liberation theology'. That theology owes much to the Council's emphasis on the centrality of the local church, but also to the fact that Vatican II 'gave the best possible theoretical justification to activities developed under the signs of a theology of progress, of authentic secularization and human advancement'.[73] The

---

[72] Edward Kilmartin, 'Reception in History: A Theological Phenomenon and Its Significance', *Journal of Ecumenical Studies*, 21 (1984), 37. Kilmartin's comment is not a judgement on specific developments after Vatican II, but on the general dangers that can threaten genuine reception.

[73] Leonardo Boff and Clodovis Boff, *Introducing Liberation Theology*, tr. P. Burns (Tunbridge Wells: Burns & Oates, 1987), 68.

emergence of liberation theology, and of new models of ecclesiology in the church of Central and South America, marked the end of the exclusive influence on the church at large of the theology and practice of European Catholics. That development underscored the fact that Vatican II, itself the assembly of the worldwide episcopate, 'was the starting point for a new Pentecost, a holy spark that released a set of movements towards the creation of a truly global community of believers'.[74]

The period after the Council may well have been one of exuberance, but it also became one of confusion. In some instances, the confusion resulted from the desire for change separating itself from anything that Vatican II had said or intended—'much of this could be likened to a spaceship that had lost contact with ground control'.[75] In some instances, the confusion arose from the meeting between new ideas and a church that had strenuously resisted new ideas during the preceding century. That history meant that the church at large had neither the theory nor the experience to discern an appropriate response to what was new. Most especially, there was no lived memory of how to involve all the members of the church as active participants in maintaining and developing the church's tradition in new circumstances.

In the 'perfect society' model, all influence and ideas flowed from the top downwards. While those at the base of the church, that is, those who were not ordained, were the recipients of the pastoral care and sacramental ministrations of the ordained, they received little, if any, formation in the 'sacred sciences', Scripture and theology. They derived their understanding of the church and its processes from their priests and bishops, whose own theological understanding, given the poverty of preconciliar theology discussed above, was not necessarily splendid. The introduction into this context of the Council's stress on, for example, the common priesthood of the faithful and on the equality of all the baptized within the people of God had the potential to create upheaval. As a result, Catholics have struggled in recent decades to translate into their local experi-

---

[74] Virgilio Elizondo, 'Emergence of the World Church and the Irruption of the Poor', in Baum (ed.), *The Twentieth Century*, 105.

[75] Kasper, 'The Council's Vision', 476.

ence Vatican II's affirmation of the complementarity between the common priesthood of the faithful and the ordained priesthood.

Those who had been for so long the passive recipients of what came from above—those whose place in the church was often summarized crudely in the mantra: 'pray, pay, and obey'—were the same people, women and men, who throughout the previous century had gradually acquired more and more rights in democratic societies. In short, members of the church in many nations were also members of societies that no longer accepted that a patrician class had a right to rule and make decisions for the rest of the society. It is hardly surprising that similar sentiments began to be transferred to the church.

The notion of a clerical elite privileged by arcane knowledge, language, and religious ceremony—to say nothing of gender and marital status—was perceived to be not only undemocratic, but a denial of the baptismal equality of every member of the church. One could argue, of course, that such views misunderstand the church's ordained ministry, but their emergence in the church was consistent with the convergence after the Council of a variety of factors: the Council's promotion of greater involvement by all the baptized in the activities of the church; the decline in the number of ordained ministers; and the perception that the Council had encouraged a new way of 'being church'.

In some instances, the immediate seat of the confusion was that the Council itself had promoted a certain vision but did not provide the wherewithal by which the church might understand how to implement that vision. Thus, for example, 'The Constitution on the Liturgy' emphasized worship as a communal celebration of the church, but did so in the context of a church that had no experience of understanding itself as a community and, therefore, did not know how to celebrate as a community.[76]

While the Council pursued the renewal of the church, it did not do so within the context of a clearly articulated theology of

[76] Rembert Weakland, 'Introduction', in Pierre Hegy (ed.), *The Church in the Nineties: Its Legacy, Its Future* (Collegeville, Minn.: Liturgical Press, 1993), p. xix.

reform or a theology of history that explained the relationship between the old and the new.[77] At first glance, that lacuna might appear to be of interest only to those concerned with theological niceties, but its practical impact emerges in stark relief when we consider that Vatican II introduced change into a church that, as has been illustrated above, not only had no lived memory of how to change, but was also suspicious of change as a threat to the faith and order of the church. In addition, the language of the Council was often alien to the prevailing practice of the church. Thus, for example, the Council used words like 'dialogue', words that had horizontal implications, even though the experience of Catholics was that everything in the church operated vertically.[78]

As has already been discussed, Vatican II's reforming vision emerged from a desire to bring the church into a more healthy relationship with the modern world. In this it was unique, as other significant moments of reform in the history of the church had focused on responding to an explicit controversy or crisis. In the past, there was a specific issue, clearly delineated opponents, who were demonized through anathemas, and a band of supporters committed to ensuring that the proposed reforms became the standard by which the church lived. All of these were absent at Vatican II: it was irenic, not confrontationalist; it was wide-ranging, not focused on a single issue; it was pastoral, not doctrinal; and it did not give birth to a group whose very survival depended on the Council's reforms taking root in the church.[79]

---

[77] For a detailed discussion of Vatican II's approach to history, see John O'Malley, 'Reform, Historical Consciousness and Vatican II's *Aggiornamento*', *Theological Studies*, 32 (1971), 573–601. For further insight into the dynamics (and divisions) within the Council—as well as for discussion of how those dynamics continue to shape the contemporary church—see Joseph Komonchak, 'Is Christ Divided? Dealing with Diversity and Disagreement', *Origins*, 33 (17 July 2003), 140–7.

[78] John O'Malley, 'Vatican II: Historical Perspectives on its Uniqueness', in Lucien Richard, Daniel Harrington, and John O'Malley (eds.), *Vatican II: The Unfinished Agenda—A Look to the Future* (New York: Paulist, 1987), 28.

[79] For a discussion of Vatican II's place in the history of reform in the church, see John O'Malley, 'Developments, Reforms, and Two Great Reformations: Towards an Historical Assessment of Vatican II', *Theological Studies*, 44 (1983), 373–406.

In addition to all of the above, it is significant that the initial reception of Vatican II took place in 'the Sixties'. Whether we locate the characteristic spirit of that era in rock music or the protest movement, it is indisputable that the 1960s were about change. In flux were perceptions of what constituted success and meaning in life, attitudes towards authority and structures, and the understanding of right and wrong. In short, just as the church was striving for a more creative response to modernity, the dimensions of 'postmodernity' were beginning to be evident—a discussion of the postmodern era will be a focus of Chapter 5—and having an impact on the church. Consequently, the church no longer offered a refuge from the turmoil of the wider culture, but actually reflected that culture in experiencing its own turmoil.

As we have seen, acceptance of authority and the proper ordering of the church were primary elements of Catholic ecclesiology in the period before Vatican II. Even if Vatican II situated authority within a broader context than had been done previously, it was anything but anarchic in its approach to the church's authority and structure. Indeed, the bishops at the Council would have had no expectation of a clash between the authority of the Pope and the faith of the members of the church. Such a clash, however, did eventuate.

Perhaps not surprisingly, the clash came in 1968, the archetypal year of the 1960s. In addition, the clash came over an issue that combined two themes prominent in debates throughout the 1960s: human sexuality and freedom. The issue, of course, was *Humanae vitae*, the encyclical in which Pope Paul VI (1963–78) ruled against the legitimacy of artificial means of birth control. In the present context, what is significant about the protests by theologians and other members of the church against *Humanae vitae* is their highlighting of the fact that authority in the church, even papal authority, was no longer unquestioned and unquestionable. As a result of this controversy, questions about the role of authority in the church, especially how it could provide leadership and challenge while being something other than absolute monarchy, became central to Catholic life. More broadly, the controversy around authority in the church indicated that reconsideration of the implications of belonging to a communion of faith had become necessary.

The other social development in the 1960s that was no less revelatory of the irreducible nexus between the church and world was the emergence of the women's movement. Not only did that movement jettison the conventional wisdom that women were the homemakers and men were the principal providers for their families, it also raised, and continues to raise, questions that relate to human sexuality and reproduction, as well as employment opportunities and policies. All of these have had an impact on the church.

As mentioned above, women in the church were perhaps the group with the most muted voice under the sacred canopy. Although women were esteemed as wives, mothers, or religious, and were elevated as models of a spirituality of trust and obedience, they had even less influence on the direction of the church than did non-ordained men. In particular, women had very little access to theological formation. In the generation since the Council, that has changed. As a result, issues of authority and structure, of human sexuality and reproduction, and even issues relating to the language of worship have all become more sensitive than ever before.

Taken together, all of the above factors form a picture of a church that is no longer a sacred canopy, under which neatness and harmony prevail. Nonetheless, the disarray of the first decades of the post-Vatican II period does not necessarily suggest a church in peril. Why, then, has such a description become appropriate?

As indicated at the beginning of the chapter, the designation of the church's contemporary situation as perilous is the product of an assessment of the inner life of the church. More than anything else, that assessment highlights the breaking down of communion within the church. That breakdown, in turn, reflects the lack of a shared, sustaining, and challenging, sense of Catholic identity, including the church's place in the world. Much of that breakdown has occurred because of divergent expectations in the post-Vatican II period.

On one hand, there are those for whom the 'phase of exuberance' declined into the 'phase of disappointment'.[80] Here, the regret is that the church's institutional inertia has resisted

---

[80] Kasper, *Theology and Church*, 167.

developing Vatican II's endorsement of collegial authority and greater participation of all of the baptized in the church's life. Indeed, the perception is that there has even been a retreat from the Council's openness, a retreat back into a more closed world:

The new Code of Canon Law [1983] shows that the ruling mentality has still not changed, nor come to accept the intentions of Vatican II. The juridical aspect still predominates in preaching and the sacraments, with emphasis on textual orthodoxy and faithful performance of the prescribed rites.[81]

The censure of liberation theology, the publication of the *Catechism of the Catholic Church* (1994), the nature of some episcopal appointments, a resistance to developments in biblical studies, a campaign to 'reform the reform' of liturgy, and trends among those entering seminaries, have also nurtured similar perceptions.[82] For many in the church, therefore, the sense of possibility that Vatican II represented has collapsed in the face of 'a wintry season' in which hope is under siege.[83]

On the other hand, there are those whose disillusionment with the post-Vatican II church leads them to regard contemporary Catholic life as impoverished, an impoverishment evident in a low level of religious knowledge, a diminished sense of

[81] Jose Comblin, *The Holy Spirit and Liberation*, tr. P. Burns (Maryknoll, NY: Orbis, 1989), 104.

[82] In the 1980s, the Congregation for the Doctrine of the Faith published two documents on the theme of 'liberation': the first, 'Instruction on Certain Aspects of the Theology of Liberation' (1984) was critical of the methods and emphases of that theology; the second 'Instruction on Christian Freedom and Liberation' (1986) was more positive towards the basic theme. For an assessment of the current state of biblical studies see Brendan Byrne, 'Scripture and Vatican II: A Very Incomplete Journey', *Compass*, 37 (2003), 3–9; for the current state of debate about the church's liturgical life see Gerard Moore, 'Fording the Impasse: Beyond the "Reform of the Reform" of the Liturgy', *Compass*, 37 (2003), 9–15; for a description of the implication of the style of contemporary seminarians, see Richard Marzheuser, 'A New Generation is on the Rise in Seminaries', *Seminary Journal*, 5 (1999), 21–31, and David Whalen, 'The Emergence of the Contemporary Traditionalist', *Review for Religious*, 61 (2002), 585–93.

[83] Karl Rahner, *Faith in a Wintry Season: Conversations and Interviews with Karl Rahner in the Last Years of his Life*, ed. Harvey Egan (New York: Crossroad, 1990), 189–200.

the transcendent, and either a rejection of or, at least, insuffi-
cient respect for, authority. Thus, to take but one example of
such a critique, much of the post-Vatican II liturgical and
spiritual life of Catholics is seen to be 'beige', to lack the
vibrancy, depth, and colour evident in what prevailed prior to
the Council.[84] For those unhappy with contemporary Catholic
life, it seems that, as a result of the importation into the church
of attitudes and values from the surrounding culture, there has
been a dilution of richness of the Catholic tradition: depth has
given way to blandness, which is unlikely to appeal to anyone
who is conscientiously seeking God and a tangible experience
of human communion.

When carried out without a prevailing spirit of justice and
generosity, clashes between those two conflicting views contribute to the church's perilous state. Such clashes divert
energy and attention from what is, perhaps, a more serious
cause of decline: the fact that, as the *Called to be Catholic*
document noted, many Catholics exist on the margins of the
church. This marginality is evident in their non-involvement in
worship, but also in a limited understanding of the purpose of
the church, and, most fundamentally, in uncertainty about
their relationship with the God of Jesus Christ and its connection to the church.[85]

THE PRESENT CHALLENGE

Clearly, then, there is an urgent need to consider how we might
'be church' today in response to the present perilous situation,
how we might nurture a communion of reconciled diversity and
engender positive engagement with the world. Those requirements, however, do not mean that we must design a church
different from what any other generation of Christians has
ever considered. In fact, today's primary challenge is the re-
reception of our tradition in the light of the present.

The next chapter will attempt to elucidate aspects of a theology of the church that might meet that need. That goal does

---

[84] See, for example, Robert Barron, 'Beyond Beige Catholicism', *Church*,
16 (2000), 8–9.

[85] Bernardin and Lipscomb, *Catholic Common Ground Initiative*, 38.

not imply that this book presents itself as holding the key that will free the church from its contemporary peril or dissolve all divisions within the church. Indeed, nothing in the following chapters will even suggest that such a magic key might exist. The book, however, does seek to find hope in a positive 're-reception' of the Christian tradition in regard to the church, especially as that tradition was articulated at Vatican II. It promotes also the willingness to embrace risk, which is essential to faith. More than anything else, what follows will emphasize that authentic ecclesial faith is a permanent project, one that challenges every member of the church to ongoing conversion.

2

An Undreamed of Possibility for Love

Definitions and descriptions of 'the church' can conceal more than they reveal. This is evident when analyses of the church's educational or welfare activities, its liturgical traditions, or its systems of governance treat those subjects as if they illuminated the full reality of 'the church'. Although each of those themes focuses on something that is important, the differences between them imply that all of them capture only an aspect of the church. In the hope of formulating a more comprehensive theology of the church, this chapter will seek to answer the fundamental question: Why the church?

A helpful answer to that question will be one that not only casts light on particular features of the church, but also situates the church in a larger framework: God's relationship to humanity. With that requirement in mind, it is possible to develop a 'job description' that details the features that must characterize any theological approach that professes to offer insight into the identity and purpose of the church.

First, it will shed light on the claim that is foundational to the self-understanding of those within the church: that the church exists because of God—more specifically, the God of Jesus Christ mediated through the Holy Spirit—and exists to be about the things of God. As a result, it should even be able to clarify why disagreements between members of the church often reach high levels of intensity. Secondly, it will be informative about what might draw people to the church and sustain their lives as members of the ecclesial community. In so doing, a helpful theology will also indicate something about the influence that membership of the church might have on how people understand themselves, their relationship with others, and their engagement with life in the wider world. Thirdly, it will explain the church's multifaceted identity. This means that such a theology must not only clarify why 'the church' can contain so many elements, that theology must also provide criteria by which to assess whether particular expressions of the church do actually manifest what they claim to embody. Fourthly, it will offer some orientation to the future; this will require it to be enlightening about how 'the church' might respond creatively to its present situation. In short, such a theology will make clear that the church is more than an historical artefact, that it is something other than a political party, sporting club, or any other group, but also that its relationship to God is not an excuse for non-involvement with the concerns of humanity.

Clearly, then, any definition or description of 'the church' that can respond to those stipulations must have texture and nuance. In its attempt to fulfil such conditions, this book will make use of both a contemporary and an ancient metaphor for the church. The contemporary metaphor comes from Juan Luis Segundo, a twentieth-century liberation theologian, who speaks of the church as 'an undreamed of possibility for love'.[1] The ancient contribution is from Hippolytus, a third-century theologian, who describes the church as 'the place where the Spirit flourishes'.[2] Although not a commentary on either Segundo or Hippolytus, this book will use their phrases to frame its exposition of the church.

While there always remains the prospect that these metaphors too will conceal more than they reveal about the church, they have the virtue of suggesting something other than a

---

[1] Segundo, *The Community Called Church*, 82–3. Segundo argues that the message of Matt. 25: 31–46 ('I was hungry and you gave me food . . .') sets the standard for how members of the church are to live. When members of the church are faithful to that message, they manifest the church as 'an undreamed of possibility for love'. Segundo observes too that when they live by some other standard, members of the church actually endanger their prospects for salvation since, unlike the people in the parable, they will not be able to claim either that they did not understand how they were supposed to act in the world or where it was that they would encounter Jesus.

[2] Hippolytus, 'The Treatise on the Apostolic Tradition', no. 35. This phrase, which Hippolytus applies particularly to the worshipping assembly, is used in the section on the church in the *Catechism of the Catholic Church*, no. 749. Gregory Dix translates the phrase as 'the place where the Spirit abounds', see G. Dix (ed.), *The Treatise on the Apostolic Tradition* (London: SPCK, 1968), 62.

one-dimensional approach to the church. In fact, the claim of this book is that they not only illuminate the purpose and identity of the church, but also indicate the qualities that ought to colour both relationships within the church and the relationship of the church to the wider world. Moreover, they can challenge members of the church to a breadth of vision and a sense of possibility, which, in turn, might facilitate the development of alternatives to 'the peril'. The two metaphors are also rich in ecumenical potential, since the Christian church can most effectively reveal God's Holy Spirit, the expression of God's unifying love, only when differences between Christians are no longer church-dividing.

Although the focus of this book is on the Roman Catholic tradition of ecclesial faith, this does not mean that its discussion of 'the church' will have no resonances for Christians from other traditions. The divided state of the Christian church means that there are aspects of the Roman Catholic tradition not shared by other Christians, but does not imply that Catholics move in an exclusive orbit. In addition, Catholics can be authentic to their tradition, which professes the unity of the church as an irreducible element of Christian faith, only if they embrace the challenge of reconciliation with other Christians.

Whatever virtues are proper to the two metaphors that are central to this book's theology of the church, a hard-headed critic might suggest that they are so vague as to be devoid of content or so unconventional as to be incapable of accommodating what people usually associate with 'the church'. In an effort to establish both the provenance of the description of the church as 'an undreamed of possibility for love' and to indicate why it is appropriate and helpful, this chapter will argue that the Christian church exists to be a symbol of the God made present in human history through Jesus Christ and the Holy Spirit. As such, the church acts as both a guarantor and a unique means of access to God's love. On the validity of that claim hangs the church's appeal, the willingness to embrace the risk of ecclesial faith, and the passion to advocate and pursue the authenticity of the church.

As the first step towards establishing this chapter's thesis, the next section will explore the notion of 'symbol'. The remaining sections will apply the theology of the symbol to

the story of God's self-revelation, especially the revelation in
Jesus Christ, which leads to the role of the Holy Spirit in
establishing the identity and purpose of the church. Chapter 3
will develop in detail the implications of understanding the
church in terms of the Holy Spirit. Chapter 4 will then investigate how those aspects of the church that loom large in popular
perception—institution, authority, and tradition—might relate
to the church's existence as the symbol of God's Spirit in
human history.

SYMBOLS AND SELF-REVELATION

In everyday speech, there is a tendency to discount the importance of symbols—'It's *only* a symbol'. This tendency owes
much to the fact that 'symbol' resists easy analysis. Symbols
are not a particular classification of objects, akin to animals,
vegetables, and minerals; in fact, symbols, *as* symbols, exist
only when they fulfil their defining function. Symbols are the
means by which we come to experience and know what we
cannot experience and know more directly.[3] While signs point
to something that is other than themselves, symbols introduce
us to something that is inseparable from the symbol itself.[4]

Symbols make accessible to our senses, which play an indispensable role in the dynamics of human knowing, what is not
directly 'sensible'. Words, objects, even persons, can operate as
symbols. In so doing, they have more levels of meaning than
'the univocal language of science'.[5] Thus, for example, a
person, object, or word can make present—symbolize—qualities such as 'love', 'courage', or 'nationhood', which we cannot
know 'in themselves'.

Since symbols involve one reality that is inseparable from
another, there are two dangers that can frustrate the effective
communication by the symbol of what it symbolizes. On one
hand, there is a danger that we might fixate on the surface
reality as if that were the whole story—this is one of the flaws

---

[3] Karl Rahner, 'The Theology of the Symbol', *Theological Investigations*, 4,
tr. K. Smyth (New York: Crossroad, 1982), 225.

[4] Louis-Marie Chauvet, *The Sacraments: The Word of God at the Mercy of
the Body* (Collegeville, Minn.: Pueblo, 2001), 72–5.

[5] Ibid. 77.

in racism and other '-isms' that portray life as if it were one-dimensional. On the other hand, there is a danger that we might fixate on what is symbolized, as if this could exist without the symbol that makes it present—the flaw in the desire to nurture 'the human spirit' while neglecting the human body. A proper appreciation of symbols, therefore, requires not only openness to possibilities beyond the empirical, but also respect for humanity's need for the concrete and tangible. Although symbols are radically ambiguous, they remain our sole means of access to what transcends the quantifiable. In other words, there is an inextricable link between symbols and the revelation of mystery.

While 'mystery' implies something hidden from us, the meaningfulness of the term suggests also the revelation of something, the turning towards us of what we are capable of knowing, even if we cannot know it exhaustively or possess it definitively.[6] In other words, our capacity to refer to mystery indicates that we have some awareness of it, an awareness that is entirely the result of the self-revelation of 'the mystery'. Even this self-disclosure, however, does not erase mystery, reduce it to limited dimensions, or obliterate its 'otherness'.

In being the gateway through which mystery becomes present to us, symbols enable us to experience that reality is not one-dimensional. Paradoxically, then, symbols open for us a depth of reality that our senses are incapable of apprehending directly, but they do so by presenting that reality to our senses. Those considerations apply pre-eminently to how we come to know God, the ultimate mystery and the one who is totally 'other':

'God' is itself the final word before wordless and worshipful silence in the face of the ineffable mystery. It is the word which must be spoken at the conclusion of all speaking... ['God'] is an almost ridiculously exhausting and demanding word. If we were not hearing it in *this* way... we would have heard something which has nothing in common with the true word 'God' but its phonetic sound.... The concept 'God' is not a grasp of God by which one masters the mys-

---

[6] Kasper, *Theology and Church*, 25. Kasper applies this idea particularly to God's self-revelation.

tery, but it is letting oneself be grasped by the mystery which is ever present and yet ever distant.[7]

Such a description of God might suggest either that it is impossible for human beings to know God or that how we know God defies any attempt to account for it. The idea that knowledge of God is impossible for us derives primarily from the fact that God is not corporeal: if our senses cannot have a direct experience of God, we cannot know God. Similarly, the difference between God and humanity is the basis for the claim that any human knowledge of God must be unlike all other instances of human knowing: God, who transcends the limitations to which human beings are subject, could determine ways of being known that are specific to God alone, ways that do not involve the usual dynamics of human knowing. That conclusion might seem to protect divine freedom, but does so at the cost of erecting two obstacles to the possibility of portraying faith in God, which includes its ecclesial dimension, as a reasonable exercise of human freedom.

First, human beings are likely to regard as capricious a God about whom they could have no sure knowledge. Thus, a God who was utterly unknowable, as likely to be malevolent as benign, would inspire more fear than love, more doubt than faith. Secondly, if our knowledge of God required the abandonment of the faculties and qualities that define us as human beings, including our rationality, then faith in God would be nothing other than fideism, which, as the previous chapter discussed, is an uncritical attitude that rejects a role for human reason in the processes of faith. While fideism seeks to ensure that human reason does not falsely claim sovereignty over God, it does so at the cost of sacrificing the possibility of demonstrating that faith in God could be authentically human. Faced with no option but fideism, it is likely that people would perceive the self-surrender required for faith as an inappropriate use of human freedom, that they would even see it as harmful to human flourishing.

In its presentation of human knowledge of God, the Second Vatican Council, drawing on an oft-reaffirmed tradition,

---

[7] Karl Rahner, *Foundations of Christian Faith*, tr. W. Dych (New York: Seabury, 1978), 51–4. The emphasis is Rahner's.

emphasized not only that God is knowable, but also that our knowledge of God does not bypass normal human dynamics. While the Council stressed the freedom of God's initiative in the process of revelation, it insisted also on both the historical nature of God's self-revelation and its symbolic dimension:

> The pattern of [God's] revelation unfolds through deeds and words bound together by an inner dynamism, in such a way that God's works, effected during the course of the history of salvation, show forth and confirm the doctrine and realities signified by the words, while the words in turn proclaim the works and throw light on the meaning hidden in them.[8]

As already indicated, symbols, which our senses can experience, provide a means of access to what we cannot know more directly. If, therefore, we can encounter God via a symbol—or, in the more explicitly theological language that will recur throughout this book, a sacrament—then it is possible for human beings to talk about God in ways that that are meaningful, in ways that do not contradict the usual processes of human knowing, despite the fact that God is not corporeal. As an illustration of what this might entail, we can turn to St Paul: 'Ever since the creation of the world [God's] eternal power and divine nature, invisible though they are, have been understood and seen through the things [God] has made' (Rom. 1: 20)[9]. For Paul, then, it was God's symbolic self-disclosure in the natural world that made it possible for all people to encounter God.

Nor does its reliance on symbols imply that our knowledge of God bears no relationship to other instances of human knowing. As suggested above, our knowledge of the deepest qualities of human life, as also of other people, is unimaginable without symbols. Indeed, our knowledge of God, who is the ultimate mystery, the other who is Other, can help us to understand more of the dynamics of interpersonal knowing, since each person is both 'other' and 'mystery'.

---

[8] Vatican II, 'Dogmatic Constitution on Divine Revelation' (*Dei verbum*), *DV* no. 2.

[9] This, and all subsequent biblical quotations, are from the *New Revised Standard Version*.

Although we can gain a limited amount of information about another person by observation—height, weight, eye colour, and so on—such features do not disclose the 'self', the deepest reality, of that person. In fact, if we want to know another as a self rather than as an object, if we want our knowledge of a person to be more than mere information about them, we require their free self-revelation or self-communication. As with our knowledge of God, then, fully human knowledge of another person has its source in their willingness to reveal—to symbolize—through their words and actions, what otherwise remains closed to us.

While symbols might provide a means by which we can expound God's self-revelation in terms attuned to the dynamics of human knowing, there remains a significant difficulty: how is it that something finite could be the symbol of God who is infinite? Similarly, there might be concern about how this self-disclosure of God meshes with the normal functioning of the universe, with the laws of physics, or with human history. In other words, we might wonder whether symbolic communication implies a cinematic God who bursts spectacularly into human history in earthquakes, wind, and fire. More fundamentally, perhaps, we might also wonder what it is that God communicates to us, and what difference it might make to how we live.

What is at issue here is the relationship of God to the created order. If the physical universe is autonomous, if the principles of causality that are internal to that universe furnish an explanation for everything, then it seems that God is locked outside. As a result, our knowledge of God must involve some irruption by God into that closed world. While such irruptions might express the unrestrained power of God available for our benefit, they also reintroduce the spectre of an unpredictable God, one who might, perhaps for some whim, disrupt all that we know of life.

The notion of a closed universe reflects the view that God as creator must be simply an instrument that causes something to exist, but has no relationship to the finished product: God, then, like an artisan, would complete a task and move on. An alternative approach, one that is more satisfactory in its presentation of both God and the working of the world, is to argue that creation is the self-expression of God, that it is not something God 'does', but is the revelation of God, the symbol that makes God known. As a result, God, without being an object in the created world, has an abiding relationship to the whole created order. Paradoxically, then, the God who transcends the finite universe is always immanent to it.[10]

Such a presence of God would imply, as St Paul observed, that the whole of the created order could be an avenue of encounter with God. In short, God's abiding relationship to creation means that the whole created universe can be a symbol for God. The universe is not God, but God is made present through it for us, who are also not God but are capable of relating to God, who sustains our existence. Thus, the primary theological task is not to insert God into an autonomous world, but to highlight the existence of the world as the permanent venue of God's symbolic presence.

The idea that the material world symbolizes God who is spirit, implies that even matter must have 'spirituality', itself the expression of God's creative self-revelation.[11] There must also, however, be degrees both of that presence of God and of the spirituality that allows created things to respond to God. This would account for the difference between seemingly inanimate objects, whose 'spirituality' is far from obvious, and human beings, in whom this spirituality is most evident in our reason, which allows us to transcend the limits of our materiality, to perceive God immanent in all of creation, and to enter into a relationship with God.[12]

If every relationship that we have expands the limits of our finiteness and offers us possibilities that we cannot provide for ourselves, a relationship with God offers us the possibilities that the Christian tradition of faith has always named 'salva-

---

[10] For examples of contemporary understandings of the relationship between God and the universe see, Karl Rahner, 'Natural Science and Reasonable Faith', *Theological Investigations*, 21, tr. H. Riley (New York: Crossroad, 1988), 16–41; John Wright, 'Theology, Philosophy, and the Natural Sciences', *Theological Studies*, 52 (1991), 651–68; Denis Edwards, *Jesus and the Cosmos* (Mahwah, NJ: Paulist, 1991).

[11] Karl Rahner, 'Immanent and Transcendent Consummation of the World', *Theological Investigations*, 10, tr. D. Bourke (New York: Seabury, 1977), 273–89.

[12] See Franz Josef van Beeck, 'Divine Revelation: Intervention or Self-Communication', *Theological Studies*, 52 (1991), 207–8.

tion', a term that encapsulates the fullness of life and the overcoming of all obstacles to that fullness. Such fullness implies communion with God, whose creative power, as exemplified in the Book of Genesis (Gen. 1: 26–7; 2: 15–23), not only brings us into being, but also establishes the possibility of transcending our finiteness.

The offer of such a possibility, as well as our response to it, does not occur only within the realm of the specifically 'religious'. What is significant is that we do not have to reach God, but that God comes to meet us where we are. God's self-communication takes place without us ceasing to be human or part of the created world:

The world becomes a locus of sacramentality at a given existential moment when a human person perceives and responds to the self-revealing God, but the human person does this in and through the uniqueness of his or her own sedimentary history and his or her own determination of significance.[13]

Were there to be contact between God and ourselves only when God made an unpredictable, albeit spectacular, entry into our history, God could not be central to how we think about everyday life. Consequently, God would be corralled within a specialist enclosure—'religion'—that most people would visit, if at all, only in extraordinary circumstances. From there, it is a small step to the conviction that a person's involvement in anything religious, including the church, must be directly proportional to their exit from the rest of life, from 'the real world'.

In its richest manifestations, the Christian tradition has not only resisted any tendency to restrict God to a specialist enclosure, it has also done more than identify creation as a symbol of God: it has insisted on the possibility of a specific, albeit still symbolic, revelation of God, one that enables human beings, collectively and individually, to have a relationship with God. The following sections will argue that that relationship has its grounding in human history, especially in Jesus Christ, and also that it has the whole of life, including the fullness of life in the eternal God, as its ambit. As we shall see, it is those features that provide both the basis on which it is meaningful to

---

[13] Kenan Osborne, *Christian Sacraments in a Postmodern World: A Theology for the Third Millennium* (Mahwah, NJ: Paulist Press, 1999), 149.

describe the church as 'an undreamed of possibility for love' and insight into how the church can realize its mission in the world.

Before addressing the issue of God's specific revelation, it is important to discuss how it is that we come to apprehend more than the surface level of a symbol. To do this, we need to explore the dynamics of faith.

THE SELF-SURRENDER OF FAITH

Since contemporary Western cultures tend to locate 'faith' only within the sphere of 'religion', the sphere of the profoundly optional, it is easy to assume that faith concerns few people or 'the real world'. Faith, however, is not about religion alone, not merely an option for those so inclined, and not disconnected from life. In fact, the need for faith is universal; it touches not simply every person, but every aspect of our lives. Faith, then, is an irreducible element of our humanity. Most particularly, the possibility of human flourishing is inseparable from the need for faith.

The centrality of faith derives from our finiteness as human beings. As a result of this finiteness, we can neither know everything nor cater for all our own needs. We need others, therefore, not only to show us possibilities, but also to provide us with what we cannot achieve on our own. Faith is the means by which we appropriate what we cannot provide for ourselves. Faith, then, is not a defective way of knowing, but a necessary aspect of our engagement with the world. As such, it is a way of affirming that life is not absurd.[14] Faith involves the surrender of ourselves to what offers us possibilities, but exceeds our capacity for control. As a result, faith contains an ineradicable element of risk. Our finiteness means that we cannot know in advance what the outcome will be when we entrust ourselves to another. This 'unknowing' and, its corollary, the risk inseparable from the need to surrender to the unknowable, are fundamental aspects of faith, but also of what it means to be human:

Faith's home is in heaven. She retires from the comfortable, sleeps lightly, eyes heavy with wanderlust. *Your* world is not *the* world, she whispers, which insists on being more, yet again more, and different,

---

[14] Kasper, *An Introduction to Christian Faith*, 75–6.

sometimes intensely and mysteriously more foreign that you can grasp or tolerate at once.[15]

The risk involved in faith does not mean that faith is irrational, especially since it can be a considered response to what we have experienced. On the other hand, while we might weigh carefully our possible actions, while we might consider the particular trajectory of all the evidence on which we rely, such discernment does not spare us the burden of decision-making, of committing ourselves, surrendering ourselves to one possible action or another.[16] Such decision-making is burdensome because it is inseparable from the need to give ourselves over to what we cannot control. This surrender highlights our vulnerability, since the outcome of our act of faith might be to our disadvantage. Every act of faith, therefore, underscores the vulnerability that is inseparable from being human.

The risk involved in faith might incline us towards wanting to live without it. While many people reject religious faith, we could live entirely without faith only if we were able to be as inert as rocks. Faith and human flourishing are inseparable because the latter derives from the embrace of possibilities that only others can provide; that embrace is an act of faith. Faith involves reaching out for what lies beyond our present situation, for what is 'more' than our present situation in life. As such, every act of faith embodies our desire to transcend the finitude of this world, a desire 'to be absolutely'.[17] This suggests the orientation of faith towards faith in God, the one who transcends the limits of time and space. It indicates also that faith is always more than an intellectual attitude; faith involves us in making choices, in taking action. Despite the fact that we cannot provide indisputable evidence to support the action we are taking, faith must be unconditional, as it requires the commitment of our whole self.[18]

[15] Michael Heher, 'Why We Still Need Theologians', in David Kendall and Stephen Davis (eds.), *The Convergence of Theology* (Mahwah, NJ: Paulist, 2001), 68. The emphasis is Heher's.

[16] John Macquarrie, *In Search of Humanity* (New York: Crossroad, 1983), 164–5.

[17] Roger Haight, *Dynamics of Theology* (Mahwah, NJ: Paulist, 1990), 21.

[18] Cf. David Pailin, *The Anthropological Character of Theology* (Cambridge: Cambridge University Press, 1990), 8.

Since so much of the 'more' of life that we cannot provide for ourselves is offered to us via symbols, there is no alternative to surrender to the symbol if we are to appropriate what it symbolizes. This surrender is an act of faith. Indeed, in its fullest realization, this self-surrender is an act of love. In authentic love, we open the whole of ourselves—the symbol and the symbolized—to another and we desire also to know the whole of the other—the symbol and the symbolized. We do this in order to enter into communion with the other, not to absorb the other into us—'for the lover loves and affirms the other precisely *as* other, certainly not seeking simply to absorb the beloved into his or her peculiar way of being'.[19] This would suggest that interpersonal love is the paradigmatic human act, the act by which we seek to make present the whole of who we are and to enter into communion with the whole reality of another person. That understanding of love as communion applies particularly to our faith in God, where the goal is not absorption into God, which would involve our obliteration, but communion and friendship with God.[20]

It is impossible, however, to realize such love without the willingness to surrender oneself, to embrace the ambiguity of the symbol. That self-surrender, of course, is not without risk or vulnerability as the object of our faith, of our self-surrender, might prove to be unworthy of it. This is why love, an act that involves the surrender of our whole self, is so demanding:

in this self-abandonment, once all antecedent considerations, verifications, and demands of reasonableness and legitimation are posited—one ventures more, and *must* venture more than these grounds seem to justify.... Every trusting, loving relationship to another human being has an uncancellable 'plus' on the resolution-and-decision side of the balance sheet—as over against the reflective side, the side that tallies up the justifiability and reasonableness of such risk and venture.[21]

[19] Karl Rahner, *The Love of Jesus and the Love of Neighbour*, tr. R. Barr (Middlegreen, Slough: St Paul Publications, 1983), 21. The emphasis is Rahner's.

[20] Kasper, *Theology and Church*, 31.

[21] Rahner, *The Love of Jesus and the Love of Neighbour*, 17. The emphasis is Rahner's.

The fact that love involves risk, the fact that it thereby engages aspects of ourselves that we do not always employ, strengthens rather than diminishes the contention that love is the paradigm of human action. Conversely, if we refuse to love, or if our efforts to love flounder because we insist on accepting only the symbol or the symbolized, then our humanity does not reach its full potential and, like the chorus in T. S. Eliot's *Murder in the Cathedral*, we are left merely 'living and partly living'.[22]

If a loving relationship, a relationship built on our surrender to the self-revelation of the other, is the highest realization of human action, its most profound expression is in our surrender to the God, whom we can neither control nor know independently of the symbols of God's self-communication. While this self-surrender is never less than a risk, it is also a response to what we have experienced and come to understand about God not just as individuals, but also as social beings who learn from others. That we can consider whether to make the surrender of faith highlights that faith in God need not be fideism, that it can be compatible with the exercise of our reason, rather than the denial of it.[23] Although such discernment will not eliminate the risk of faith, it does ensure that faith is less of a leap into the dark than a leap into what we hope will be the light.[24] Faith in God, then, can be a legitimate exercise of human freedom, rather than the abrogation of it. Indeed, it can be authentic faith only when it is a response that we choose freely.

This analysis of faith as self-surrender has implications for an understanding of the church: if the church is a symbol for God's self-revelation in human history, then the fullness of what it offers will not be accessible independently of such a self-surrender. What this might mean, and what the obstacles to it might be, will emerge later in this chapter and in Chapter 3.

---

[22] T. S. Eliot, *Murder in the Cathedral* (London: Faber & Faber, 1958), 19.

[23] The compatibility of faith and reason has been affirmed strongly by the Catholic tradition. The most recent major discussion of the relationship between faith and reason is Pope John Paul II's 1998 encyclical *Fides et Ratio*.

[24] For the notion of hope as surrender of oneself to what we trust is the source of possibility see Karl Rahner, 'On the Theology of Hope', in *Theological Investigations*, 10, tr. D Bourke (New York: Seabury, 1977), especially 251–6.

Before moving on to focus specifically on God's self-revelation in human history, it is important to acknowledge one further aspect of faith. So far, the emphasis has been on the nexus between being human and the need for faith, on the dynamics of the act of faith, and on the risk and vulnerability inseparable from faith. A comprehensive analysis of faith, however, requires some reference to the impact that context might have on the possibility of faith. It will be clear that context is important: particular moments of history or particular societies seem to make it either easier or more difficult not only to appraise positively what faith in God or the church might mean, but also to move towards acts of faith.

Nonetheless, even an environment that seems conducive to faith—because of, for example, high levels of religious practice—does not make the surrender of faith either easy or inevitable. Nor does the opposite necessarily apply when society at large has little sympathy with religious faith. There will be more detailed exploration of this issue in Chapter 5, which will investigate specifically what influence the present moment of history might have on the possibility of faith, on commitment to God and, derivatively, to the church.

Having examined the factors that would express a healthy human relationship with God, we need now to look at the dynamics that actually apply in the story of the relationship that we claim to have with God. The following section will portray that relationship as both inviting and enabling human beings to live well. In order to do so, our relationship with God must not only be able to respond to our failures and ambivalences, it must also promote a deeper involvement with life. This means that it is human history, rather than 'religion' in a narrow sense, which must be a primary venue both for the presence and action of God and for our response to God.

GOD'S SYMBOLIC SELF-REVELATION

The oldest literary strands of the Judaeo-Christian tradition locate the relationship between God and humanity at the centre of life itself. For the writers of the Book of Genesis, that relationship was not a philosophical problem requiring analysis, it was simply the core of life. Although Genesis begins in

classic story-telling style—'Once upon a time . . . / In the beginning . . .'—it aims to do more than set the scene for a single
incident. In fact, it wants to identify God as the source of all
that is and, consequently, to establish that a right relationship
with God is fundamental to human well-being.

Thus, God's self-communication to humanity, and humanity's response to it, is the thread connecting the diverse collection of books that we know variously as 'The Old Testament',
'The First Testament', or 'The Hebrew Bible'. What is primary to that self-revelation is the invitation to a relationship
with God, not the passing on of information about God. The
relationship with God is expressed in a covenant, which God
not only initiates, but also renews consistently when humans
show that they are incapable of sustaining it.[25] Nor does the
covenant focus exclusively on religion in a cultic sense: relationship with God is inextricably linked with relationship with
others and the shape of everyday life.

In addition, God's covenant is with a particular people who
understand their history as the locus of God's presence, even
though God remains transcendent. God's self-revelation, then,
is inseparable from the history of that people. The people know
God through charismatic patriarchs and judges, who oversee
the emergence of a people to be God's own, through the Law,
which orders right relationships both with God and between
people, and through the prophets, who interpret history and
culture in the light of the covenant. In short, the people know
God through concrete symbols, which emerge from everyday
life and invite engagement with that same life.

By means of history, law, poetry, moral exhortation, and
other genres, the scriptures map the relationship between
God and Israel. The story of that relationship manifests the
dynamics of authentic interpersonal communication. That
communication, although it involves always more than one
person, begins with 'the generous inner freedom of the mature',
which initiates and sustains personal presence to another.[26]

---

[25] The book of Genesis details covenants between God and Noah (Gen. 9:
1–17), God and Abraham (Gen. 15: 18–21; 17: 2), and with Moses, the
representative of the people of Israel (Gen. 19: 1–24: 8).

[26] van Beeck, 'Divine Revelation', 217.

The influence of the mentor enables the younger or less mature to embark on the process of self-discovery and self-expression, which entails awareness of self, self-correction, conversion, and growth:

> Encounters in which significant others reveal themselves to us are appreciated by us only to the extent that encountering them, we find ourselves revealed to ourselves . . . encounters in which we meet significant others as truly other are inseparable from authentic self-experience.[27]

As a result of such encounters, our life in the world becomes an affirming witness of the contribution made by significant others. We live, therefore, not with 'functional indebtedness' to them, but with 'grateful self-awareness' of those significant others.[28] This can involve us attributing to significant others things that they did not actually do or say, but which we cannot imagine ourselves doing or understanding without them. As a result, we do not see their self-communication as something that comes from outside, but as something immanent, not as the communication of information, but as the experience of finding our deeper selves engaged and enhanced.[29]

This means that the benchmark of authentic self-communication, and human relationship, is not 'Big Brother', who dominates every aspect of the other and whose communication aims at control, but parental love, which gives freely to the child, aims at the emergence of the child, and promotes a relationship with the child, a relationship within which the child remains free and 'other'. Within such a relationship, children come to know themselves, feel free to express themselves, to learn, to acknowledge failure, and to begin anew after failure. Children can also recognize how much they have received from their parents, cherish the indelible 'stamp' of their parents that marks all that they are and do, but know too that they are free, that they are distinct from their parents, and that their parents do not seek to absorb them.

It is hardly surprising, then, that the love of a parent for a child resounds through the descriptions of God's relationship to Israel. The language is often poignant, capturing the com-

---

[27] van Beeck, 'Divine Revelation', 218.   [28] Ibid.   [29] Ibid. 219.

mitment that does not falter, even in the face of the child's fickleness:

> When Israel was a child, I loved him,
> and out of Egypt I called my son.
>
> The more I called them,
> the more they went from me,
> they kept sacrificing to the Baals,
> and offering incense to idols.
>
> Yet it was I who taught Ephraim to walk,
> I took them up in my arms;
> but they did not know that I healed them.
>
> I led them with cords of human kindness,
> with bands of love.
> I was to them like those who lift infants to their cheeks.
> I bent down to them and fed them. (Hos. 11: 1–4)

The story of the Old Testament is the story of Israel coming to understand more and more of God. This understanding, however, is not the product of clinical experimentation or academic research, but of learning from their own experience, their own history. Like the relationship between parent and child, the relationship between God and Israel moves through numerous phases: the initial stages of the parent's exuberant self-giving and the child's total dependence; a growth in the child's desire for independence and, the corollary of that desire, resentment at being the child rather than the adult/parent; the child blaming the parent for misfortunes that were actually the result of the child's own choices and actions; the child feeling that its failings have forced the parent to turn away definitively; and the child coming to recognize the need for change in its life in order to facilitate appropriation of the love and self-giving of the parent, which is not only crucial to the child's well-being, but, always available, even if the child cannot always accept it.

The books of the Old Testament highlight God's passion for Israel and the intensity of God's self-giving to Israel. While that self-giving takes place without obliterating the freedom of Israel to reject it, it is not dependent on Israel's acceptance. In other words, God who gives birth to Israel remains faithful to Israel. What God seeks is the welfare of Israel, the key to which is a right relationship with God and neighbour. Over and over,

God encourages Israel to a way of living that reflects trust in the God who has given the people life and assures them a secure future. As Israel changes, as it grows, learns—learning that occurs, often, via a process involving the rejection of God and a subsequent recognition of the need for conversion—and encounters new situations that call for new responses, so also is there a development in the symbols of God's presence to Israel. Thus, there is movement from the diffuse presence of God in nature, to a closer, more explicit presence in the Law, and, ultimately, a more personal presence in the prophets, who offer guidance or challenge in the context of changes in Israel's circumstances.

God's self-communication to Israel, then, is something other than a once-for-all, one-size-fits-all event: it is a presence attuned to the needs and the capacity of those who receive it. This fact not only establishes a history for God's self-communication, it creates the expectation that there is more to come. This 'more' also concerns the relationship between God and Israel. The longing of Israel was for certainty that God would always be with them. That desire for certainty had its origins in Israel's fear that God would ultimately abandon them on account of their sinfulness and ambivalence towards God. This fear of Israel became palpable in particular moments of its history, such as the Exile and destruction of the Temple by the Babylonians, when God seemed not merely distant, but angry and vindictive. In such an environment, the prophetic word promised Israel a saviour, a Messiah who would be the guarantee that their future was secure with God and would make an unbreakable covenant between God and the hearts of the people (Isa. 60–3; Jer. 31: 1–34; Ezek. 36: 16–38).

This Messiah or saviour, however, was not to be merely a cipher, but the ultimate symbol of God's self-communication and commitment to the relationship with Israel. Since the Messiah had the unique task of being the symbol of God's irrevocable commitment to humanity, the unsurpassable expression of God's self-communication, it suggests that the identity of the Messiah as symbol was also unique:

The whole movement of this history of God's self-communication lives by virtue of its moving towards its goal or climax in the events by which it becomes irreversible, and hence precisely by virtue of what we are calling the absolute saviour. Therefore, this saviour, who constitutes the climax of God's self-communication to the world, must be at the same time *both* the absolute promise of God to spiritual creatures as a whole *and* acceptance of this self-communication by the saviour for otherwise, of course, history could not have reached its irreversible phase. Only then is there an absolutely irrevocable self-communication on both sides and only then is it present in the world in a historical and communicable way.[30]

In order to elucidate that claim, we need to turn to God's self-communication in Jesus, the one whom the Christian tradition names the Saviour and the study of whom—Christology—is foundational to Christian self-understanding. By clarifying what salvation might mean, a focus on Jesus will not only provide insight into what 'an undreamed of possibility for love' might entail, it will also lay the foundations for identifying the church as the symbol of that possibility.

In the contemporary world, any theological discussion of Jesus needs a few prefatory remarks. This is because theology, in approaching Jesus from the perspective of faith and drawing on biblical texts as its support, seems to be at odds with two significant trends in intellectual life. On the one hand, there is the impact of the burgeoning interest in the historical reality of Jesus, which prescinds any doctrinal concerns in the search for the 'real' Jesus. On the other hand, there is the fact that the impact on biblical scholarship of such developments as the growth in historical consciousness and literary theory has cast a shadow over any form of Christology that might approach biblical texts as an unproblematic source of historical or doctrinal material. Taken together, those two influences challenge Christology to establish that it is neither historically nor biblically naïve. More fundamentally, perhaps, they challenge Christology to clarify its purpose. Clarifying that purpose, and addressing the legitimacy of Christology's sources and method, will be the concern of the next section, which provides a bridge to the exploration of Jesus' centrality to Christian faith.

---

[30] Rahner, *Foundations of Christian Faith*, 195. The emphasis is Rahner's.

JESUS, HISTORY, AND THE INTERPRETATION OF FAITH

Christology's primary concern is faith in Jesus Christ as the self-revelation of God; it seeks to articulate both the basis for and the meaning of that faith. Since its focus is theological, Christology views Jesus in the context of Christian faith, it proceeds by:

asking about his relations to God on the one hand and to the human race on the other, and asking how we must think of a person who can sustain these relations. It is this further theological question (or group of questions) that seems to demand the formulation, 'Who *is* he?', rather than 'Who *was* he?'.[31]

This means that Christology distinguishes between the 'historical Jesus', the product of historical research and reconstruction, and the 'historic Jesus', as he is 'existentially appreciated' by someone who encounters the historical figure.[32] For that reason, the Catholic tradition, in particular, has always stressed that 'the interpretation of Jesus takes place through more sources than historical research: Jesus is mirrored in the lives of the saints, proclaimed in paradigmatic Gospel stories, and is actualized in the liturgical calendar commemorating the key mysteries of his life'.[33]

On the other hand, since Christian faith has its grounding in the life of Jesus, it cannot blithely bypass history. As a result, both faith and theology must address 'the uncertainties that arise as soon as we investigate any event of the past, and especially an event so distant and so obscure as the career of Jesus Christ'.[34]

This does not necessarily mean, however, that Christology would be richer—or empirically verifiable—if there existed

---

[31] John Macquarrie, *Jesus Christ in Modern Thought* (London/Philadelphia: SCM Press/Trinity Press International, 1990), 5.

[32] These terms, and the definition of them, come from Roger Haight, 'Appropriating Jesus Today', *Irish Theological Quarterly*, 59 (1993), 247.

[33] Francis Schüssler Fiorenza, 'The Jesus of Piety and the Historical Jesus', *CTSA Proceedings*, 49 (1994), 94.

[34] Macquarrie, *Jesus Christ in Modern Thought*, 6. For a survey and critical assessment of the significant names in research into 'the historical Jesus' see Ben Witherington, *The Jesus Quest: The Third Search for the Jew of Nazareth* (Downers Grove, Ill: Inter Varsity Press, 1995).

today a fuller historical record, more facts, about Jesus. While such facts might enable us to locate Jesus in context, the distance of two millennia between Jesus and the present, to say nothing of linguistic, cultural, and other differences, mean that even those facts would be subject to a variety of interpretations. Theological statements about Jesus—including the gospels as well as the church's creeds and doctrines—rely on the raw material of history, but are always interpretations of that material. The key question is whether they provide a valid interpretation of Jesus. For the Christian tradition, the answer to that question depends less on historical information that the statements convey than it does on their capacity to mediate— indeed 'symbolize'—a present encounter with Jesus Christ as the one who communicates God's life-giving love.[35]

Accordingly, the church's dependence on the gospels and other New Testament documents expresses the conviction that those texts are a valid interpretation of Jesus:

The gospel texts are accounts of Jesus' life and ministry, death and resurrection. The early communities' respect for these texts and their placement in the Canon (as well as the exclusion of others) not only reflects the faith of those communities, it also inherently claims that the included texts are the best, most accurate interpretations of the meaning of Jesus' life.[36]

This claim does not ignore the fact that the texts have different backgrounds and perspectives, still less that there can be for us today significant difficulties, such as gender or cultural issues, in accessing what the various documents of the New Testament have to offer. Nonetheless, the radical claim of Christian faith is that the texts can mediate for us in the here and now, no less than for people in other eras in the church's history, the love of God that Jesus made present and—the key

---

[35] It is worth noting that numerous synods and councils in the early church, including the Council of Chalcedon (451), which formalized the church's christological faith, described their credal statements as a *symbolum*; this indicated that they were the expression of living faith, that they were more than a statement of facts. For examples of these ancient creeds see Neuner and Dupuis (eds.), *The Christian Faith in the Doctrinal Documents of the Catholic Church*, 4–13.

[36] James McEvoy, 'Narrative or History?—A False Dilemma: The Theological Significance of the Historical Jesus', *Pacifica*, 14 (2001), 279–80.

claim of this chapter (and book)—that the church exists to make present. While Chapter 4 will grapple with how we might understand the unique role of the Bible in the church, the following section draws on the gospels to develop a portrait of Jesus as the revelation of God. In so doing, it aims to illustrate the faith of the New Testament in Jesus as saviour, a faith that is common to the various texts, irrespective of the historical and contextual differences between them.

JESUS AND THE FULLNESS OF LIFE

Just as Israel used its present experience as a lens through which to view the whole of life and to identify God as creator, the writers of the gospels read the life of Jesus through the lens of their conviction that Jesus was indeed the Messiah, the saviour, that he was *Immanuel*, the revelation and presence of God in human history. As a result, their writings are not merely reports on events in the life of Jesus, still less are they attempts at biography. In fact, they have an explicit theological purpose, the articulation of which is clear in John's Gospel: 'that you might come to believe that Jesus is the Messiah, the Son of God, and that believing you might have life in his name' (John 20: 31).

In order to understand not only how they arrived at such a conviction, but also what 'life in his name' might imply, the best approach is to review their exploration of what, particularly in the gospels of Matthew, Mark, and Luke, is central to the life of Jesus: his preaching and action on behalf of the Kingdom or the reign of God. As we shall see, it is this focus that connects God and human flourishing.

The gospels do not give a precise definition of the Kingdom, but refer to it through symbols and images—a mustard seed (Matt. 13: 31; Luke 13: 18), yeast (Matt. 13: 33; Luke 13: 20), a treasure (Matt. 13: 44), a seed that grows unseen (Mark 4: 26), or a wedding feast (Matt. 22: 2 ff.). Through those images, the writers of the gospels portray the God who turns to humanity in order to reveal the depth of the divine love for humanity. They express, therefore, both a sense of abundance and a sense of gift. The reign of God is synonymous with abundance because it is synonymous with God's own life and with the invitation to communion with God. It is synonymous with a sense of gift as, in fulfilment of the promise that God had made to Israel, it offers more than anyone could pay for, even if payment were required:

> The Kingdom is a gracious gift from God, who comes with uncondi-
> tional love to seek out humankind and to offer ultimate salvation to
> all . . . It is a gift from God which people can only receive in gratitude
> and awe. God is coming toward us as unconditional love, seeking
> communion and intimacy. Since it is a gift of love, the only concrete
> description can be in terms of symbols and images.[37]

Entry to the Kingdom of God, then, does not come via our achievements, but via our willingness, itself the product of God's action, to allow God to love us, our willingness to accept the reconciling love that Jesus makes present. Thus, the Gospel of Mark begins with Jesus calling people to repentance as a preparation for the coming of the Kingdom (Mark 1: 15). This repentance is about opening our heart to God, about expressing the desire to receive the gifts of God rather than depending on our own, ultimately unreliable, strength. The gospels depict acceptance of what God offers in Jesus as the source of 'salva-tion': connection to Jesus opens possibilities beyond the limits imposed by human sinfulness and fickleness (Luke 1: 77; Luke 19: 1–10). As such, it reinforces the notion of the Kingdom as God's work, as the fulfilment of God's promises made in the midst of Israel's desolation and exile, when Israel was no longer clinging to the illusion that it might be able to secure its own future.

The gospels emphasize that Jesus is not merely a messenger who talks about the Kingdom or promises that God will bring it about at some indeterminate point in the future: Jesus is the one who actually makes present the hope and possibility that the Kingdom expresses. The capacity of Jesus to do this sug-gests a particular intimacy between God and Jesus, an intimacy captured in Jesus' use of *abba* (Mark 14: 36):

> The *Abba* experience of Jesus, although meaningful in itself, is not a
> self-subsistent religious experience, but is also an experience of God

---

[37] John Fuellenbach, *The Kingdom of God: The Message of Jesus Today* (Maryknoll, NY: Orbis, 1997), 97.

as 'Father' caring for and offering a future to his children, a God, Father, who gives a future to the person who from a mundane viewpoint can be vouchsafed no future at all. Out of his *Abba* experience Jesus is able to bring to a person a message of hope not inferable from the history of our world, whether in terms of individual or socio-political experiences—although the hope will have to be realized even there.[38]

The parables and miracles of Jesus offer the best illustrations of the connection between Jesus' intimacy with God and his capacity 'to bring to a person a message of hope not inferable from the history of our world'. The parables, the most famous examples of which are the Good Samaritan (Luke 10: 25–37) and the Prodigal Son (Luke 15: 11–32), reveal the compassion and mercy of God, which are infinitely more generous than what we might be prepared to practise. Similarly, the miracles of Jesus show God's unlimited power to provide for our needs—Jesus feeding the crowds from scant resources (Matt. 14: 13–21) and turning water into wine (John 2: 1–11)—and to overcome anything that threatens us, be it because of our fragile humanity—Jesus curing the sick (for example, Matt. 15: 29–31)—or even the effects of our sinfulness—Jesus' acts of forgiveness (for example, Matt. 9: 2–13).

In short, Jesus' words and actions make present the unrestrained and unconditional love of God originally promised to a people enduring an exile they knew to be the outcome of their own failures. These words and actions of Jesus, therefore, are the embodiment of what John's Gospel articulates as the mission of Jesus: 'I came that they may have life, and have it abundantly' (John 10: 10).

As already noted, the appropriation of what God offers in Jesus depends only on a readiness to receive. While it is easy to assume that all human beings would display this receptivity and be eager to accept unconditional love, human experience reveals that self-assertion is often a more attractive option than receptivity. In the gospels, a consequence of that tendency is that Jesus' message arouses a positive response in a small group, but opposition in many people. Accordingly, the

---

[38] Edward Schillebeeckx, *Jesus: An Experiment in Christology*, tr. H. Hoskins (New York: Crossroad, 1981), 267–8.

'stars' of many events in the gospels are not the great people, not the wealthy, the powerful, or the clever, not even the religiously articulate, but the poor, those who hunger for the acceptance or forgiveness that Jesus offers, those who know the limits of self-assertion. It is also significant that these people, like Zacchaeus (Luke 19: 2–10) or the woman caught in the act of committing adultery (John 8: 3–11), often fall below acceptable standards of behaviour, standards of behaviour that Jesus' contemporaries accepted as God-given.

Jesus' words and actions, therefore, not only put him at odds with his society, but also appear to be subversive of God's ordering of that society. Ironically, then, the upholders of that society condemn Jesus, the one whose life embodied the hope and possibility of God's Kingdom, as a threat to the things of God.

In terms of the concepts developed in this chapter, one aspect of the condemnation of Jesus is that it expresses an inability to accept that a human being could be the symbol of God's self-revelation in history—'Is this not Joseph's son?' (Luke 4: 24). The rejection of Jesus expresses also a demand that God should conform to humanity's prescriptions for ordering life. Far from confirming God's willingness to accept such a secondary position, Jesus presents God not as a 'kindly grandfather', but as the one who challenges human narrowness, who offers possibilities to those whom conventional wisdom dismissed as 'sick' (Mark 2: 15–17) or 'lost' (Luke 15: 1–7).[39] Jesus, then, symbolizes a renewed invitation from God to Israel, an invitation to a broader community, one that includes sinners and the poor. In all of this, Jesus stands alone, since not even his disciples were able to accept that the righteousness of the rich could possibly be inferior to that of the poor (Mark 10: 23–7).[40] There is, then, a thread running between the story of Adam and Eve (Gen. 2–3), which highlights humanity's resentment of its dependence on God and its demand for equality with God, and the rejection of Jesus, which also highlights humanity's unwillingness to accept God's gifts.

---

[39] Ibid. 143.
[40] Cf. Juan Luis Segundo, *The Historical Jesus of the Synoptics*, tr. J. Drury (Melbourne: Dove Publications, 1985), 118.

Since Jesus was no mere cipher, the rejection both of his words and actions, and of the likelihood of his connection to God, challenged his own commitment, especially when that rejection threatened his own life: Why be faithful to a God who seems unwilling or unable to preserve you from destruction? As we have already seen, the story of the covenantal relationship between God and humanity shows human beings as, at best, ambivalent in their attitude to God: faithlessness was often humanity's dominant response to the faithfulness of God. In Jesus, however, there is a radically different sense of how human beings might live. In Jesus, the faithfulness of God found an echo:

Jesus experienced the unfathomable mystery of God and God's will, but he endured the darkness in faith. This extremity of emptiness enabled him to become the vessel of God's fullness. His death became the source of life. It became the other side of the coming of the Kingdom of God—its coming in love.[41]

While the death of Jesus manifests rejection of all that he embodied, that death was for Jesus himself the expression of his willingness to trust unconditionally in God, rather than to demand that God produce an environment more congenial to trust. As such it is an act of self-surrender rather than of self-assertion. It is also a refusal to place his own survival above his connection to others. In all of this, the death of Jesus manifests the deepest meaning of the Kingdom: 'a struggling and protesting "no" to the powers of dehumanization'.[42] Thus, it challenges people in every age to 'de-etherialize' and 'de-individualize' our understanding of what it might mean to be a follower of Jesus.[43]

Nonetheless, if Jesus' death had been the last word in his story, it would be difficult to sustain the link between faith in Jesus and human flourishing. If his death had been the last word, Jesus could be no more than a noble and inspiring, albeit failed, figure in the long history of people who have promoted

---

[41] Walter Kasper, *Jesus the Christ*, tr. V. Green, (London/New York: Burns & Oates/Paulist, 1976), 118–19.

[42] William Thompson, *The Jesus Debate: A Survey and Synthesis* (Mahwah, NJ: Paulist, 1985), 208.

[43] Ibid.

and worked for a better world only to be betrayed or frustrated by the beneficiaries of the status quo. What makes Jesus more than that, what establishes the meaningfulness of Christian discipleship, and what opens the way to the church and its mission, is that the full story about Jesus is incomplete without the Resurrection.

The Resurrection is God's response to the life and death of Jesus. It does not return Jesus to the life he lived before his death, but frees him from the limits of death and reveals him within the fullness of God's own life. The Resurrection, then is not simply another event, not simply what comes after the death of Jesus, but is what transforms the story of Jesus. Thus, while the gospel writers had no doubt that it was Jesus, the crucified one, who had been raised from the dead, they were also at pains to illustrate that this did not mean that everything returned to the way it had been before his death. The gospels try to illustrate this difference by describing how the risen Jesus seemed to be at different places at the same time, how he could appear to his disciples even when they were in locked rooms, or how even those who knew him best could fail to recognize him (see, for example, Luke 24: 13–39; John 20: 19–22).

Although the 'mechanics' of the Resurrection are endlessly fascinating, the interest of the gospels, and especially of St Paul and the earliest Christian writings, is not in speculation on the 'how' of the Resurrection, but in its meaning. In that regard, there are two foci: What does the Resurrection reveal about Jesus? What does it mean for humanity, indeed for the whole of creation? The answer to both of those questions comes in the proclamation that the Resurrection reveals that Jesus is the Christ, the anointed one of God, that he is Lord and Saviour, that he is the Messiah: 'the vehicle and bearer of a definitive message that can basically no longer be transcended, a message in which God definitively "commits [Godself]" '.[44]

For the writers of the gospels, the proclamation of Jesus as Christ and Lord performed five key functions. First, it provided a caption to cover the whole identity and life of Jesus. The gospels, therefore, emphasize intimacy with God as consti-

---

[44] Rahner, *The Love of Jesus and the Love of Neighbour*, 28.

tutive of the identity of Jesus, even though it was the Resurrection that revealed Jesus to be the Messiah. It was, as noted earlier, this conviction that underpinned the writing of the gospels, which aim to show how each moment, each word and action of the life of Jesus, was a revelation of God, even if its witnesses only understood it all after, and because of, the Resurrection. Thus, for Mark, the unique relationship of Jesus to God is evident from his first public appearance (Mark 1: 9–13); for Matthew and Luke it is evident even in his conception and birth (Matt. 1–2; Luke 1–2); and for John, the most dramatic of the four, that uniqueness, even if revealed at a particular moment in history, resided in the eternity of God (John 1: 1–18).

Secondly, the titles encapsulated the effect of the life and death of Jesus. In other words, the fact that it was Jesus who had been raised from the dead was not a random occurrence that defied all attempts at explanation. Jesus was Lord because he alone had lived and died with faith, he alone had handed his life over to God. As a result, he had inherited the reward of the faithful servant of God (Isa. 52: 13–53: 12).

Thirdly, the titles highlighted that God was not only trustworthy, but also able to transcend all limits, including, most crucially, the limit of death. Jesus, then, was Lord because the love of the God in whom he trusted was stronger than death. The Resurrection showed that God's promises to Israel had not been empty words. It showed too that God was not a vindictive judge, but one who longed to offer life and reconciliation to an alienated creation.

The Resurrection reveals also the meaning of God's Kingdom in the present: the life of God is shown to be present in powerlessness, wealth in poverty, love in desolation, abundance in emptiness, and life in death.[45] In other words, if the life of Jesus showed that the love of God could reach sinners, the sick, and foreigners, those who, according to the prevailing socio-religious norms had no place, the Resurrection shows that God's love, the source of the fullness of life in the Kingdom, could reach us even in the face of death, the obstacle inimical to every human endeavour.

[45] Cf. Kasper, *Jesus the Christ*, 119.

Fourthly, the titles proclaimed that the risen Jesus was indeed the means of reconciliation between God and the whole of creation—'to believe in Jesus as the Christ, means to confess and actually to recognize that Jesus has a permanent and constitutive significance in the imminent approach of the kingdom of God and thus in the all-embracing healing of men and women and making them whole.'[46] If Jesus in his life and death returned to God the love that had brought creation into being, then the Resurrection expressed not only God's willingness to ensure the future of the whole of that creation, but also the fact that the future was inseparable from the risen Jesus. In the Resurrection of Jesus, God made present the future of creation. Through the Resurrection, God in Jesus Christ was revealed to be, as St Paul notes, 'all in all' (Eph. 1: 23). The Resurrection, then, renewed God's initial creative act and covenant, but in a way directed towards the consummation of that creation and covenant in Jesus Christ—'[Jesus] is the fulfilment of God's intentionality for creation: God's final and unambiguous self-communication to humankind.'[47]

Thus, if everything about Jesus expressed God's passion for humanity, the Resurrection of Jesus established him, and identified him, as the means by which human beings could have access to that passionate love, both in the present and for eternity. In short, the risen Jesus is the one in whom God's promise of a Messiah for Israel has its fulfilment (Acts 2: 14–36; 3: 13–26). Consequently, the Resurrection means that God's assurance of victory over sin and death becomes the patrimony not simply of Israel or the contemporaries of Jesus, but of all people and all times. Indeed, St Paul writes of the entire creation groaning in anticipation of the fulfilment of all life that God will accomplish in the risen Jesus (Rom. 8: 22).

Fifthly, the proclamation of Jesus as Christ and Lord linked him, inextricably, with God's self-communication— 'the truth, both about God and the salvation of humankind inwardly dawns on us in Christ, who is himself both the mediator and

---

[46] Edward Schillebeeckx, *Interim Report on the Books 'Jesus' and 'Christ'*, tr. J. Bowden (New York: Crossroad, 1982), 131.

[47] Fuellenbach, *The Kingdom of God*, 215.

fullness of all revelation.'[48] In thus identifying Jesus as central to humanity's relationship to God, the proclamation of Jesus as Lord was also an affirmation that humanity itself could be the vehicle for God's self-communication:

The altogether human reality and history of Jesus is not just the material through which a divine 'I', God himself, manifests himself... Obviously, this subjective human personality in reality has a relationship to God as fully active as that of any other human being, and *thus* (without being diminished thereby) belongs to God as God's own reality. The radical oneness of this human reality (along with its subjectivity) with the divine reality of the eternal Word, far from diminishing this subjectivity of the human being, Jesus, actually enhances and radicalizes it. For the nearer one is to God, the more one is a human being, in all human freedom.[49]

Reflection on Jesus as the one whose humanity made God present led the followers of Jesus to a startling conclusion: 'only God could be so human'.[50] Those who knew their well-being to be inseparable from faith in the risen Jesus, the Christ, proclaimed him to be not simply an unusually gifted or generous human being, but the self-expression of God. In Jesus, the Word had become flesh (John 1: 14)—'the humanity of Christ *is* the "appearance" of the Logos itself, not something in itself alien to the Logos and its reality.'[51] In Jesus, then, God had become present to humanity in the most intimate way possible, in one who was the 'Son of God':

To declare Jesus to be the Son of God is, I suggest, to declare that he was not only produced, but effectively, indestructibly, 'absolutely' cherished. If we take 'loving production' to be part of what we mean by 'true parenthood' and if, in declaring Jesus to be the Son of *God,* we declare 'parenthood' to be a divine attribute, then we are thereby declaring our conviction, derived from reflection on his fate, that being lovingly produced, being effectively cherished with a love that transcends destruction in mortality, is an aspect of what it ultimately is, means, and will be to be human.... 'Jesus is Son of God' is a

---

[48] *Dei verbum*, *DV* no. 2.

[49] Rahner, *The Love of Jesus and the Love of Neighbour*, 33. The emphasis is Rahner's.

[50] Leonardo Boff, *Jesus Christ Liberator*, tr. P. Hughes (Maryknoll, NY: Orbis, 1979), 179.

[51] Rahner, 'Theology of the Symbol', 238. The emphasis is Rahner's.

confessional utterance declaring our faith in his resurrection and our hope for the resurrection of all mankind. If 'parenthood' is a divine attribute, then the destruction of the product is not the last word concerning the human condition.[52]

With the revelation of the full identity of Jesus, the breadth and depth of 'an undreamed of possibility for love' also become clearer. First, it must open for us God's own life. Secondly, it must be available to us where we are and as we are, since it is the expression of the God who comes to meet us rather than demanding that we reach what is beyond us. Thirdly, it must involve a free gift of God, a gift that is universal rather than exclusive, a gift that is healing and reconciliation for those who are broken, and a gift that is an opportunity and a future for those who believe they have neither. Fourthly, it must be a gift that is human and personal: it must be for me as an individual, but also for me as a person whose deepest identity is bound up with others. Fifthly, it must open us to what transcends the immediacy of our experience, must make us more aware that to be human is to be capable of receiving God, capable also of being the means by which the love of God reaches other human beings. Sixthly, in being those things, it must involve us in a relationship with Jesus, the Christ, the one who is both symbol and guarantor of God's unconditional love.

The question, of course, is whether the church can meet those requirements. Clearly, the likelihood of such being the case depends entirely on whether there is a connection between Jesus and the church. Since a comprehensive answer to that question depends on understanding the role of the Holy Spirit, it requires a full chapter. As a prelude, however, the final section of this chapter will address a more primordial issue: whether there is even a need to consider anything beyond Jesus.

THE CHURCH AS AN UNDREAMED OF POSSIBILITY

Even in a non-religious age, Jesus remains an attractive figure. Although people in contemporary Western societies might be

---

[52] Nicholas Lash, 'Son of God: Reflections on a Metaphor', in E. Schille- beeckx and J. B. Metz (eds.), *Jesus, Son of God?* (*Concilium* no. 153), (Edinburgh: T. & T. Clark, 1982), 15. The emphasis is Lash's.

sceptical about miracles, uninterested in Jesus' focus on God, and even alienated by explicitly religious claims, such as referring to Jesus as the fully human–fully divine 'Saviour', it is, nonetheless, likely that the story of the good Samaritan will resonate with them, that they will appreciate Jesus' promotion of forgiveness and reconciliation, and find admirable his willingness to give of himself. That appreciation will not necessarily translate into acceptance of the uniqueness of Jesus or, more radically, into an act of faith in Jesus as Lord, but it establishes a positive connection between Jesus and the universal human struggle to live a good life. Establishing a sympathetic openness to the church is a more demanding task.

While Jesus attracts as an affirming, albeit challenging, human being, the attractiveness of the church is less obvious. This is so because some aspects of ecclesial life seem inimical to human flourishing. Indeed, for many people, any reference to the church invokes images of 'dogmatic spoon-feeding, magisterial baby-minding, thought police and thought control, even of sanctions against dissenters, inquisitions and heresy trials'.[53] In addition, if more were needed, the perception that the church is afflicted by chronic 'institutional sclerosis' suggests that it might be best to avoid the church or, at least, to keep it at arm's length.[54] It would seem, then, that while there might be some hope, even in a postmodern world, for the promotion of faith in Jesus Christ, there is little prospect of a positive appropriation of the church.

Consequently, any desire to apply 'an undreamed of possibility for love' to the church seems doomed, especially since the description can be valid only if the church is an irreducible element of God's self-communication in Jesus. That condition means that the problem is not just the flaws of the church, but the fact that the whole idea of the church seems superfluous. If Jesus is God's unsurpassable self-communication to humanity and if the Resurrection of Jesus marks God's irreversible commitment to the fulfilment of creation, why is there a need for anything beyond Jesus? Why replace the human reality of Jesus

---

[53] Kasper, *An Introduction to Christian Faith*, 135.

[54] Leonardo Boff, *Church: Charism and Power*, tr. J. Diercksmeier (New York: Crossroad, 1990), 49.

with the impersonal structures of the church? How could such a move be anything other than a loss, a settling for second prize?

To have any prospect of providing satisfactory responses to those questions, any theology of the church must not only illuminate the link between Jesus and the church, it also must show that 'the church' refers to something more than an institution. Most particularly, that theology must be the product of engagement with the concrete history of the church. To be helpful, therefore, ecclesiology, the branch of theology that focuses on the church, cannot approach the church as an abstract, as an ideal that we could design and build in a vacuum. Rather, it must draw its understanding of the church from the story of the church, especially from its beginnings. Ecclesiology, then, gives 'reflective expression to the practices of believers'.[55] As we shall see in later chapters, that approach also provides the tools for efforts to ensure the authenticity of particular expressions of the church's life.

The focus on the concrete reality of the church, however, does not mean that ecclesiology is simply a sociological study of the church, an exploration of group dynamics as they operate within the church, or a catalogue of the impact of the wider society on the church. While such studies are far from irrelevant for the church, since it is both a human reality and one that is immersed in history and culture, ecclesiology seeks ultimately to locate the church in relation to God's self-communication. Nor does this mean that ecclesiology can never be other than a pious exercise. In fact, the most significant critics of the church are those whose faith leads them to highlight the ways in which the church fails to be what it claims to be, those for whom criticism of the church is inseparable from commitment to it.[56]

Faith, then, neither ignores the weaknesses of the church nor accepts that only what is perfect could be a vehicle for God's presence. Part of the reason why the scriptures portray human

---

[55] Christian Duquoc, *Provisional Churches: An Essay in Ecumenical Ecclesiology*, tr. J. Bowden (London: SCM, 1986), 2.

[56] Cf. Avery Dulles, *The Craft of Theology: From Symbol to System* (New York: Crossroad, 1992), 66.

insight into God's self-communication as the product of retro-spection, of reflection on experience, rather than of anticipa-tion, is that God's self-giving does not announce itself in ways that compel our affirmative response to it. Since God's pres-ence does not distinguish itself clearly from the everyday shape of human history, it follows that it is not just what is splendid that can be a symbol of God. The fact that God can bring life from death would seem to endorse the veracity of that conclu-sion.

Although it would be more economically rational if God compelled our acceptance of divine self-communication, either by abandoning symbols or by ensuring that any symbols were less ambiguous, such a tactic would eliminate human freedom and the surrender of faith. While God's chosen method is messy, it allows faith to be a genuinely human act, part of which includes the vulnerability inseparable from risk.

Accordingly, if the church is indeed part of God's self-revelation, we can expect that it too will not have flashing lights that identify it immediately and unequivocally as revelatory of the presence of God. Paradoxically, then, the fact that the church manifests the messiness of the human condition does not necessarily disqualify it from being the expression of God's presence. The fact that the characteristics of the church are not what we might design for a symbol of God reinforces also the centrality of faith to all that concerns our experience of God. Nor does this imply that we ought to be quiescent in the face of any aspects of the church that distort the presence of God. It does suggest, however, that we ought at least to hesitate before asserting that the God of Jesus Christ could have no connection to a flawed church.

While those points suggest the importance of maintaining a willingness to consider the church and its claims, we are likely to nurture that openness only if we accept that there can be a connection between the church and Jesus. Attempting to make that case will be the concern of the next chapter, which will focus on the Holy Spirit as the link between Jesus and the church.

3

Where the Spirit Flourishes

In the register of 'foundation myths', the church's entry is far from spectacular. The Christian story does not begin with noble patriots who pursued their vision with courage and single-minded dedication. True, the annals of 'the early church' have many stories of martyrdom and holiness, but they emerge only after the opening chapter has already begun. What comes first, according to the gospels, little resembles anything heroic and inspiring. Where we might have expected a zealous commitment by the friends of Jesus to his 'cause', there was only despair in the face of the Crucifixion, a sense that the death of Jesus was also the death of possibility—'But we had hoped that he was the one to redeem Israel' (Luke 24: 21). Overwhelmed by sadness and disappointment, the disciples went into hiding (John 20: 19) or attempted to return to life as it had been before the advent of Jesus (John 21: 3).

'The church', therefore, does not begin as the dream of a band of activists united by a shared passion. Nor is it true that the church in the period that history knows as 'primitive Christianity' was either a model of organizational brilliance or of untroubled serenity. Thus, the New Testament communities reflect anything other than an ideal church, one that was simply following the perfect blueprint bequeathed by its 'founder'. In fact, those communities faced numerous crises that challenged them to discern the shape of authentic discipleship in situations that they had not anticipated. The deconstruction of any notion of a timeless, perfect church not only highlights that the risks inseparable from ecclesial faith are far from being merely a modern-day issue, it can also nurture the expectation that the contemporary church will likewise experience circumstances that call for discernment and imagination.

Nonetheless, there still remains the need to account for the emergence of the church from those followers of Jesus who had lost heart in the face of his death. In order to meet that need—indeed, in order to gain insight into the constellation of issues that orbit around the identity of the church—it is necessary to develop a theology of the Holy Spirit, especially of the Spirit's relationship to the church.

Accordingly, it is that relationship that is the central theme of this chapter, which will begin by outlining the connection between the revelation of the Holy Spirit and the transformation of the followers of Jesus into a community of witnesses to Jesus as the Christ. Following that exposition, the chapter will explore the role of the Spirit in establishing the symbolic reality of the church, the relationship between communal and individual faith, and between the health of the church's communion and the health of its mission in the world. More than anything else, the goal of this chapter is to indicate the qualities of the church's life that express the flourishing of the Holy Spirit.

THE SPIRIT OF REVELATION AND TRANSFORMATION

As the New Testament develops it, the followers of Jesus changed from people dominated by their fears to people alive with faith in Jesus as the Christ, the faith that is the foundation of the church. That transformation of the disciples had two distinct phases. The final scenes of each of the gospels capture the first phase, the shorter of the two. The focus of those scenes is on encounters with the risen Jesus, since it was through such encounters that the disciples came to believe that Jesus had been raised from the dead (Matt. 28: 1–15; Mark 16: 9–14; Luke 24: 1–53; John 20–1).

Flowing through the narratives of those encounters—the 'appearance stories'—is the conviction that the Resurrection of Jesus signals that sin and death are not the equals of God; consequently, human beings do not need to live in fear. Furthermore, those who have found life and hope in Jesus Christ do not need to cling anxiously to Jesus since their faith frees them to turn outwards: to offer hope to others through the same Jesus Christ (Matt. 28: 16–20; Mark 16: 14–20; Luke 24: 44–53; John 20: 19–23). Thus, in the synoptic gospels, the encounters with the risen Jesus conclude with the story of the Ascension of Jesus, the event that is associated with the commissioning of his followers to act in his name—'Go into the world and proclaim the good news to the whole creation' (Mark 16: 15). Central to that event is the promise that they will receive 'power from on high' (Luke 24: 49) to enable them to fulfil their mission.

The second phase in the process of transformation centres on the disciples' proclamation of the risen Jesus as Lord and Messiah; the story of this movement constitutes the Acts of the Apostles. Unlike the first, however, this phase has no closure. Indeed, the emphasis here is on beginnings, rather than on a completed story. Thus, the disciples emerge from fear and begin to live in a way that corresponds with the message of hope characteristic of the encounters with the risen Jesus. In addition, there is an emphasis on the connection between missionary zeal and the development of a common life, which celebrates and nurtures that shared faith, among those who profess faith in Jesus as the Christ. It is in that common life and shared mission of proclamation that the outline of the church is evident.

For the author of Acts, it is, unequivocally, the reception of the Holy Spirit by the disciples at Pentecost (Acts 2: 1–36) that brings about the transformation of the disciples of Jesus. The gift of the Spirit also fulfils the promise of Jesus about power from on high and inspires the proclamation of the Good News. As a result of such effects, the Christian tradition has associated the coming of the Spirit with the birth of the church.

The Pentecost story, then, is primarily a description of the profound change effected by the presence of the Spirit (Acts 2: 1–4). While the nature of that presence is as unsubstantial as that of the wind or of fire that symbolize it, its effect is as unambiguously clear as, again, that of wind and fire. What Pentecost supplies, therefore, is insight into the impact of the Spirit, into the outcomes of an encounter with Spirit. The Acts of the Apostles affirms constantly (see, for example, Acts 4: 31, 8: 26–40, 19: 1–6) not only that the Spirit's presence is beyond human control, but also how effective that presence can be. It follows, then, that the effects of the Spirit must hold the key to revealing the identity of the Spirit. More than anything else, that identity concerns the revelation of Jesus as the Christ.

After, and because of, Pentecost, the relationship of the disciples to Jesus acquires a new dynamism. What they came to recognize and understand through the Spirit related exclusively to Jesus: that as the one who had made God present in an unsurpassable way, Jesus was one with the Father; that in his Resurrection he had become the Christ, the guarantor of a future for creation. Through the Spirit, the disciples knew that Jesus could be who he was only if the distinction between the Father and himself did not imply any separation. Thus, this new understanding did not simply expand their supply of information about Jesus: it led them to a new understanding of God's own identity.

In addition, the disciples' new understanding was not simply intellectual conviction, but brought about in them the willingness to surrender themselves in faith to the God of Jesus Christ, to reorder their lives in response to that faith, to deepen the bonds they had with one another, and to become passionate about sharing with others their faith in Jesus as the Christ. The fact that those elements are fundamental to the identity and mission of the church, amplifies the reasons why the Christian tradition regards Pentecost as marking the beginning of the church.

Like the author of Acts, St Paul too stressed the power of the Spirit to bring about a new way of living (Rom. 8: 1–7; 2 Cor. 3: 3–6; Gal. 3: 1–5). For Paul, faith in Jesus as the Christ, the faith that enabled the proclamation 'Jesus is Lord' (1 Cor. 12: 3) was the product of the Spirit. The Spirit, then, was the source of insight into God's revelation in Jesus. It was also the Spirit who, by uniting humanity with Christ, enabled human beings to acknowledge God as *abba*, the one who promised that all the children of God would share in the inheritance of Jesus Christ (Gal. 4: 3–7).

Since the Spirit made present the full truth about Jesus, this suggested a union between Jesus and the Spirit. Accordingly, while Luke-Acts develops an unfolding narrative in which the revelation of the Spirit to the disciples occurs first at Pentecost, the author also makes it clear that the relationship between Jesus and the Spirit predates humanity's awareness of it. In fact, both Luke's Gospel and Acts identify Jesus as the one anointed by the Spirit.[1] To highlight the relationship between

---

[1] For a detailed discussion of the identity of Jesus as the one anointed by the Holy Spirit see David Coffey, *Grace: The Gift of the Holy Spirit* (Manly, NSW: Catholic Institute of Sydney, 1979), 120–44.

Jesus and the Spirit, Luke's Gospel weaves the Holy Spirit through all of the events associated with the birth of Jesus (Luke 1–2) and also the beginnings of the ministry of Jesus (Luke 3: 21–2, 4: 14–30). In so doing, the writer of the gospel also connects both Jesus and the Spirit to the long history of God's creative love in the covenant with Israel.

Although the emphasis on the Spirit is a particularly prominent Lucan theme, the other synoptic gospels also portray Jesus as the one who lived a life filled with the Spirit (cf. Matt. 3: 16; Mark 1: 4–13). In John's Gospel, which does not have a story of the Spirit's coming at Pentecost, the emphasis on the Holy Spirit is hardly less prominent than is Luke's. In John too, the connection between Jesus, the Spirit, and the Father reaches out to include the disciples. Thus, Jesus assures them that they will never be alone, that, even if he dies, his Father will send them an Advocate, 'who will teach you everything and remind you of all that I have said to you' (John 14: 26). The role of the Spirit, therefore, is to keep the followers of Jesus united to him so that through him they might be led to the God whom Jesus acknowledges as his Father. Just as the Prologue to John's Gospel (John 1: 1–18) can speak of the eternal union between God and the Word that becomes flesh in Jesus, so too the Spirit is never less than the expression of the mutual love between the Father and Jesus (John 14: 8–17).

The gospels, then, acknowledge not only the relationship between Jesus and the Spirit, but also that the Spirit expresses the Father's love for Jesus (Mark 1: 10–11; Luke 3: 21–2), the love that is the source of Jesus' words and actions. Most importantly, it is the love of the Father communicated by the Spirit that sustains Jesus' willingness to entrust himself to the Father in the face of his own death (John 15: 23–16: 28). Since that trust is a return of love by Jesus to the Father, it follows that it too is the expression of the Spirit. From reflection on those dynamics, Christian theology has identified the Spirit as the embodiment of the mutual love of the Father and Jesus in a way that reveals the relationship between the Father and the Son within the Trinity.[2]

---

[2] For the parallel between the relationship within the Trinity and within the life of Jesus see ibid. 91–143.

Just as the coming of the Holy Spirit not only transformed the disciples, but also opened the way to a deeper understanding of God's own life, so too can an exploration of the relationship between the Spirit and the church transform the questions about the church. As we shall see in the following section, a focus on the Spirit evokes explicitly theological questions about the church, questions that relate to the possibility of seeing it as the product of God's design, rather than simply as an institution or human society.

THE SYMBOLIC REALITY OF THE CHURCH

What Pentecost makes obvious is that the primary outcome of an encounter with the Spirit is not acquisition of knowledge about the Spirit. Indeed, the Spirit emerges not just as the one whose movement human beings cannot predict or anticipate, the one who 'breaks in', but as the one whom human beings never know as an object distinct from what it is communicating. The Spirit enables us to understand the identity of Jesus, even the relationships within the Trinity, but in so doing the Spirit remains beyond human control:

> The light of faith and the impulse of the Spirit do not permit of being isolated for inspection by a reflexive process in which attention is turned back upon itself and withdrawn from the object of faith. They are the brightness which illuminates the object of faith, the horizon within which it is contained, the mysterious sympathy with which it is understood and not properly the object directly regarded, not a sun which we can immediately contemplate.[3]

Even the use of 'Spirit', which suggests the lack of an individual form and is not a proper name or even a title, indicates immediately that the presence of the Spirit must be diffuse, that it is not as explicit as the human reality of Jesus. Although 'Spirit' might imply what is invisible, what eludes our examination, the New Testament is adamant that the presence of the Spirit is discernible, even if we cannot isolate it as we can isolate an object or even another human being. The story of Pentecost, for example, associates the coming of the Spirit with

---

[3] Karl Rahner, 'The Development of Dogma', *Theological Investigations*, 1, tr. C. Ernst (New York: Crossroad, 1982), 51.

events 'like the rush of a violent wind' and 'divided tongues, as of fire' (Acts 2: 3). While those descriptions are far from precise, they highlight that something happened to the disciples, a 'something' that came to be understood as the revelation of the Spirit.

Since the purpose of the Spirit is to make present the love of God revealed in Jesus Christ, the love that, as a result of the Resurrection, is unlimited in scope and extension, the presence of the Spirit cannot be restricted to one place or one form, which might make it unlikely that most people would have access to it. Only a love that is universally accessible could be the expression of the risen Christ, who is not bound by the limits to which Jesus, as fully human, was subject during his life.

Thus, whatever allows us to know ourselves as loved and forgiven unconditionally, whatever allows us to hope that all will be well, even though we might be unable to find a specific ground for that hope, can indicate the Spirit, who makes present the risen Christ, the source of hope that derives from humanity's reconciliation with God. Similarly, it is valid to claim the presence of the Spirit in whatever allows us to recognize our connection to one another, helps us to appreciate one another as something other than competitors, and, most especially, encourages us to reach out to one another in ways that enhance life not only by promoting justice and peace, but also by nurturing the whole of creation. In other words, God's love, the expression of God as one-in-three and three-in-one, is present in whatever promotes communion—of humanity with God, between human beings, and between humanity and the whole of creation.

Nonetheless, the fact that God's revelation in Jesus was neither invisible nor anonymous, as well as the fact that the gift of the Spirit to the disciples brought about a public proclamation of the identity of Jesus, suggests that it must be possible for us to have an explicit sense of where we might not only encounter the Spirit, but respond to such encounters through communion with others and life-giving action in the world, all in the name of Jesus Christ. In other words, the 'logic' of God's revelation in Jesus Christ implies the existence of a particular symbol for the Spirit, a symbol that can express the freedom of the Spirit only if it is itself the work of the Spirit, rather than of human beings.

To do justice both to the Spirit and to the dynamics of human existence, such a symbol would not only need to be apprehensible in time and space, it would have to offer a sure means of encounter with the Spirit, but without obliterating either the mystery or the freedom of the Spirit. As such, it would need to be the work of the Spirit, rather than simply one that the Spirit 'adopts'. That symbol, then, could be the guarantee of the Spirit's activity in human history. Although the existence of such a symbol need not imply that the Spirit works only through that particular symbol, its existence provides the criteria that enable human beings to recognize the presence of the Spirit; this suggests that all other symbols of the Spirit have an orientation towards that primary symbol.

Here, then, we arrive at the central claims that Catholic faith makes about the church: the church is the product of the Holy Spirit, who forms it as the communion of faith in Jesus Christ; the church exists as the unique instrument of the Spirit, who leads people, in Christ, to that communion with the Father that is the fullness of the Kingdom; through the Spirit, the church exists both to proclaim Christ and to be the means of a real, yet symbolic or sacramental encounter with Christ in history.

For the Christian tradition, the fact that even the development of a notion of 'the church' depends entirely on an experience of the Spirit led inexorably to the conclusion that the church must be an aspect of the process of God's self-revelation. Indeed, the Second Vatican Council argues, in its document on the church, that there is 'no mean analogy' between the identity of the church as an aspect of the mystery of God and the identity of Jesus as the incarnate Word of God.[4] This is not an attempt to place the church on the same level as Jesus, to claim that it represents a further incarnation of God. It is, however, a consequence of the fact that those who formed the church, even though they existed already as human beings, came to exist as 'the church' only because of a response to what the Spirit

---

[4] Vatican II, 'The Dogmatic Constitution on the Church' (*Lumen gentium*), *LG* no. 8.

initiated. While human decisions and actions are central to the foundation and development of the communion of faith, the initiative for the formation of that communion resides fully with the Spirit:

> Thus is established a parallel between the sacred humanity (of Jesus) and the Church. However, it should be remembered that while both were created by the bestowal of the Holy Spirit, they were not created in exactly the same way. The sacred humanity was created absolutely, from nothing, but the Church was created only relatively, i.e. from an existing group of men and women.[5]

That analogy applies primarily to the existence of the church as a communion of believers, rather than to any particular structure or doctrine. The Spirit, the expression of the communal love between Jesus and the Father, brings about a communion of faith whose sole purpose is to be a means of access to that love.

The Spirit, then, brings the church into being as the symbol or sacrament of what God offers to humanity in the risen Christ: 'an intimate union with God and of the unity of all humanity'.[6] As such, the church, in all of its aspects, exists to be 'an undreamed of possibility of love', to be the place 'where salvation from God is thematized or put into words, confessed explicitly, proclaimed prophetically and celebrated liturgically'.[7] It is in being a communion of people united by their common faith in Jesus Christ that the church is most revelatory of the presence of the Spirit. In addition, all aspects of the church's life as a communion of faith exist to communicate the Spirit—'the Church's gospel, doctrine, sacraments, and structure—which come from Christ—are fully grasped only when they are also appreciated as gifts of communion "in the Holy Spirit".'[8]

Locating 'the church' primarily in terms of the communion of faith brought into being by the Spirit provides a context in

---

[5] Coffey, *Grace*, 161.

[6] 'Dogmatic Constitution on the Church', *LG* no. 1.

[7] Edward Schillebeeckx, *Church: The Human Story of God,* tr. J Bowden (New York: Crossroad, 1980), 13.

[8] Richard Marzheuser, 'The Holy Spirit in the Church: A Truly Catholic *Communio*', *New Theology Review*, 11 (1998), 63.

which to situate every aspect of the church, including its institutional elements.[9] In later sections of this chapter, and in the next chapter, there will be further explorations of the church's existence as a communion, of the relationship between communion and mission, and between communion and structure. There will also be consideration of the implications of the church's failure to fulfil its mission, a failure that must always be possible since the communion of faith, despite being the product of the Spirit, is also a communion of finite human beings.

The existence of the church as a communion in the Spirit means too that faith in the church has its foundation in, and depends totally on, faith in Jesus Christ. Just as the Spirit leads not to itself, but to Christ, the church, as the work of the Spirit, exists not for its own sake, but to lead people to the God of Jesus Christ: 'the Church radicalizes the vacancy of the place of God. To accept its mediation is to agree that this vacancy will never be filled.'[10]

As a result, the self-surrender we make in relation to the church derives from, and depends on, our primary act of faith, which is in the God of Jesus Christ. Ecclesial faith, however, prevents our faith in Jesus becoming an abstraction. It helps to ensure that that faith remains fully human: embodied, social, and historical. Although the self-surrender of faith thereby connects us to the institutional reality of the church, the authenticity of the church's institutional dimension depends totally on the degree to which it expresses the

---

[9] In recent years, there has been a considerable amount of theological reflection on the church as a communion; see, for example, Walter Kasper, 'The Church as Communion', *New Blackfriars*, 74 (1993), 232–44; Thomas Rausch, 'The Ecclesiology of Communion', *Chicago Studies*, 36 (1997), 282–98; Susan Wood, 'The Church as Communion', in P. Phan (ed.), *The Gift of the Church: A Textbook on Ecclesiology* (Collegeville, Minn.: Michael Glazier, 2000), 159–76. For more exhaustive studies, see Denis Doyle, *Communion Ecclesiology* (Maryknoll, NY: Orbis, 2000) and Jean-Marie Tillard, *Flesh of the Church, Flesh of Christ: At the Sources of the Ecclesiology of Communion*, tr. M. Beaumont (Collegeville, Minn.: Pueblo, 2001).

[10] Louis-Marie Chauvet, *Symbol and Sacrament: A Sacramental Reinterpretation of Christian Existence*, tr. P. Madigan and M. Beaumont (Collegeville, Minn. Pueblo, 1995), 178.

implications of faith in Jesus Christ. Ecclesial faith, then, does not require either that we approach the church as if it were divine or deny that:

[The church] is not omniscient and omnipotent, not self-sufficient and autonomous, not eternal and sinless. It is not the source of grace and truth; it is not Lord, redeemer, and judge, and there can be no question of idolising it. The Church is the often threatened and endangered fellowship of the faithful and the obedient which lives from God and for God, which places its trust in [God], which believes in God.[11]

That disclaimer not withstanding, it remains true that the uniqueness of the church is that it exists only because it is the symbol of the Spirit. This means, in turn, that the existence of the church guarantees the presence of the Spirit in human history.

This does not imply that the church owns the Spirit or that we can encounter the Spirit only if we have an explicit relationship to the church. It does not even require that such encounters must always be in a context that is obviously 'religious'. What it does imply, however, is that the concrete reality of the church gives us a human means by which we can know—in the sense of the knowledge that derives from the self-surrender of faith—that the Spirit is operative in our history. Every encounter with the Spirit, then, as 'non-religious' or 'anonymous' as it might be, relates in some way to the church where the Spirit makes a home. In short, all encounters with the Spirit have an orientation towards the revelation of their full meaning and purpose: they have an orientation towards the church.[12] Clearly, such a claim will ring alarm bells for many in contemporary Western societies, alarm bells to which Chapter 5 will respond.

Although the reality of the church's chequered history casts a shadow over the claim that the church is the primary symbol of the Spirit, the claim must also respond to two objections of a

---

[11] Hans Küng, *The Church,* tr. R. and R. Ockenden (New York: Image Books, 1976), 57.

[12] For the relationship of the church to the presence of the Spirit in the wider world, see Karl Rahner, 'The New Image of the Church', *Theological Investigations*, 10, tr. D. Bourke (New York: Seabury, 1977), 3–29.

more specifically theological nature. The first is a concern that the focus on the centrality of the Spirit to the church undermines any identification between the Jesus of history and the church. The second is that efforts to establish a necessary connection between faith in Jesus Christ and the role of the church as a communion of faith are irrelevant because we can each have our own relationship with Jesus. The next two sections will address those objections.

THE SPIRIT OF JESUS' CHURCH

The Catholic tradition of apologetics has often promoted a narrow interpretation of the notion that Jesus is the founder of the church, an interpretation that has sought to identify specific founding words and actions of Jesus. That narrowness has affected even the reading of the gospels. Thus, there has been a tendency to interpret a text such as Matt. 16: 13–19, which involves Jesus describing Peter as 'the rock' on which he will build the church, in the light of later developments in ecclesial life, thereby suggesting that those developments were the direct outcome of a particular statement by Jesus.

Such an approach not only concertinas the flow of history, it is also in danger of obliterating the Holy Spirit by implying that only the life of Jesus is relevant to the development of the church. In the light of those dangers, we need to approach with some caution the identification of Jesus as the founder of the church. In addressing this theme, the challenge is not only to do justice to the link between Jesus and the church, but also to the role of the Spirit in the church. In order to achieve that balance, we need to recognize the limits of the claim that 'Jesus founded the church':

Does *Jesus* refer only to the earthly Jesus during his public ministry? Or does it include his passion, death, and resurrection? Does *found* mean to establish a consciously planned social institution with specific rules and administrative structures? Or does it mean to provide the dynamism and energy (the 'Spirit') to inspire others to carry on the movement begun by Jesus? And does *Church* describe a social institution over against other groups and the wider society, an organization with structures that remain unchanged throughout its history? Or does it describe more simply and basically ... *the Jesus movement?*[13]

The gospels do not present Jesus as the founder of an institution, but they do show him gathering a group around him (Matt. 4: 18–22, 10: 1–4; Mark 1: 16–20; Luke 5: 1–11; John 1: 35–51), initiating the members of that group into the life of faith and prayer (Matt. 6: 1–15; Luke 11: 1–13), and sending them out to be agents of the Kingdom (Matt. 10: 1–23; Mark 6: 7–13). Clearly, in all of those events we can see something of the nature and purpose of the church. We cannot, however, understand the church simply by saying that it exists to continue what Jesus commissioned his disciples to do during his life. This is so because their mission did not include proclamation of Jesus as the Christ, which, as we have seen, is constitutive of the church's identity and mission as it emerges after Pentecost. To expect, then, that events in the life of Jesus will provide even a rough outline for every aspect of the church is to leave no room for the whole story: Jesus living, crucified, risen, and present in the Spirit. Significantly, the adoption of that broader perspective does not render unintelligible any notion of Jesus as founder of the church:

Jesus founded the church by freely and unreservedly opening himself to God's self-gift in Word and Spirit—from that emerged a transformed humanity shaped by the Word and animated by the Spirit and a community of believers dedicated in faith and discipleship to bringing about a new humanity.[14]

Thus, viewing the emergence of the church from the perspective of the Resurrection and Pentecost does not imply the absence of a connection between the church and the life of Jesus. Indeed, as we have stressed, the Spirit's mission is inextricably linked with the mission of Jesus. There is, then, no serious suggestion that the first Christian communities understood themselves as existing for any purpose other than

---

[13] Daniel Harrington, *The Church According to the New Testament: What the Wisdom and Witness of Early Christianity Teach Us Today* (Franklin, Wis.: Sheed & Ward, 2001), 20–1. The emphasis is Harrington's.

[14] Bernard Cooke, 'Jesus of Nazareth, Norm for the Church', *CTSA Proceedings*, 49 (1994), 35.

witnessing to the Kingdom that Jesus had both proclaimed and embodied.

Since the consummation of that mission lies in the future, when the Christ will appear as 'all and in all' (Col. 3: 11), the Spirit's role is not simply to direct the gaze of the church back to the life of Jesus. The Spirit guides the members of the church as they discern, in the present, the shape of a faithful response to Christ. To accomplish that task, the Spirit inspires the development of the church and the promotion of new forms of ecclesial life according to the needs of each age:

If the church were just a creation of Jesus . . . it would not change, nor could it. Anything history added to it would be casual and value-less; it would have entered history only by accident . . . If the church proceeds from the Holy Spirit, however, its condition is different. It springs up in an infinite variety of human situations, as a community made up of communities of faith, hope and mutual love. Each com-munity bears the marks of its historical origin; it springs from the history of those who founded it. Each community is subject to the history of its members and the history of their coming together; each community is made by history.[15]

The Spirit, then, is a creative force, one whom Yves Congar describes as the 'co-instituting principle' of the church, without thereby detracting from Jesus.[16] In other words, we do the Spirit an injustice if we assign to the Spirit no role except 'to animate an institution that was already fully determined in all its structures'.[17]

It is, however, not just a theological understanding of the Spirit's role that ought to make us cautious about equating Jesus as 'founder of the church' with the idea that Jesus sup-plied a particular blueprint for structures and a constitution. History is equally telling against such a view, especially if we consider the church from the perspective of the complex struc-ture with which we are familiar today.

Thus, in the Pauline corpus, 'church' is more likely to refer to an event, an assembly of Christians in a particular place and

[15] Comblin, *The Holy Spirit and Liberation*, 89.

[16] Yves Congar, *I Believe in the Holy Spirit*, tr. D Smith (New York/London: Seabury/Geoffrey Chapman, 1983), ii. 9.

[17] Ibid.

time (Rom. 16: 1–16; 1 Cor. 1: 2; Gal. 1: 22), rather than a structure. Alternatively, it might even refer to a heavenly reality, not a historical assembly (Eph. 3: 10, 21). In Acts too, 'church' is a local gathering in, for example, Jerusalem (Acts 5: 11, 11: 22), Antioch (11: 26, 13: 1), Derbe and Lystra (16: 5), or Ephesus (20: 17).[18] In short, the New Testament concern is not with foundations and a particular historical connection to Jesus, but with the life of a group of people attempting to live according to the message, and Spirit, of Jesus Christ.[19]

The second objection to linking the church to faith in Jesus Christ is that it represents the imposition of an unnecessary medium between the individual and that faith. In part, that objection can be an appeal for the primacy of the individual over the group, an appeal for direct access to Jesus Christ, but it can also express a desire for a 'pure' faith in Jesus Christ, a faith that transcends all that is unattractive about the church. In responding to those issues, the following section will focus on the Spirit not only as the source of connection between communal and individual faith, but also as the stimulus to authenticity in the church. In doing so, however, it will not neutralize the fact that ecclesial faith involves the risk of committing ourselves to a communion with others as the avenue to a communion with the Spirit of Jesus Christ.

INDIVIDUAL AND COMMUNAL FAITH

The tension between the individual and the group is a universal feature of human enterprises; not only is it present within families and local communities, it can also be central to conflicts in world politics. The clash between communism and capitalism, which affected much of the world for much of the twentieth century, is an example of that tension, as is the contemporary struggle between the advocates of national identity and supporters of globalization. As with many such tensions, the truth in the contest between the individual and the

---

[18] See Raymond Collins 'Did Jesus Found the Church? Which Church?', *Louvain Studies*, 21 (1996), 361.

[19] For a useful overview of the issues associated with the question of the church's foundation see Roger Haight, 'Ecclesiology from Below: Genesis of the Church', *Theology Digest*, 48 (2001), 319–28.

group does not lie simply on one side of the divide: human beings are individuals, but they are also social beings defined by their relationships with others.

If faith in God touches the ultimate concerns of human beings, if it involves the deepest meaning of our existence, it is unlikely that it would have no implications beyond what is merely individual to each of us. What is more likely is that religious faith will connect us with each other, will involve us in giving and receiving.[20] The fact, then, that faith in Jesus Christ has an irreducibly communal dimension does not mean that it has only one mode of existence: the dominance of a 'repressive collective' that crushes individuals.[21] Indeed, the goal is a genuine communion, one that not only nurtures the thriving of each of its members, but also does not define itself by hostility to other communities.[22]

That there is a church, a communion of believers, not just isolated individuals who all claim to believe in Jesus as the Christ but have no connection to each other, is a reflection of the fact that 'no great human meanings and values can exist without the language, symbols, and shared convictions of a community.'[23] More specifically, the existence of the church expresses the fact that our knowledge of Jesus as the Christ depends on others identifying the Christ for us. Indeed, in the startling language of Louis-Marie Chauvet:

> [Ecclesial faith] requires a *renunciation of a direct line*, one could say a Gnostic line, to Jesus Christ. It is impossible to truly recognize the Lord Jesus as living without giving up this illusory quest . . . which irresistibly leads us to desire to see, touch, find, that is, finally to prove, Jesus. For exactly like the women or the disciples running to the tomb, what could we see, what are we *expecting* to see and to know, if not the corpse of Jesus?[24]

Although each of us is the recipient of the Spirit, of grace, through a variety of symbols that are not necessarily religious in

---

[20] Cf. Karl Rahner, 'Courage for an Ecclesial Christianity', *Theological Investigations*, 20, tr. E. Quinn (New York: Crossroad, 1986), 9.

[21] Maurice Wiles, *Faith and the Mystery of God* (London: SCM, 1982), 81.

[22] Ibid.

[23] Tony Kelly, *Seasons of the Heart* (Blackburn, Vic.: Dove, 1984), 68.

[24] Chauvet, *Symbol and Sacrament*, 172–3. The emphasis is Chauvet's.

an explicit way, we need the witness of the Christian community in order to identify the Spirit who speaks to our heart, the
Spirit who reaches us through those symbols, as the Spirit of
Jesus Christ. Since God's revelation in Jesus was historical,
access to Jesus as the Christ must also take place in history. The
church, the communion of faith, is both the guarantee that we
can know the Christ and also, as we saw earlier, the place
'where salvation from God is thematized or put into words,
confessed explicitly, proclaimed prophetically and celebrated
liturgically'.[25]

Since we can know Jesus Christ explicitly only through the
proclamation of the community of faith, entry into the church
involves a certain 'self-expropriation', a surrender of one's own
private judgement 'in favour of the mind of Christ, perpetuated
in and through the church'.[26] While we are yet to explore the
dynamics that apply within the church in regard to issues such
as authority or the gap that inevitably exists between the articulated faith of the community and the faith of individual
members, that exploration too will confirm the primacy of the
community's faith, but without discounting the indispensable
role of personal faith. There is, then, an irreducible tension
between the fact that Christian faith must always be personal,
must become 'my faith', and the fact that it is a communal faith,
'our faith', which none of us is able to construct according to
our own desires or interests. That situation, particularly the
need for 'self-expropriation' highlights the challenge—and
risk—inseparable from ecclesial faith.

While ecclesial faith is a challenge to individualism, it ought
not to be inimical to individuality, to particular responses to the
Spirit by individual members of the communion of faith. This
is so as that Spirit, though one, is given to each of us in different
ways for the good of the whole body (Rom. 12: 4–8; Eph. 4:
1–16). If it is the Spirit that brings the community of the
church into being as the primary witness to Christ, then only
faithful response to the Spirit by everyone in the church can
save the church from becoming either a form of dictatorship,

---

[25] Schillebeeckx, *Church*, 13.
[26] Avery Dulles, 'The Ecclesial Dimension of Faith', *Communio*, 22 (1995),
420.

which would exterminate individuality, or a cacophony, which would render impossible both the sharing of faith and communal witness to that faith.

As already noted, it is not only its communal nature that can make ecclesial faith seem daunting. More daunting still can be the fact that being part of a community of faith connects us to 'inhuman aspects' of the church's history.[27] These suggest that ecclesial faith, because it is tainted by the whiff—indeed, at times, even the stench—of various forms of corruption, is detrimental to human flourishing. The fact that aspects of the church's life can seem to have little connection to the Spirit highlights a central truth about the church: since it exists only as the creation of the Spirit, the authenticity of the church depends on its becoming transparent to the Spirit. The church, then:

is the proclaiming bearer of the revealing word of God as (God's) utterance of salvation to the world, and *at the same time* she is the subject, hearkening and believing, to whom the word of salvation of God in Christ is addressed.[28]

In other words, only an affirmative response to the offer of the Spirit by all those who form the church can prevent the development of an unbridgeable gap between what the Spirit enables in the church, between what the church exists to be as the sacrament of the risen Christ, and the lived reality of the church.[29] Despite this fact, it is not possible to escape the concrete church in the hope of finding a church without flaws, a communion of faith through whose members the Spirit will always shine diaphanously.[30] Thus, the only church that we can know is the one that exists in history—'The Church community as mystery cannot be found behind or above concrete, visible reality. The Church community is to be found *in* this reality which can be demonstrated here and now.'[31]

---

[27] Rahner, 'Courage for an Ecclesial Christianity', 9.

[28] Rahner, 'What is a Sacrament?', *Theological Investigations*, 14, tr. D. Bourke (London: Darton, Longman and Todd, 1976), 143. The emphasis is Rahner's.

[29] See Coffey, *Grace*, 159–62.

[30] Cf. Rahner, 'Courage for an Ecclesial Christianity', 12.

[31] Schillebeeckx, *Church*, 213. The emphasis is Schillebeeckx's.

Although we cannot bypass the historical reality of the church, the need to engage with it does not oblige us either to license mediocrity in the church or tolerate what is destructive. It does, however, make more urgent the conversion of all those who form the church. Thus, the communion of the church, and each member of it, remains always dependent on the very mercy of God that it exists to symbolize. Nonetheless, the fact that we cannot escape the church for a more direct connection to the Spirit of Jesus Christ, suggests that the ultimate risk of ecclesial faith arises because the Spirit leads our relationship with the God of Jesus Christ though a relationship with people who are as flawed and fallible as we are.[32] It means too that ecclesial faith is genuine faith: a surrender of ourselves to what we cannot control.

While such surrender is a risk, a radical act, it could not be an authentically human act if it were absurd, if it required the rejection or denial of reason. It will be clear that ecclesial faith is a risk, but is it equally clear that it is not absurd? As a way of addressing that concern, this chapter has focused on highlighting the congruence between the church and what we know of the dynamics of God's self-communication, especially the role and activity of the Spirit. In so doing, the aim has been to suggest that the more we understand the connection between the Spirit and the church, the more we can grasp something of both the appeal of the church and of its constant need for reform. With that in mind, the next task is to detail the qualities that characterize a Spirit-filled Christian communion. As we might expect, the Spirit's presence does not lead to passivity, does not aim at creating a tableau of the church, but promotes dynamism in the church.

THE FLOURISHING OF THE SPIRIT

The best summary of the effect and flourishing of the Spirit in the church is the list of features or 'marks' of the church that is part of the ancient formulae of Christian faith: the church is one, holy, catholic, and apostolic. Since the presence of the Spirit is independent of our achievements, this suggests that

---

[32] See Chauvet, *Symbol and Sacrament*, 186.

the 'marks' are a fact, that they are always characteristic of the church. On the other hand, since we are capable of quenching the Spirit (1 Thess. 5: 19), the church can be one, holy, catholic, and apostolic only if faithfulness to the Spirit is the hallmark of those who form the church's communion. The marks, therefore, are both a gift and a project for the church. Since they all express something of the one Spirit, it means too that they are also interconnected. Thus, in the formulation of Yves Congar, 'the unity of the church is apostolic, holy and catholic, its catholicity is holy, one and apostolic, its apostolicity is catholic, one and holy, and its holiness is apostolic, catholic and one.'[33]

Unity expresses the presence of the one Spirit of the one Christ who forms the one body of Christ, the church (cf. 1 Cor. 12: 12–13; Eph. 4: 1–6). Since this unity comes as a gift from God through the Spirit, it is a reflection, and symbol, of the unity of God in the Trinity.[34] As such, it is indicative of a communion, a unity of difference, rather than uniformity, where unity depends on the obliteration of difference. Since the communion of the church expresses and points to the communion of God, it is more than a way of ensuring that the operation of the church runs smoothly. It is, in fact, both a foretaste and a reminder of humanity's ultimate orientation:

The grace of our Lord Jesus Christ, the love of God, and the communion of the Holy Spirit enable the one church to live as sign of the reign of God and servant of the reconciliation with God, promised and provided for the whole creation. The purpose of the church is to unite people with Christ in the power of the Spirit, to manifest communion in prayer and action and thus to point to the fullness of communion with God, humanity and the whole creation in the glory of the Kingdom.[35]

Since communion is essential to both the authenticity of the church's mission in history and its orientation to the fullness of

---

[33] Congar, *I Believe in the Holy Spirit*, ii. 27.

[34] For a discussion of Vatican II's exposition of the link between the communion of the Trinity and the communion of the church see Kasper, *Theology and Church*, 150–6.

[35] The Faith and Order Commission of the World Council of Churches, 'The Unity of the Church as *Koinonia*: Gift and Calling' (Canberra, 1991), in G. Gassmann, *Documentary History of Faith and Order: 1963–1993* (Geneva: WCC Publications, 1993), 3–4.

the Kingdom, the church needs to be 'the home and school of communion'.[36] We know, however, that such is not always the case. Indeed, not only are we more familiar with 'churches'— not in the New Testament sense of particular, local communities in communion with one another, but as divided groups, which are often in conflict with each other—rather than 'the church', but we are also aware that the church has often resisted diversity and pluralism in order to impose uniformity. The unity of the church, therefore, is not simply a gift of the Spirit, but also an invitation, a project, and a challenge.

Just as the manifestation of the church's Spirit-given unity depends on a universal openness to the Spirit, who alone can ensure that diversity does not become disunity, so the manifestation of the church's Spirit-given holiness (1 Cor. 6: 11) depends on the same openness. Vatican II attributes the holiness of the members of the church, which discloses itself in love of both God and neighbour, explicitly to their new birth in the Spirit of Christ.[37] This resonates with a variety of sources from the New Testament that, without directly describing the church as 'holy', refer to it as the 'Bride of Christ' (Eph. 5: 25–7) and 'God's holy temple' (1 Cor. 3: 16–17), whose members are 'saints' (Rom. 12: 13; Acts 9: 13) and form 'a holy priesthood' and 'a holy nation' (1 Pet. 2: 5,9).

Such appellations, however, ought not to promote smugness among Christians, since we know that the story of the church— in the present as well as in the past—is not one of unequivocal witness to the holiness that reveals the Spirit. We need, then, to develop an understanding of the church's holiness in tandem with exploring the impact of sin in the church. The experience of sinfulness in the church gives rise to two fundamental questions: Does the fact of sin in the church destroy any claim to holiness for the church? Does the sinfulness of members of the church mean that the church as a whole is sinful?

Since the holiness of the church expresses the presence of the Spirit, who is the guarantee that God's victory over sin and death in Jesus Christ is definitive, it follows that sin in the

---

[36] John Paul II, *Novo Millennio Ineunte* (Strathfield, NSW: St Paul Publications, 2001), no. 43.

[37] Dogmatic Constitution on the Church, *LG* no. 9, no. 40.

church cannot imperil the ultimate outcome of humanity's relationship to God. Nonetheless, the manifestation of sinfulness is, as Hans Küng expresses it, 'a dark paradox', part of the 'un-nature' of the church, rather than the expression of what is proper to the church.[38] Such sinfulness, therefore, remains inseparable from human existence, and the church, even as we seek to be faithful to the Spirit of Jesus Christ. As a result, the church, which 'awaits the arrival of the new heavens and the new earth in which justice dwells', cannot separate itself from 'the figure of this world which is passing'.[39]

Despite its status as a flawed pilgrim to the fullness of God's Kingdom, the church remains a vehicle for grace, for an encounter with the Spirit, especially through the scriptures and the sacraments, whose holiness derives from their existence as the work of the Spirit.[40] Properly understood, therefore, even when sinfulness disfigures it, the church remains holy with the holiness proper to the Spirit, the holiness that is beyond the destructive reach of sinful human beings.[41]

Sinfulness in the church also underscores the implications of the church's sacramental existence: it reinforces the notion that while the church is indeed a sacrament, it is no more than a sacrament.[42] In other words, there is always a gap between the church as symbol and what it exists to symbolize. Accordingly, sinfulness highlights the church's need for conversion in order that the presence of the Spirit might become more obvious.

In the light of the sinfulness that can blight the church's witness to the presence of the Spirit, it is worth noting something of the radical nature of symbols, and the equally radical act of accepting the mediation of the symbol. If the flawed church does not cease to be the creation of the Spirit, it must mean that the capacity of the symbol to symbolize what is other than itself is something objective—in the case of the church,

---

[38] Küng, *The Church*, 422–3.
[39] Dogmatic Constitution on the Church, *LG* no. 48. For the acknowledgement of the church as both holy and in need of conversion, see *LG* no. 8.
[40] Cf. 'Dogmatic Constitution on the Church', *LG* no. 39.
[41] See Karl Rahner, 'The Sinful Church in the Decrees of Vatican II', *Theological Investigations*, 6, tr. K.-H. and B. Kruger (New York: Crossroad, 1982), 290–2.
[42] Chauvet, *Symbol and Sacrament*, 186.

this refers to the fact that it is something God-given or, more explicitly, something Spirit-given—rather than something that depends on the aesthetic, utilitarian, or any other, value of the symbol itself.[43] This indicates that the act of faith, which involves surrender to the symbol and provides the only means of access to what is symbolized, is never less than a radical act, a hoping-against-hope.

In other words, even the most beautiful symbol cannot render unnecessary the surrender of faith that is an irreducible element of appropriating the deeper meaning that the symbol conveys. This is so as the surrender of faith embraces both the symbol and the symbolized, not just the symbol. Indeed, there is always the danger that we can fall in love with the beautiful symbol and neglect what it symbolizes. In addition, it is important not to impose on God's action a human standard, such as maintaining that only 'the unviolated and unspoiled' can ever represent God.[44] If God is present only in the beautiful and unsullied, then it places in doubt the centrality of the crucified Jesus to the Christian dispensation. On the other hand, there is no particular virtue in a symbol that makes the act of faith more difficult than it is intrinsically. It is the latter fact that argues for the conversion of the symbol so that it might promote, rather than discourage, the surrender of faith.

While the evident sinfulness of the church does not disqualify it from being the symbol of the Spirit's presence, the holiness of the church makes it more likely that people will recognize that the Spirit gives life to the church. This means that it is saints, those who stand as symbols of what the Spirit can accomplish in human beings, who are the best expression of the relationship between the symbol and the symbolized in the church.[45]

---

[43] For the idea that the effectiveness of the symbol is not dependent on its aesthetic value see Chauvet, *The Sacraments*, 84–5.

[44] Anne Loades, 'Word and Sacrament: Recovering Integrity', in N. Brown and R. Gascoigne (eds.), *Faith in the Public Forum* (Adelaide: ATF, 1998), 31–2.

[45] Karl Rahner, 'On the Significance in Redemptive History of the Individual Member of the Church', *Mission and Grace*, 1, tr. C. Hastings (London: Sheed & Ward, 1963), 139. See also, Walter Kasper, *Faith and the Future*, tr. R. Nowell (New York: Crossroad, 1982), 62 and Congar, *I Believe in the Holy Spirit*, ii. 58.

Since those who form the church, including those who represent it officially, are sinners, is it valid to conclude that the church itself is sinful? It is easy to see how that question can become entangled in apologetic concerns, such as the desire to save 'the good name' of the church when its representatives are mired in scandal, as with clerical sexual abuse. The danger, however, is that an apologetic focus produces unsustainable contortions, which amount to claiming that the church is always holy because it exists independently of those who form it. If the church exists only as a communion of believers, then there can be no separation between 'the church' and its members. In that respect, there is surely a proper sense in which sinful members result in a sinful church. On the other hand, as we noted above, saints also represent the church. In short, there is a need for an even-handedness that recognizes that while the triumph of the Spirit does not colour every aspect of the church's life, it is also not absent from every aspect. While 'the sinful church' is an appropriate term for some situations, the hope remains that it is not the most fitting description for what every member of the church produces on every occasion.[46]

Just as any allusion to the unity and holiness of the church is problematic because we experience their opposites in the concrete church, so too the focus on the catholicity of the church confronts us with contentious issues of identity. Since catholicity implies universality, not just in a geographical sense, but also in the sense of being able to embrace God's presence in a multitude of forms, it is at odds with the denominationalism and centralization that seem to dominate the historical reality of the church. Nor does 'catholic' seem an appropriate designation for a church that seems, often, to define itself by what it opposes in the world, rather than what it affirms. As we might expect, however, the catholic Spirit challenges any tendency either to sectarianism or flight from the world.

For this reason, Pentecost (Acts 2: 5–11) stands as the ultimate expression of catholicity. There, the Spirit spoke through

---

[46] For a valuable discussion of the impact of sinfulness on the church see Francis Sullivan, *The Church We Believe In: One, Holy, Catholic and Apostolic*, (Dublin: Gill & Macmillan, 1988), 76–7, 82–3.

the disciples in a variety of languages, demonstrating that the good news about Jesus as the Christ was not the preserve of any one nation, but could unite the members of every group.[47] The presence of the Spirit, then, and the sharing by all Christians of the one Spirit in baptism means that 'multiculturalism already is a given in the Church, a reality and a gift to be cherished, a place where all the displaced are welcomed by a common baptism into a common home (cf. Gal. 3: 27; 4: 6).'[48]

That emphasis on the universal, and the unexpected, continues throughout the Acts of the Apostles as the Spirit becomes present to the gentiles, even to Roman conquerors (Acts 10). In addition, the Spirit leads the communion of the church to recognize the authenticity of such developments, to recognize that faith in Christ is not the same as subscribing to particular cultural norms, even ones that boasted of God's sanction (Acts 15).

Nonetheless, achieving a truly catholic church is demanding. It requires the willingness to accept that God's Spirit can choose freely how and where to make itself present. Catholicity, therefore, requires us to recognize that the Spirit's practice can transcend what we have assumed to be the boundaries of the Spirit's domain. An authentically catholic church, therefore, does not define itself by its opposition to the new, the unusual, or the individual, but by its expectation that the Spirit will always appear in surprising ways:

The catholic spirit is prepared to learn from all parties, seeking out the truth in every opinion and the merit in every cause . . . To be truly catholic means to call into question the self-interest of any group, even that of the church itself, and to maintain critical distance from every passing vogue. In short, catholicity seeks to foster a vision and coherence as deep and comprehensive as God's creative and redemptive plan made known to us in his Son.[49]

---

[47] Marzheuser, 'The Holy Spirit in the Church', 65.

[48] Maxwell Johnson, *The Rites of Christian Initiation: Their Evolution and Interpretation* (Collegeville, Minn.: Pueblo, 1999), 267. The references to Galatians form part of Johnson's text.

[49] Avery Dulles, *The Catholicity of the Church* (Oxford: Clarendon Press, 1987), 180.

Since the Spirit alone can support such a degree of openness, it
will be clear that a lack of trust in the Spirit reveals itself by a
narrowing of attitudes in the church, just as the same lack of
trust reveals itself in disunity and sinfulness. While a later
chapter will discuss the irreducible tension between claiming
the Spirit as the source of the church's abiding truth and also as
the source of change that moves the church towards becoming
more catholic, there can be no doubt that the genuinely catholic
is not reconcilable with a blanket rejection of change, an implacable opposition to what is new, or, no less crucially, with a
denial of the Spirit's presence in what has been received from
the past.

Similarly, efforts at imposing uniformity in the church
through excessive centralization are inimical to both the unity
and catholicity of the church. The logic of Pentecost dictates
that the church can reflect the Spirit only when it is a communion, but it can be a communion only when it is a union of
difference. As we shall see in Chapters 4 and 6, this principle
has implications for the relationship between 'the universal
church' and 'the local church'. Here too, however, we should
not expect the neat and one-dimensional to disclose the Spirit's
presence. The catholic Spirit is more likely to be at home in the
'both . . . and' than in the 'either . . . or':

Through the mission and gift of the Holy Spirit, the Church was born
universally by being born manifold and particular. The Church is
catholic because it is particular, and it has the fullness of gifts because
each has his own gifts.[50]

The Spirit who promotes catholicity within the church promotes also a 'catholic' outlook towards the world from the
members of the church. In order to understand that claim we
need to recall that while the church is the primary sacrament of
the Spirit, the Spirit is not captive within the church. In other
words, the church is the sacrament of what God, through the
Spirit, intends for all people: that they might recognize the love
of God that has become irreversibly and invincibly accessible to
humanity through Jesus Christ. While human beings know the
identity of the Spirit only because of, and in, the church, it is

---

[50] Congar, *I Believe in the Holy Spirit*, ii. 27.

nonetheless true that, once we understand the mission and purpose of the Spirit, we ought to expect that the Spirit is operative beyond the confines of the church.

Although its history reveals that it has not always achieved the goal, the church must strive to realize itself as 'a dialogistic sacrament'.[51] In other words, the church must remain open to dialogue with the world because it recognizes in the world, albeit in a fragmentary way, the truth that is its *own* truth, the truth of Jesus Christ. While the church knows too that not everything in human history will be reconcilable with life in Christ, it must remain open to dialogue with 'the partial cath-olicities' of philosophy, science, politics, economics, and the arts, which also offer a vision for the whole of human reality, a vision that is not necessarily in conflict with faith in Christ.[52] If they are to participate effectively in such dialogue, the members of the church must strive continually to deepen their grasp of their own identity, including recognizing faith in Christ as a source of possibilities. In order to deepen that identity and retain a sense of possibility, the members of the church must maintain a positive appreciation of the apostolic dimension of their faith.

The 'apostolic' dimension of the church refers to the fact that the communion of faith, in every era, remains dependent on the witness of the disciples of Jesus. If it is true that there is no access to the life, death, and Resurrection of Jesus outside of the church, which exists to proclaim him as the Christ, it is more explicitly true that that proclamation depends, in every age, on those who testified from their own experience to God's action in Jesus. The church, therefore, lives always from what it has received from the apostles.

Since it is the Spirit who inspired that original witness, it is also the Spirit who keeps it alive through the history of the church. In order to keep that witness alive, however, the Spirit does not simply encourage us to refer back to something set in concrete or frozen in time. Since each member of the church, through baptism, shares the same Spirit bestowed at Pentecost, that Spirit empowers and inspires each person in the church to

---

[51] Kasper, *Theology and Church*, 140.
[52] Dulles, *The Catholicity of the Church*, 178.

take up the missionary mandate given to the apostles, to be about service, witness, suffering, and struggle for the sake of the Kingdom inaugurated in Jesus Christ.[53] In short, faithfulness to the apostolic inheritance of the church is not simply about statements of faith, but also includes the willingness to place service, even martyrdom, above comfort, a prospect that only the Spirit could enable us to face positively.[54]

Although a genuinely apostolic church is one that is in continuity with the witness of the apostles, it is not one that is merely backward-looking. Since the mandate given to the apostles implied a movement into the future, apostolicity is likewise oriented to the future, to the fulfilment of God's Kingdom—a point that the next chapter will develop further. Just as any rejection of our dependence on the foundations of the church's identity and mission would subvert the apostolic nature of the church, so too does denial of its eschatological orientation, the orientation to the fullness of the Kingdom. Such a denial suggests either that the fullness of the Kingdom lies in the past or that it will never come, both of which imply that the apostolic faith is ultimately futile.

The eschatological orientation is especially important when we consider issues of 'apostolic succession'. Here, the danger is that we claim the support of the Spirit for what is merely able to show a connection with the past—a literal sense that traces particular aspects of the church, especially the role of the bishop, back to the apostles—rather than for what brings about the life that comes from the Spirit, the life that characterized the apostles themselves:

> Apostolic succession is therefore a question of a continual and living confrontation of the Church and all its members with this apostolic witness; apostolic succession is fulfilled when this witness is heard, respected, believed, confessed, and followed.[55]

It will be clear from all of the above that the flourishing of the Spirit is inseparable from our willingness, our Spirit-generated and Spirit-sustained willingness, to be open to what exceeds our capacity for control and ordering. This means

---

[53] Congar, *I Believe in the Holy Spirit*, ii. 45.

[54] Cf. Comblin, *The Holy Spirit and Liberation*, 102.

[55] Küng, *The Church*, 458.

that the triumph of regulation and 'juridical consciousness' in the church can bury the Spirit as effectively as disunity.[56] If the fact that the church cannot exist without a definite structure—a theme that will be prominent in the next chapter—is not to negate the claim that the church is the symbol of the Spirit, then even what seems fixed and formal in the church must be something other than petrified, must retain the dynamism that both derives from and reveals the Spirit.

This means that one role of the Spirit, one aspect of its flourishing, is that it acts as 'the element of dynamic unrest, if not of revolutionary upheaval'.[57] The Spirit, therefore, is responsible for both authentic conservation and authentic change in the church. In short, the Spirit is responsible for all dimensions of the church's apostolicity. This twofold theme of conservation and development, and the Spirit's relationship to both aspects, will be central to Chapters 4 and 6.

It is important to remember that while unity, holiness, catholicity, and apostolicity express the flourishing of the Spirit, that flourishing aims to produce something other than a church that is merely externally attractive. In fact, the goal is the building up of the church as a communion of faith better equipped to witness to the Kingdom or reign of God that has begun in Jesus Christ. It is, therefore, a holy and united church, a church sure of its identity and of its faith, that is more able to be a wholehearted witness in the world to Jesus Christ as the source of hope and of the promise of God's irreversible commitment to humanity. Such a church is the most powerful symbol of the Spirit's flourishing.

The final task of this chapter, then, is to explore the connection between the communal life of the church and the mission of the church in the world. This is crucial since the world is the venue in which the church is to make present the hope and love that have their foundation in Jesus Christ. With this in mind, the following section has a twofold aim: to show the connection

---

[56] Ludwig, *Reconstructing Catholicism for a New Generation*, 2. Ludwig suggests that many young people see the church as the place where such a consciousness dominates.

[57] Karl Rahner, 'The Individual in the Church', *Nature and Grace*, tr. D. Wharton (London: Sheed & Ward, 1963), 79.

between communion and mission and to identify the Spirit as
the source of both aspects of the church's life.

THE MUTUALITY OF COMMUNION AND MISSION

The best way to gain insight into the relationship between
communion and mission is to begin with what exemplifies the
connection between the two: the Eucharist. In its document on
the liturgy, Vatican II, in one of its most oft-quoted passages,
characterized the celebration of the Eucharist as 'the high point
towards which the activity of the Church is directed, and,
simultaneously, the source from which all its power flows
out'.[58] Central to that description is the fact that the Spirit is
at the heart of the Eucharist.

Since the communion of the church is a communion in the
one Spirit of Jesus Christ, the eucharistic assembly is not a
random gathering, but the assembly of those baptized into the
Spirit of Christ. Nor does that fact simply provide an identifying badge. As we have already seen, the Spirit does more than
connect us to the life of Jesus as an historical event: the Spirit
makes present the crucified and risen Christ. As a result, the
Eucharist, which is the sacrament of the death and Resurrection of Jesus Christ, is the principal means by which we enter
into communion with the Spirit. That communion not only
invites us to a deeper trust in God's love expressed in Jesus
Christ, it also connects us more deeply with one another.

The measure of an authentic response to the multiple dimensions of the Eucharist is not so much the growth of our internal
conviction about God's love for us in Jesus or even individual
piety; while those are not irrelevant, they are not ends in
themselves. What is crucial is the impact that the Eucharist
has both on how we act towards one another within the communion of the church and on how we live in the world. The
Eucharist, then, promotes an embrace of the invitation to make
the healing, forgiving, and reconciling love of God in Jesus
Christ accessible to others:

---

[58] 'The Constitution on the Sacred Liturgy' (*Sacrosanctum concilium*), *SC*
no. 10.

The Eucharist is subversive: it subverts any illusions we might have
that faith in the God of Jesus Christ is reconcilable with self-suffi-
ciency, self-absorption, or the pursuit of a pain-free life. The Eucharist subverts all of this only so that we might know both the limitless
power of God to give life and the equally limitless desire of God to
give life to all people, not simply to a few. Only a Church which is
similarly committed to life, similarly committed to all people, can
worthily celebrate the Eucharist and so be 'a sacrament of intimate
union with God and of the unity of all humanity'.[59]

In short, the Eucharist confirms that the existence of the
church is for the sake of witnessing to the Kingdom. A church
that is genuinely holy and united, a church free from the
dissipation of energy through internal struggles, a church that
has a strong sense of its shared faith, a church that celebrates
that faith in a life-giving liturgy, is one that is able to fulfil its
mission, which is 'to be the channel of the gift of grace'.[60] This
mission involves the proclamation of the Gospel, a proclamation linked to embodying the reign of God in history. The
church's promotion of God's Kingdom is also inseparable from
a willingness to include sinners and those marginalized by
society, a sense of solidarity with all forms of human suffering,
a rejection of the division between rich and poor, a reverence
for creation as the expression of God's wisdom, the wisdom
made manifest above all in Jesus, and the expectation of a
future beyond human calculation or control, a future that is
always more than we can even imagine.[61]

In other words, a church grounded in the Spirit encourages
sympathy for the world and its sufferings, since the Good News
of God's love for us in Jesus is intended for the whole world,
not just those within the church. Members of the church,
therefore, need to keep in mind, as Vatican II's 'Pastoral Constitution on the Church in the Modern World' emphasized,
that:

---

[59] Richard Lennan, 'The Eucharist: Sacrament of the Church', in Mar-
gareb Press (ed.), *The Eucharist: Faith and Worship* (Strathfield, NSW: St
Paul Publications, 2001), 36. The quote in the last line is from *LG* no. 1.

[60] Paul VI, *Evangelii Nuntiandi* (1975), no. 14.

[61] This presentation of the dimensions the Kingdom follows that of Francis
Schüssler Fiorenza, 'Thy Kingdom Come', *Church*, 10 (1994), 6–7.

Their community is composed of people united in Christ who are
directed by the holy Spirit in their pilgrimage towards the Father's
kingdom and who have received the message of salvation to be communicated to everyone. For this reason it feels itself closely linked to
the human race and its history.[62]

If members of the church approach the needs of the world as
their own needs, there is a greater likelihood that their faith will
reflect God's own commitment to humanity in the incarnation
of Jesus.[63] What is also likely is that their relationship with the
needs of the world will not express the sort of 'charity' that
Charles Dickens subjected to mordant criticism for its lack of
humanity, to say nothing of its failure to embody the Spirit of
Jesus: 'It is a remarkable Christian improvement, to have made
a pursuing Fury of the Good Samaritan; but it was so in this
case, and it is a type of many, many, many.'[64]

There ought to be, then, no division between authentic
Christian communion and the authenticity of the communion's
interaction with the world. All members of the communion,
therefore, share the responsibility both for communion and
mission:

Central to the church's mission in and to the world is its own living of
communio as fully as possible. The better it does the latter, the more
effectively it accomplishes the former. Therefore, whatever contributes to the church's ordering and living its life of communion can be
seen, not necessarily as turning inward and away from the world, but
rather as ways in which the church sharpens its ability to be a visible
and credible sign in the world of the way God wishes the whole of
humanity to live. The more the church is truly and fully the church,
the more it serves and witnesses in the world.[65]

This link between communion and mission also has implications for Christian spirituality. It suggests that love of neighbour has a socio-political, not merely a personal and individual,
dimension:

[62] 'The Pastoral Constitution on the Church in the Modern World' (*Gaudium et spes*), *GS* no. 1.

[63] See John Paul II, *Novo Millennio Ineunte*, no. 43.

[64] Charles Dickens, *Our Mutual Friend* (Oxford: Oxford University Press,
1998), 506. The original publication was in 1864–5.

[65] H. Richard McCord, 'Participation by Laity in Church Life and Mission', *Chicago Studies*, 39 (2000), 55–6.

Demands of Christian non-violence, environmental protection, responsible family planning, health care, political responsibility, and so forth, can be of at least as much moment as the particular injunctions of Christian love of neighbour that have been reflected upon and preached in the past as the content of the commandment to love one's neighbour.[66]

In order to ensure that its life in the world does express Christian discipleship, there are two specific dangers that the church must avoid. The first is that those who form the church might perceive the world as alien territory defined by the absence of God. In the light of that perception, the church measures its virtue by its lack of interchange with the world. Such an attitude ignores the fact that the Spirit is at work in the whole of creation. It ignores too that the church's proclamation of the Gospel 'can be helped greatly in various ways by the world, whether by individuals or by society and their resources and activities'.[67] In short, the church can provide an opportunity for people to recognize the Spirit in the communion of faith, to share the means that the church offers to enrich one's life in the Spirit, and to be part of the church's profession of faith, only if it maintains a strong connection to the whole of life.

The second danger, the opposite of the first, is that the church will attempt to control life in the world. The problem here is not simply one of a lack of competence, although that is not an insignificant issue, but the fact that the specific role of the church in the world is to be a sacrament, a reminder and means of encounter with the love of God that will have its fulfilment in God's Kingdom. The accomplishment of that role does not require that representatives of the church must be in charge of everything. Indeed, the moments in the church's history when its representatives have attempted to run the world have not only been less than golden for both the church and the world, they have often done damage to the church's witness to Jesus Christ.

Since the Spirit alone can determine the outcome of the church's witness and since that witness is to the Kingdom,

---

[66] Rahner, *The Love of Jesus and the Love of Neighbour*, 74.
[67] 'The Pastoral Constitution on the Church in the Modern World', *GS* no. 40.

whose fullness is beyond both human history and human calculation, it follows that the 'success' of the church's mission
does not depend on the church appearing successful according
to everyday measures of success. In other words, factors such as
size, wealth, power, or popularity do not indicate that the
church is helping to bring about the Kingdom. In fact, paradoxically, they might even become obstacles to the fulfilment of
the church's mission. What counts, then, is the genuineness
of the church's communal life and the quality of its presence in
the world.

The ultimate task of the church is to remind all people that
our future and our fulfilment are in God, not in anything that is
less than God. This means that the church needs to witness to
the fact that it is a pilgrim church whose home is in God, not an
earthly kingdom.[68] In concrete terms, the church's orientation
to the fullness of life in God's trinitarian communion means
that Christians need to distinguish between the coming of the
Kingdom and proposals for a perfect world. That distinction,
however, ought not to blind us to the fact that earthly progress
can 'contribute to a better ordering of human society [and so is]
highly relevant to the Kingdom of God'.[69]

THE SPIRIT AND THE AUTHENTICITY OF THE CHURCH

A later chapter will explore the particular challenges and opportunities for the mission of the church in the contemporary
world, but it is sufficient for now to reinforce that the existence
of the church as the Spirit-formed sacrament of Jesus Christ
summons it to develop a genuine communion, to be and
become one, holy, catholic, and apostolic, and to be good
news for those in need. All of that, in turn, depends on the
willingness of every member of the church 'to accede to another
way of being'.[70] This new way of being is a response to God's
self-communication in Jesus Christ. It is a way of being for
which the Spirit is both the catalyst and the enabler. It is also a

---

[68] See Vatican II's 'Constitution on the Church', *LG* nos. 48–51.
[69] 'The Pastoral Constitution on the Church in the Modern World', *GS* no.
39.
[70] Chauvet, *The Sacraments*, 91.

way of being that involves a relationship with God, with others in the communion of faith, and with the whole of life in the world.

This chapter has stressed the Spirit's role as the one who reveals the love of God made visible in Jesus Christ, the love that both inaugurates the Kingdom in history and guarantees its future fulfilment. It has stressed too that, through the Spirit, the church exists both to make present in human history that same love and to maintain an orientation to the fullness of God's Kingdom, which is yet to come. In order to accomplish its mission, the church must not only engage with human history, the sole venue for the revelation of the Kingdom, but also understand itself as the agent of the Kingdom, not its realization. Each person who is a part of the communion of the church is a recipient of the Spirit who initiates them not only into the hope founded in Jesus Christ, but into the mission of making that same hope accessible to others.

While the chapter has identified the Spirit as central to the life of the church, it remains to make explicit the manifold ways in which the Spirit communicates life within the communion of faith. This means exploring the Spirit's connection to the concrete life of the church, it means considering whether the church's structure and organization can be the work of the Spirit, and discerning the relationship between individual faith and the claims of the church's authorities. This will also involve examining the relationship of the Spirit to permanence and development, to the capacity of the church to adapt to a changing world. Those issues will be the focus of the next chapter.

4

This Church

At the beginning of the twenty-first century, few qualities rate more highly in Western cultures than the capacity to respond to emerging demands: multiskilling, multifunctioning, and adaptability rule. Underpinning that priority is the need to keep pace with the complexity of contemporary life. What matters is 'now'; 'identity' is no more than the ability to change identities. While memory might be an asset in computers, it can be an obstacle to change for businesses and governments. In 'the real world', continuity is an illusion. In such an environment, the church appears decidedly alien.

In a world that esteems change and 'the new', the church seems to be irrelevant to the times: burdened by a commitment to what derives from 'tradition', as well as by arcane institutions and organs of authority, the church is passé. As a result, the only place for the church is at the periphery of society, where it keeps company with typewriters and record-players—to say nothing of records!—as well as other curiosities that are salient warnings to those who might neglect the need to modernize.

At the heart of that assessment of the church are two common assumptions: that there is a symbiosis between the perceived irrelevance of the church in contemporary society and the role of tradition, institution, and authority in delineating a specific identity for the church; that it is not possible for the church to address contemporary society in any ways that make a connection to today's people and questions. Although those assumptions might have wide currency, they ought not to pass without some scrutiny. Accordingly, this chapter will explore the role of tradition and institution, the elements that make the church *this* church. In so doing, the aim will be to determine whether those elements might result in something other than the fossilization of the church. The next chapter of the book will investigate whether the church, without loss of its identity, might be anything other than irrelevant to the present environment.

It is worth noting immediately that nothing from the previous two chapters would support the view that the church is either inflexible or nailed to the past. Indeed, those chapters constructed a theology of the church that highlighted the dynamism of the church, which derives from the presence of the Holy Spirit, who promotes the pilgrimage to the fullness of God's Kingdom. Nonetheless, there might be a suspicion that even the Holy Spirit cannot survive an encounter with the juggernauts that carry 'tradition' and the church's institutional elements, particularly its forms of authority.

In exploring tradition and authority, this chapter aims to show not only why those two features are necessary for *this* church, but also that neither of them, when properly understood and appropriated, are synonymous with the production of a petrified church. In order to realize its aims, the chapter will stress that tradition and the church's structures of authority do not exist in an orbit that is alien to the movement of the Holy Spirit. This suggests that the church becomes closed or authoritarian only if the Spirit finds no place in it; such a development, of course, would negate the true identity of the church.

In the first half of the chapter, the focus will be on various aspects of 'tradition': its universal application to human activities; the claim that the Christian tradition is a vehicle for an encounter with Jesus Christ in the Holy Spirit; the symbolic reality of tradition; the Bible as a primary expression of tradition; and the openness of the Christian tradition to development—discussion of particular possibilities for change will be a feature of Chapter 6. The second half of the chapter will undertake a similar analysis of the institutional dimension of the church, with a particular emphasis on the relationship between authority and the communion of faith.

THE GIFT AND CHALLENGE OF TRADITION

In contemporary Western societies, it is probable that 'tradition' has more detractors than friends. That situation is largely the inheritance of the Enlightenment, which regarded reverence for tradition as indicative of a slavish dependence on the past, a dependence invariably toxic to the creative potential of the human intellect. From there, it was only a small step to the conviction that 'tradition' implies opposition to any change and, its corollary, a lack of receptivity to whatever is new. In addition, since 'tradition' is not an abstract, since it is inseparable from particular realities—'traditions'—it became common to regard any reference to tradition as expressive of an excessive concern with historical minutiae, fear of experiment, and hostility towards those who do not conform to received ways of thinking and acting.

That critique of tradition was particularly influential when applied to the church since its history is replete with examples of different groups fighting against one another, or against the wider society, in defence of specific traditions. As those struggles can appear to be little more than disputes over words, styles of worship, or other incidentals, they confirm the suspicion that those in the thrall of tradition are irrational and bigoted. As a result, the church's concern with tradition can alienate those who might value the church's communal dimension or its promotion of justice and peace, but have no desire to accept the burden of what they perceive as arcane and outdated.

While it might seem that only in the church does 'tradition' continue to play a role today, such is not the case. Indeed, in human endeavours as diverse as politics, sport, and the arts, various expressions of tradition remain central. Ironically, then, even contemporary culture preserves some openness to the value of tradition. In the light of that openness, it is important to clarify the meaning of 'tradition', especially to emphasize its positive aspects and applicability to all human endeavours. After that, the task will be to examine tradition's contribution to the construction of *this* church.

To be authentic, the quest for a positive reception of tradition cannot shrink from the fact that all aspects of 'tradition', which include particular 'traditions', and the process of 'traditioning', the passing on of a tradition, connect us to the past. That connection, however, does not necessarily confirm the Enlightenment's critique of tradition, does not imply that the inhabitants of the present are abrogating responsibility for their own lives by looking to the past for answers. On the other hand, by putting the present into a context, by helping us to recognize that this moment of history is not entirely the product of its own creation, an appreciation of tradition affords us insight into our own situation:

to understand our present experience, we have to be able to put it into relation or harmony with our past experience—with our vocabularies, our stories, our patterns of thought or ways of thinking, our self-understanding, and our understanding of others.[1]

This suggests that tradition, even though it is a bequest of the past, is also 'one to be invested in the present so that we may reap dividends in the future'.[2] The value of a tradition, then, does not reside exclusively in its antiquity, but in its capacity to inform a creative understanding of, and response to, the present and, even more importantly, to open paths to the future. Furthermore, to anticipate a critique that a later section of the chapter will develop, the claim that something from the past can be effective in the present and future does not suggest that it possesses magical properties. Rather, the claim has its basis in the possibility that there can be a relationship between the human project in different eras and cultures.

Although all moments of history, all individuals, and all communities are unique, human beings share, in every age and culture, the common tasks of meaning-making and truth-seeking. Our uniqueness, therefore, does not imply that we are monads or that there can be no commonality between us, or even between our forebears and ourselves. The common search for truth and meaning, then, holds the key to the possibility that what comes from the past can remain life-giving across diverse periods of history—the next chapter will discuss whether that principle remains applicable in the present era of Western culture, when even the concept of 'truth' is under threat. Thus, the various traditions that affect us in all areas of life witness to the relational dimensions of our existence.

---

[1] William Sweet, 'The Future of Tradition', *Science et Esprit*, 54 (2002), 305.

[2] Paul Lakeland, *Theology and Critical Theory: The Discourse of the Church* (Nashville, Tenn.: Abingdon Press, 1990), 160.

Those traditions, which involve symbols that manifest a
common identity and norms that enable shared wisdom to
express itself in action, highlight the enduring influence of
those who have opened up possibilities for life and given us
insights into how to live well.[3] When we share such insights,
when we preserve them in particular ways of acting, and 'translate' them into contexts far removed from their origins, they
help to form the identity of individuals and groups:

> By conveying a worldview and by distinguishing 'our' path from
> other paths, traditions distinguish our community from other
> communities . . . Traditions provide a sense of stability, a communal
> space in which people can dwell, and a set of practices that shape how
> the participants live in the world . . . [4]

A tradition, then, can provide a platform on which to build in
the present for the future. While it cannot inoculate us against
the need to make decisions and take actions in our unique
context, a tradition can guide that decision-making and action.
It does so by putting at our disposal language and symbols with
which we can identify and that can act as norms for our choices.
In this way, a tradition connects us with others: with our
contemporaries who subscribe to the same tradition, but also
with those from whom we have inherited the tradition. Shorn
of all traditions, we would be prisoners of the present. Traditions offer us a broader vista:

> [W]e must learn from the past if only to generate critical dissonance
> with the present, to open up new vistas and walkways, generate new
> insights, negotiate dead-ends, endure experiences of profound alien-
> ation, and live with changing criteria.[5]

A tradition, however, can enrich us only if we are receptive to
it, only if we open ourselves to what it offers. That openness
presumes the willingness to recognize that our present moment
of history is not self-sufficient. It depends too on an implicit
acknowledgement of our finitude, of the fact that others can

---

[3] For the notion of tradition as providing common identity and norms see
van Beeck, 'Divine Revelation', 220; see also Sweet, 'The Future of Tradition', 299–301.

[4] Terrence W. Tilley, *Inventing Catholic Tradition* (Maryknoll, NY: Orbis,
2000), 43.

[5] Loades, 'Word and Sacrament', 34.

add to our lives what we cannot provide for ourselves. In other words, to appropriate a tradition we need to approach it as a 'Thou', as something that is outside of us and not under our control, as something that we must receive, not seek to dominate.[6] This suggests that there is a parallel between our relationship to a tradition and our relationships with one another: both require openness, even surrender of the self, if we are to experience the enrichment they offer. Both, then, involve the risk of self-surrender, the risk that is characteristic of faith.

We cannot, of course, know in advance the outcome of our surrender to the inalienable 'Thou' of the other. On the other hand, as the discussion of 'faith' in Chapter 2 emphasized, we make that surrender on the basis of our hope that it will open for us possibilities that exceed our imagining. That surrender, however, does not mean that we become merely passive or renounce the right to question whether the relationship with the other is truly conducive to our well-being. Nonetheless, even such questioning presumes some receptivity to 'otherness'. While a tradition is not a person, it is certainly 'other', something beyond our control. This implies that a relationship with a tradition is impossible if there is no willingness to receive what we cannot dominate or determine.

While the otherness of a tradition, like the otherness of the rest of humanity, could be oppressive, a restriction on our freedom to shape the world according to our desires, it is also possible to understand that otherness as highlighting the nature of human freedom. That freedom exists only in relation to what we have not chosen, in relation to factors such as birth, bodiliness, the existence of others, the physical world, and a creator God, rather than in a realm that is entirely of our own making. In short, that freedom does not exist in a vacuum, where it could remain unfettered by any considerations other than itself. It is, rather, a responsive freedom, one that can never demand the first word.[7]

[6] For the notion of tradition as a 'Thou' see Hans-Georg Gadamer, *Truth and Method*, 2nd edn. (London: Sheed & Ward, 1979), 324.

[7] Karl Rahner, 'Baptism and the Renewal of Baptism', *Theological Investigations*, 23, tr. J. Donceel and H. Riley (New York: Crossroad, 1992), 201.

Accordingly, to insist that human beings remain free of the
fetters of any traditions is to misunderstand both the nature of
human freedom and the implications of our social and historical
existence. Traditions connect us to one another, they order our
universe, and give symbolic form to our understanding of the
meaning of life and of truth. As a result, 'to be outside all
traditions is to be a stranger to enquiry; it is to be in a state of
intellectual and moral destitution.'[8] This means, ironically, that
even the Enlightenment's view on the absurdity of tradition
provides the basis for another tradition, another claim to express the truth, rather than representing, unquestionably, *the*
truth that all people ought to accept. Clearly, if we accept that
there is *the* truth, as distinct from mere perspectives on it, there
will inevitably be friction between traditions since all lay claim
to that same truth—the implications of that fact for a positive
appreciation of 'tradition' will be a topic for further discussion
in the next chapter.

The analysis in this section promotes the conclusion
that 'tradition' and human flourishing are mutually inclusive.
The next few sections will examine whether that positive
appraisal is applicable to the role that tradition plays within
the church. As the first step in that direction, the following
section will address the specific meaning that 'tradition' has
in the church, particularly its connection to Jesus and the Holy
Spirit.

A 'ONCE-FOR-ALL' TRADITION

While life in the church is replete with traditions, the key to
appreciating their individual role and the connection between
them lies in establishing their relationship to 'the Tradition':
'by *the Tradition* is meant the Gospel itself, transmitted from
generation to generation in and by the church, Christ himself
present in the life of the church'.[9] If God's revelation in Jesus

---

[8] Alasdair MacIntyre, *Whose Justice? Which Rationality?* (Notre Dame,
Ind.: University of Notre Dame Press, 1988), 367.

[9] The Faith and Order Commission of the World Council of Churches,
(Montreal, 1963), in G. Gassman (ed.), *Documentary History of Faith and
Order 1963–1993*, (Geneva: WCC Publications, 1993), 10.

Christ were no more than an event in the past, the emphasis on tradition would imply that Christians live primarily by memory. In fact, as the previous two chapters have argued, Christian faith not only lives from a present encounter with Christ, but also has, through the Holy Spirit, an eschatological orientation.

Christian faith, then, understands the 'Christ-event' not as one event among many in the sequence of time (*chronos*), but as a 'once-for-all' event, a decisive moment (*kairos*) that 'recapitulates' what God has done over time and includes all that God will do in the future of humanity.[10] As a result, the Christian Tradition is 'a kind of epiphany of this insertion of the *kairos*, accomplished *once-for-all*, into the flow of history'.[11] This means that in order to do justice to God's revelation in Jesus Christ it is necessary to hold together its past, present, and future dimensions.

The insistence on the once-for-all nature of God's revelation in Jesus Christ can never validly be an argument for a fossilized faith—'Turned lovingly towards the past where its treasure lies, it moves towards the future, where it conquers and illuminates.'[12] Consequently, Christian faith must be capable of expressing itself in ways that respond to contemporary needs and challenges. Nor does this require that the church must abandon its traditions and begin from scratch in every new era. If the traditions of the church are genuinely symbols of the Holy Spirit, they must also be vehicles for the generative power of that Spirit, must promote the pilgrimage to the

[10] This distinction between *chronos* and *kairos* as ways of measuring time comes from Jean-Marie Tillard, 'Tradition, Reception' in Kenneth Hagen (ed.), *The Quadrilog: Tradition and the Future of Ecumenism* (Collegeville, Minn.: Michael Glazier, 1994), 333. The notion of everything coming under the headship of Christ, which was a key theme in patristic exegesis, has its origins in Eph. 1: 20–3.

[11] Tillard, 'Tradition, Reception', 334. The emphasis is Tillard's. Vatican II's 'Dogmatic Constitution on Divine Revelation' makes a similar point with its description of Jesus as 'both the mediator and the fullness of all revelation'; see 'Dogmatic Constitution on Divine Revelation' (*Dei verbum*), *DV* no. 2

[12] Maurice Blondel, 'History and Dogma', in *'The Letter on Apologetics' and 'History and Dogma'*, tr. A. Dru and I. Trethowan (London: Harvill Press, 1964), 267. The original was published in 1904.

fullness of the Kingdom.[13] The church's traditions, therefore, ought not to stifle the life of the Spirit in the community of faith, but facilitate it. Included in such a process of facilitation is stimulating creative responses to new questions—a later section of this chapter, as well as parts of Chapter 6, will develop this claim more fully.

From the fact that 'the Tradition' expresses the once-for-all event of God's revelation in Jesus Christ, it is possible to derive four attributes that will be common to authentic traditions in the church. First, authentic traditions have their foundations in the apostolic witness to Jesus Christ. As we saw in the analysis of 'apostolicity' at the end of the previous chapter, the apostolic witness grounds the church in the historical reality of God's revelation in Jesus Christ. That grounding, however, does not imply a church fixated on the past, but one that understands itself and its mission in terms of the Good News of Jesus Christ:

> The apostolicity of the Church is not just a matter of teaching what the apostles taught or having a sense of purpose and mission in the world; it means continuously and vitally being the same Church as the Church of the apostles, led through history by the same Holy Spirit to proclaim the same Good News and to bring the same salvation.[14]

Secondly, authentic traditions symbolize the presence of the Holy Spirit; they provide a means of encounter in the present with God's life-giving love, the love that Jesus Christ revealed. In short, the value of what the first generation of Christians passed on to their successors does not derive from its unique beauty or from the fact that it expresses more wisdom than anything that believers in subsequent generations might have been able to devise, but from the fact that it remains a vehicle for the Spirit. The emphasis, then, is not on the superficial, on the symbol alone, but on the symbol in its relationship to what it symbolizes.

Accordingly, the church accepted as 'the Canon' of Scripture those texts through which the Spirit of Jesus Christ was made

---

[13] Cf Jean-Marie Tillard, 'Faith, the Believer and the Church', *One in Christ*, 30 (1994), 217

[14] John Wright, 'The Meaning and Structure of Catholic Faith', *Theological Studies*, 39 (1978), 709.

present to challenge, to console, and to convey the certainty of God's faithfulness. Similarly, the formalization and codification of 'the sacraments' grew out of the community's experience that the Spirit was among them in those actions as the source of the encouragement, reconciliation, and hope that had their origin in Jesus Christ. To be authentic, therefore, traditions in the church must be more than merely awe-inspiring or ancient rituals, but avenues of encounter with the Spirit of Jesus Christ:

In the Spirit, the inner disposition of Jesus' historical life becomes the inner disposition of the historical life of believers; the narrative of Jesus' life becomes the narrative continued in the lives of those who live with him. Nothing short of the fullness of that life is the Christian tradition.[15]

This experience of the Spirit is one that we can have only in our present. In other words, we must bring the questions and concerns of the present to what is embedded in 'the classic events, images, persons, rituals, texts and symbols of a tradition'.[16] This meeting between a tradition and the present, a meeting that the philosopher Hans-Georg Gadamer refers to as the 'fusion of horizons', takes place in all areas of human life.[17] Clearly, a tradition that cannot accommodate the questions and concerns of the present, a tradition that is merely about the past, is dead; such a tradition could not be an authentic expression of the Spirit.

Thirdly, authentic traditions promote and nurture the pilgrimage towards the fullness of God's Kingdom, thereby highlighting that neither our history nor our present embodies that fullness:

Christian life issues out of an inheritance, lives in the present, but unerringly must look to the future in God. Landscapes will change and it is vital that as a community we understand the mechanism of that change if future vision is not to be usurped by past ideals or

---

[15] Arthur Vogel, 'Tradition: The Contingency Factor' in Hagen (ed.), *The Quadrilog*, 266–7.

[16] D. Tracy, *The Analogical Imagination: Christian Theology and the Culture of Pluralism* (London: SCM, 1981), 104.

[17] Gadamer, *Truth and Method*, 273.

overtaken by an obsession with novelty. That is the nature of a Spirit-filled tradition.[18]

Fourthly, authentic traditions also stimulate discipleship. Central to the deeper communion with God and other people, which is a product of a positive response to the Spirit through authentic traditions, is the call to follow Christ in the world by acting in ways that manifest the Kingdom. This following comprises the essence of discipleship.

In the context of the church, the meeting between the tradition and the issues of the present, the eschatological orientation of tradition, and the call to discipleship all converge in the task of theology: 'the role of theology in the Christian community is essentially...critical mediation between the Christian faith as it is handed down in the tradition and the contemporary living experience of Christians.'[19] The need for theology, for reception and interpretation of the tradition in light of the present, reinforces the fact that ascribing a normative role to the apostolic tradition does not imply that the subsequent history of the church is irrelevant or merely an extended period of passive acceptance of what comes from the earliest centuries. Indeed, the reception of the apostolic tradition presents its own significant challenge:

In attending to what is proclaimed from the Bible, or to what is celebrated in liturgy, or what is passed on in a tradition, the church needs to listen keenly for a word that speaks from a deeper experience of redemption than do the paradigmatic patterns of speech adopted from patriarchal, hierarchical, or technological cultures.[20]

Although there is a danger of confusing particular cultural expressions with the living Spirit at the heart of the tradition, a church that sought to exist independently of any traditions would have no support for a claim to connection with the Spirit

---

[18] Stephen Platten and George Pattison, *Spirit and Tradition: An Essay on Change* (Norwich: Canterbury Press, 1996), 41.

[19] James Byrne, 'Theology and Christian Faith', in Claude Geffré and Werner Jeanrond (eds.), *Why Theology?* (*Concilium*, no. 1994/6) (London: SCM, 1994), 11.

[20] David Power, 'The Holy Spirit, Scripture, Tradition, and Interpretation', in Geoffrey Wainwright (ed.), *Keeping the Faith: Essays to Mark the Centenary of* 'Lux Mundi' (London: SPCK, 1989), 167.

of Jesus Christ. Nor would such a church have grasped the implications of existing as a communion of people. Like any group of people that is more than a random gathering, the people who form the church need to be able to identify one another, to know what binds them together as a group, to have opportunities and means to share their life together, to be able to resolve differences, and also to pass on their faith.[21] While such mechanisms can come about only in history, while they involve, necessarily, particular words and action, while they are the product of particular decisions, the argument of this section has been that such particularity can be the language of the Spirit, can express the once-for-all nature of God's revelation in Jesus Christ.

Authentic traditions, therefore, do something other than provide information about Jesus Christ. In being the means for a present encounter with the Holy Spirit, they express the identity of the church itself. In other words, what the church in every age receives from the apostolic tradition, and passes on, is everything that is necessary for its own life:

The expression 'what has been handed down from the apostles' includes everything that helps the people of God to live a holy life and to grow in faith. In this way the church, in its teaching, life and worship perpetuates and hands on to every generation all that it is and all that it believes.[22]

This link between tradition and the faith of the church gives rise to what is probably the most controversial claim about the church's traditions: that they are the product of divine institution. The next section will examine possible meanings and legitimations for that claim.

DIVINELY INSTITUTED TRADITIONS?

In order to enable members of the church 'to live a holy life and to grow in faith', what has developed from the apostolic witness

[21] T. Howland Sanks, 'The Church: Context for Theology', in T. Howland Sanks and Leo O'Donovan (eds.), *Faithful Witness: Foundations of Theology for Today's Church* (New York: Crossroad, 1989), 109.

[22] Vatican II, 'Dogmatic Constitution on Divine Revelation' (*Dei verbum*), *DV* no. 8.

must symbolize the Holy Spirit, as the Spirit is the source of holiness. Since human beings cannot control the Spirit, it follows also that what symbolizes the Spirit must be the work of the Spirit. That conviction is at the heart both of 'divine institution' and the particular claims made for the apostolic witness:

> Thus it would not be correct to say that God's founding of the Church consists simply in conserving it in existence; rather we must say that an essential part of God's conserving it in existence consists in God having founded it at a particular moment in time. God, then, as founder of the Church has a unique, qualitatively not transmissible relationship to the Church's first generation, one which God does not have in the same sense to other periods of the Church's history, or rather has to the latter only through the former.[23]

While the conviction that there is a 'unique, qualitatively not transmissible relationship' between God and the churches of the first generation underscores much that is central to the Christian church, it presents its own challenges to belief. In part, that challenge arises from flawed uses of 'divine institution', such as its invocation in support of dysfunctional arrangements in the church or to compel unquestioning acceptance of such arrangements. The more fundamental challenge, however, is that of articulating the relationship between divine activity and human activity.

To assert that features of the apostolic churches express 'divine institution' can give the impression that those traditions are both timeless and independent of any human involvement. This could suggest either that they are perfect embodiments of the words or actions that the gospels attribute directly to Jesus or that they are the product of a unique intervention by the Spirit in human history, an intervention that not only transcended the usual dynamics of that history, but also excludes any possibility of development for such traditions. Since those interpretations are at odds with the church's history, they can make it difficult to appropriate 'divine institution' as other than a magical notion.

Inevitably, an exclusive focus on God's activity as the sole explanation for historical realities gives birth to the opposite

---

[23] Karl Rahner, *Inspiration in the Bible*, tr. H. Henkey (New York: Herder & Herder, 1964), 45.

viewpoint: an exclusive emphasis on human activity, From the latter perspective, 'divine institution' is not a meaningful concept: the church's traditions are simply human traditions, which Christians might have developed as attempts to respond to Jesus Christ, but which have no specific connection to Jesus or the Spirit. For the adherents of the minimalist interpretation of God's activity, all traditions, since they are historically contingent, can change whenever members of the church choose to change them.

What is missing from the two extremes is any attempt to bring together God's activity and human choices and history. A consequence of that absence is that both views are unable to understand change or development as other than a radical discontinuity: for those who emphasize only God's activity, such changes would be tantamount to the rejection of God's will; for those who acknowledge only human activity, changes mean simply that new human priorities replace earlier ones.

To do justice both to the historical reality of the church and to the claims that its tradition expresses the divine will, we need to investigate whether there might be possible alternative meanings of 'divine institution'. The measure of such alternatives would be that they do not make human and divine activity mutually exclusive.

One way of avoiding a dichotomy between the divine and the human is to insist that 'divine institution' is something other than either a legal or a dogmatic concept. Through the legal lens, 'divine institution' would imply that particular words of Jesus made something mandatory, leaving believers with no option except unequivocal acceptance. Similarly, the dogmatic approach implies that those who truly believe will accept that aspects of the church came directly from God without the need to consider any human agency. A more fruitful approach comes from considering 'divine institution' as a hermeneutical concept, as a way of understanding and interpreting aspects of the church's life within the framework of the whole relationship between God and humanity.[24]

---

[24] See Francis Schüssler Fiorenza, *Foundational Theology* (New York: Crossroad, 1984), 164.

From a hermeneutical perspective, affirming the divine institution of various traditions in the church is a recognition of the
deepest dimensions of the Christian community's history. In
other words, the community of faith, as the result of its own
history and reflection on that history, came to regard some
developments in its history, such as the authoritative role of
the episcopate in articulating the faith of the community, as the
expression of God's will for the church and as connected to
faith in Jesus Christ. The key to such a conviction was that the
particular developments were in continuity with the gospels'
portrayal of the relationship between Jesus and his disciples.[25]
Such developments could even be accepted as representing
something that needed to be part of the identity of the church
for all time, even if they needed also to be able to develop in
response to the challenges of history.[26] In other words, 'divine
institution' can be reconcilable both with human actions and
with openness to the implications of the church's historical
existence:

There would still be irreversible elements in the life of the Church,
but their status would not rest in the fact that they are the furthest
from being products of human freedom, development and creativity,
but rather because they are precisely the most truly human. They go
to the core of what it means to be human and so are capable of imaging
the divine.[27]

The value of such an approach is that it preserves the identity
of the church as a communion of faith dependent on the inspiration of the Spirit, without thereby sacrificing the importance
of human activity or the community's history and discernment
of what constitutes an authentic tradition. Furthermore, since
faith in Jesus as the Christ, the faith that is the product of the
Holy Spirit's presence, was prior to the development of any

[25] Francis Schüssler Fiorenza, *Foundational Theology*, 169.

[26] For an example of an attempt to link the Spirit and the historical development of structures within the community of faith see, Roger Haight, 'The
Structures of the Church', *Journal of Ecumenical Studies*, 30 (1993), 403–14.

[27] Michael Raschko, 'Issues Orbiting Church Authority', in Gary Cham-
berlain and Patrick Howell (eds.), *Empowering Authority: The Charism of
Episcopacy and Primacy in the Church Today* (Kansas City, Miss.: Sheed &
Ward, 1990), 120.

particular traditions, including even the composition of what the church now accepts as canonical gospels, it follows that the 'primeval' faith of the church includes the capacity to develop. Indeed, it was this faith that 'led the testimony of the apostles to a more explicit awareness of itself, and of all that it implied, even while this testimony was fashioning a corporate faith'.[28] In short, such faith is 'fertile and living, thus developing and unfolding throughout the ages'.[29] There is, therefore, no necessary contradiction between 'divine institution' and human activity. The best example of those dynamics is in the formation and interpretation of what is central to the apostolic tradition: Scripture.

THE HUMAN WORD OF GOD

A focus on Scripture highlights in two important ways the issue of the relationship between human and divine activity: first, it raises the question of how something of human composition could be 'the word of God'; secondly, it emphasizes that human freedom can choose to submit itself to what it acknowledges to be symbols of God. In short, the focus on Scripture underscores that an appreciation of how 'tradition' shapes the life of the church is inseparable from an appreciation of its complex and demanding nature.

The description of Scripture as 'the word of God' can conjure up immediately visions of angels whispering in the ears of scribes, who were mere ciphers. Seen in that light, Scripture is God's work in a unique way, a way that puts it not only beyond human tampering, but also, some would argue, beyond the normal mechanisms of human interpretation.

On the other hand, it is important to acknowledge that the words that form the books of the Bible, like the objects used in

---

[28] Yves Congar, *Tradition and the Life of the Church*, tr. A. N. Woodrow (London: Burns & Oates, 1964), 21. For more on how the experience of God can be richer and deeper than the efforts to express it, see Karl Rahner, 'Theology in the New Testament', *Theological Investigations*, 5, tr. K-H Kruger (New York: Crossroad, 1983), 23–41.

[29] Joseph Ratzinger, 'Revelation and Tradition', in Karl Rahner and Joseph Ratzinger, *Revelation and Tradition*, tr. W. J. O'Hara (New York: Herder & Herder, 1962), 46.

the church's sacraments and the people who represent the church in particular ministries, neither lose their everyday meaning nor acquire an encrypted meaning when used in a sacred context. That fact obliges those who wish to talk about Scripture as 'the word of God' to provide some indication of how the words of Scripture might communicate something more than what appears in print.

That challenge raises a dilemma: on the one hand, the attempt to explain the working of the Spirit could imply that faith had become unnecessary; on the other hand, the invocation of faith without any attempt at clarification could be a resort to fideism, which, as Chapter 2 argued, is not authentic Christian faith. As a way of resolving that dilemma, it is possible to demonstrate that words are capable of bearing multiple levels of meaning. This approach suggests that it is possible to use 'the word of God' in a way that neither claims to specify the mechanics of the Spirit's activity nor relies on magic to expound God's connection to human experience.

In our everyday experience, words can have multiple levels of meaning. Thus, for example, we recognize that context affects what our words convey. While we could, in theory, use the same words to compose a computer manual, a film review, or a love-letter, the words would communicate something quite different in each case. They would also have a different impact on us. This reflects something about how we use words, rather than that words, chameleon-like, can transmogrify themselves. The same words, therefore, can convey, in different contexts, raw facts or embody and express personal, even life-changing, decisions.[30] This distinction is especially evident in the difference between the use of 'love' in a philosophical analysis of the subject and in the phrase 'I love you', when one person speaks or writes it to another. In the latter instance, the words do not merely convey information, but are an event: they make present how one person feels about another, invite acceptance of the self-offering of that person, and call for a response, which, in its fullest form, reciprocates the self-offering of the speaker.

In the church too, words function in a variety of ways: from those used in a theology lecture or papal encyclical, which

---

[30] Rahner, 'What is a Sacrament?', 140.

attempt to construct an understanding of God or of some aspect of the divine-human relationship, to those that convey God's forgiveness in sacramental form or, as in the gospels, express God's promise of eternal life in Jesus Christ. In everyday usage, language as an event—'I love you'—represents the fullest realization of language's potential, since it calls for the greatest involvement of both speaker and hearer. So too in the church, the fullest realization of language is that which provides the opportunity to encounter and respond to the Spirit:

The truly kerygmatic or ecclesiastical word achieves the full realization of its nature when it has an *exhibitive* character, that is, when it effects what it signifies, when it is brought about *through* the Word or addressed to the hearers in ways that bring salvation to them.[31]

In such instances, language is sacramental: the words make present the Spirit, who offers us God's unconditional love in Jesus Christ and opens our hearts to respond to that love. Like any symbol, then, the words are an irreducible aspect of the process of communication, even though the content of the communication exceeds anything that an analysis of the words could explain. The classification of Scripture as 'the word of God', therefore, does not put that word beyond our understanding:

The term [God's word] is analogous, indicating that God's redemptive power works in human lives and human history through the convergence of the Spirit at work in the heart with that which in the flawed forms of human speech appeals to the heart and points to, or testifies to, the redemptive power of God in certain events that have been recorded for us.[32]

While faith alone can name the Spirit as the source of the impact that texts of Scripture can have, it does not require the same act of faith to accept that the possibility of such an impact beyond the time and place from which the texts originate. In fact, while the claim that Scripture can mediate an experience of God is unique, literary theory acknowledges the capacity of different types of texts to 'speak' beyond their own time and place. Indeed, part of what defines literary classics is their

[31] Ibid. The emphasis is Rahner's.
[32] Power, 'The Holy Spirit, Scripture, Tradition, and Interpretation', 170.

'excess of meaning', which enables them to be accessible beyond the context, or even the intention, of their authors.[33] Thus, readers from times and cultures far removed from the original setting of a text can make a connection to such texts. Once again, this does not suggest a secret code, but a connection based on shared humanity and shared concerns. It also assumes a willingness to listen, to ask questions, to expect something more than what is immediately obvious:

the classical text is not in some timeless moment which needs mere repetition. Rather its timelessness as permanent timeliness is the only one proper to any expression of the finite, temporal, historical beings we are.... The classic text's fate is that only its constant reinterpretation by later finite, historical, temporal beings who will risk asking its questions and listening, critically and tactfully, to its responses can actualize the event of understanding beyond its present fixation in a text. Every classic lives as a classic only if it finds readers willing to be provoked by its claim to attention.[34]

In response to the mediation of God's self-communication through Scripture, the church has always accorded Scripture a unique reverence, which is explained by, and summarized in, describing it as 'the word of God'. Scripture, therefore, 'stands as the church's support and strength, affording her children sturdiness in faith, food for the soul and a pure and unfailing fount of spiritual life'.[35]

Nonetheless, there was a long-running—and often bitter, even violent—controversy between the Catholic and Protestant communions over whether the church lives by 'Scripture alone' or 'Scripture and tradition'. At the heart of that controversy was not simply Scripture's status as manifestation of divine will for the church, but the contrast between that status and what were regarded as merely human traditions.

The Reformers' emphasis on 'Scripture alone' was, in part, an effort to reassert the primacy of Scripture as a source of challenge and reform in the church. In order to do so, there was a need to free Scripture from what they perceived to be both its subjugation to ecclesiastical authorities and its relegation to a

---

[33] Tracy, *The Analogical Imagination*, 102.   [34] Ibid.
[35] 'Constitution on Divine Revelation', *DV* no. 21.

lesser place than that held by some of the plethora of the church's traditions. Pursuit of that goal, however, often obscured the fact that Scripture, since it is the product of tradition, both in its composition and its history of interpretation, does not exist independently of the faith, worship, and ministerial life of the church.[36]

Today, there is less likelihood of isolating the Bible from any human considerations. This is so as there is general recognition that Scripture's unique role is not compromised by acknowledging that the text is the product of human beings, who used 'their own powers and faculties, in such a way that they wrote as authors in the true sense, and yet God acted in and through them, directing the content entirely and solely as he willed'.[37]

While that claim represents another aspect of the church's life that only the surrender of faith could make fully accessible, it is consistent with the anthropology and theology of symbolic revelation that Chapters 2 and 3 developed. Taken together, those arguments support the contention that it is possible to understand Scripture as a symbol of the Spirit without implying that human traditions are not evident in the Bible's composition and interpretation:

Though the precise extent of its occurrence may be disputed, no biblical scholar could now possibly deny how deeply a developing tradition has helped shape the thinking of the biblical writers. Not only John, but also the synoptics do not simply pass on such material as they have inherited but creatively adapt it to address new circumstances ... Add to that the extent to which the thought of the biblical writers is reliant on earlier assumptions and the case for a cumulative tradition appears overwhelming.[38]

Nor do those processes belong only in the past, only to the formation of the canonical texts of the Bible. Indeed, the story of Scripture in the church is a story of ongoing interpretation. In addition, the process of reception of Scripture is not an

---

[36] For discussion of the ways in which the emphasis on 'Scripture alone' overturned traditional ways of understanding Scripture's relationship to other aspect of the church's life of faith see Ratzinger, 'Revelation and Tradition', 26–31.

[37] 'Constitution on Divine Revelation', *DV* no. 11.

[38] David Brown, *Tradition and Imagination: Revelation and Change* (Oxford: Oxford University Press, 1999), 113.

abstract process, but takes place in the multiple dimensions of the community's life of faith:

The church, indeed, does not regard the Bible simply as a collection of historical documents dealing with its own origins; it receives the Bible as word of God addressed both to itself and to the entire world at the present time. This conviction, stemming from the faith, leads in turn to the work of actualizing and inculturating the biblical message, as well as to various usages of the inspired text in liturgy, in *'lectio divina'*, in pastoral ministry and in the ecumenical movement.[39]

The recognition of Scripture as foundational to every aspect of the church's life echoes the efforts that the Second Vatican Council instituted to bridge the historical divisions between Protestants and Catholics. The Council stressed that Scripture and tradition form 'a single sacred deposit of the word of God, entrusted to the church'.[40] In this, Vatican II's emphasis differed significantly from that of the Council of Trent, which, in order to distance Catholics from the Reformers, argued that 'the whole truth of salvation and rule of conduct' had passed from Jesus Christ to the church not only by means of 'written books', but also by 'unwritten traditions'.[41] Although the latter could refer both to the faith of the church and the process of transmission, rather than material additional to the content of Scripture, the polarized environment of the Reformation era received 'unwritten traditions' as an assertion of the prerogatives of the church's teaching authority above those of Scripture.[42]

Vatican II, on the other hand, reaffirmed the responsibility of the church's teaching authority for safeguarding the authenticity of what the church had received from the apostolic tradition, without thereby implying that the teaching authority had access to a body of knowledge that was independent of Scrip-

---

[39] The Pontifical Biblical Commission, 'The Interpretation of the Bible in the Church', *Origins*, 23 (6 Jan. 1994), 520. The document was released in 1993.

[40] 'Constitution on Divine Revelation', *DV* no. 10.

[41] Council of Trent, Session no. 4 (8 April 1546), 'First Decree: Acceptance of the Sacred Books and Apostolic Traditions'.

[42] For a survey of the ways in which 'unwritten traditions' had been understood prior to Trent see Congar, *Tradition and the Life of the Church*, 18–21.

ture. Indeed, the Council stressed the accountability of the church's teaching office to what was not subject to its disposal:

[that office] is not above the word of God but stands at its service, teaching nothing but what is handed down, according as it devotedly listens, reverently preserves and faithfully transmits the word of God by divine command and with the help of the holy Spirit.[43]

While Vatican II was no less committed than Trent to the central role of the teaching authority, its formulation ensures that nothing obscures the dependence of the whole church on Scripture.[44] Similarly, Vatican II's claim that 'God's wise design' made provision to ensure a connection between Scripture, tradition, and the church's teaching authority, helps to focus attention on the single reality of the apostolic tradition, which includes, of course, Scripture.[45] As this chapter has emphasized, the purpose of that tradition is not simply the preservation of what is ancient, but the preservation of the church in the faith of the apostles, the faith that leads to life in Christ, through the Spirit.

One aspect of that faith is that it brings about a communion of believers, who are to reflect the unity within the Trinity. Although the faith of the church professes that the Spirit alone is the source of its unity, as Chapter 3 discussed, it also connects the activity of the Spirit to its structures and organs of authority. As the beginning of this chapter acknowledged, however, it is those very structures and authorities that critics of the church see as the sources of reaction and intransigence in the church. The following sections will explore both whether it is possible to locate 'authority' within the understanding of the church as a communion and whether the exercise of such authority can be anything other than reactionary. Since this discussion of authority examines the church's institutional life, it will be useful to preface it by considering whether 'institution' belongs rightly in the same sentence as 'the church'.

[43] 'Constitution on Divine Revelation', *DV* no. 10.

[44] The import of Vatican II's claim is well expressed by Joseph Ratzinger: 'What can be unambiguously recognized from scripture, whether by scientific methods or by simple reading has the function of a real criterion, the test of which even the pronouncements of the magisterium itself have to meet.' See Ratzinger, 'Revelation and Tradition', 49.

[45] 'Constitution on Divine Revelation', *DV* no. 10.

INSTITUTION AS GIFT AND CHALLENGE

The fact that human beings can never experience the Spirit independently of symbolic or sacramental forms, suggests that the aspects of the church that give it visibility, that structure its life as a communion, and that express its interface with the wider society, are not necessarily injurious to the presence of the Spirit in the church. The challenge, then, is to show how there can be a symbiosis between the Spirit and the manifold expressions of the church. This is vital as the church can symbolize God's self-communication to humanity only if the Spirit is constitutive of all aspects of its life, including its institutions.

Although that conclusion is consistent with the argument of the previous two chapters, it might appear too sweeping to be satisfactory: Does it imply that the Spirit is responsible not simply for the existence of the church, but also, for example, for the particular offices that help to shape the church as *this* church? What guides the determination that something is or is not of the Spirit? Who can make such a determination? If the Spirit is responsible for the structures of *this* church, does it put them beyond any possible need for reform?

Underpinning such questions is a twofold concern about claiming too explicit a link between the Spirit and particular manifestations of the church. The first aspect of that concern is that such an association might limit 'the overflowing fruitfulness' and 'incalculable creativity' of the Spirit.[46] Clearly, the Spirit can be the Spirit only if it is free to operate where it will, rather than requiring permission from ecclesial overlords. If Christianity at large has not always been good at witnessing to the freedom of the Spirit, it is likely that the record of the Catholic church would be particularly vulnerable to such criticism:

The Catholic Church has often given—and still gives—the impression of behaving as though it had the Holy Spirit constantly at its command. It sees itself as a sort of vast warehouse of the Spirit, which it distributes in the form of sacraments, dogmas, and acts of authority.[47]

[46] John O'Donnell, *The Mystery of the Triune God* (London: Sheed & Ward, 1988), 93.
[47] Comblin, *The Holy Spirit and Liberation*, 103.

Secondly, there can be a fear that acceptance of a connection between the Spirit and particular structures might either give aid and comfort to some dysfunctional exercises of authority in the church or issue in assertions that those structures are perfect, that their God-given form is never likely to be in need of reform. Since such outcomes would be likely to nurture denominationalism, buttress intolerance of what is new, and affirm those who regard secular culture as irrelevant to the things of God, they are far from appealing.

In light of the church's history, both forms of concern are reasonable. While both would dissolve if 'the church' and 'structure' were mutually exclusive, an amorphous church could be neither a fully human reality nor reflect what we know of God. There could be, for example, no connection between such a church and the dynamics of God's relationship with humanity, a relationship characterized by the mediation of the social and historical, rather than reliance on the private, the invisible, or the purely interior. In addition, it would be remarkable if the church's claim to be the product of the Spirit, whose own identity is particular since its task is to reveal Jesus as the Christ, did not involve the development of a particular identity and organs to maintain and promote that identity.

Nonetheless, it is important to acknowledge that just as 'tradition' can strike terror into the hearts of those with a delicate constitution, so too can 'institution' be frightening. At its worst, 'institution', like 'authority' and 'tradition', lends its name to an '-ism' that suggests hostility towards freedom and creativity. Even apart from the damage done by that extreme form, it is difficult to imagine how 'institution' and 'authority' could ever evoke 'an undreamed of possibility for love':

The real and irremovable scandal of faith, the cross of Jesus Christ, has been obscured by superficial and unnecessary scandals. Here we shouldn't think in the first place of moral scandals, but of the scandal of many of the Church's structures, which seem to many people obstacles both to human emancipation and happiness and to Christian freedom, and an encouragement to immaturity and authoritarian attitudes.[48]

---

[48] Kasper, *Introduction to Christian Faith*, 135.

The challenge, therefore, is to establish that 'institution' in the church can have a mode of operation that is other than destructive. Part of that process involves highlighting the irreducible link between the very existence of the ecclesial community and the role of institutions within that community:

> We cannot collaborate, we cannot function as a community in time and space without some institutional forms. . . . The shape of those institutions, the way they are administered, the distribution of authority within them and among them, the struggle to prevent them from becoming obsessed with their own continuance rather than furtherance of the mission, all these are absolutely essential concerns. What works in one time and in one set of circumstances may be destructive in another time and place. But this is an invitation to pay greater care and attention to our ecclesial institutions, not to dismiss them or drop out of them or seek that chimera, a purely spontaneous, noninstitutional community.[49]

That argument supports the effort to show that the mere existence of institutional forms in the church is not destructive of the Spirit's presence. On the other hand, it does not imply that the exercise of authority in the church expresses, always and everywhere, the love that the Spirit makes present in human history. Nonetheless, if God's self-communication attunes itself to our humanity—a notion that this book has used as a refrain—then the fact that there is an institutional dimension to the church is far from convicting the church of being at odds with the Spirit. Equally, of course, it does not oblige members of the church to affirm that any particular aspect of the church's institutional life always serves well the promotion of faith in the God of Jesus Christ or acts as a reliable beacon of hope.

There is, then, a tension, itself irresolvable, between the need for structure in the church and the danger that the structure might become dysfunctional. While such a situation might seem less than satisfactory, it reflects the fact that '[a]ll things human are ambiguous, and what can serve the greatest good can wreak the greatest harm. But that is the way of things in a world of creatures marked by sin and redeemed by grace.'[50] As

---

[49] Michael Himes, 'Church Institutions: A Theological Note', *New Theology Review*, 14 (2001), 14.

[50] Ibid. 15.

a result, the church's institutional forms, which make the church something other than a disembodied ideal, share with every aspect of its life the obligation to ensure that they do not mask the presence of the Spirit. Concretely, this means that those who exercise authority in the church are not immune from the need for conversion, not simply as individual believers, but as people who exercise authority.

Only when all aspects of the church's institutional life remain open to that conversion, to the realization of the church's mission to be a symbol of the Spirit, can there be hope that members of the church will not regard 'the institution', no less than 'the tradition' that it exists to support, as alien to the concerns of ecclesial faith. While suspicion of institutions might be ineradicable, that suspicion will decline when there is not only a clear link between the practices of the institution and the beliefs held by those who are subject to it, but also 'an obvious fairness' between the burdens imposed on individuals to ensure the functioning of the institution and the rewards that derive from being a part of it.[51] Recognition of the church's pilgrim status, however, means that we ought not to expect that controversy will be unknown or that the church's institutions, like those of every human enterprise, will never alienate some members or fail to live up to what they expect in disciples of Christ.[52]

That analysis suggests that criticism of the church's structure and authorities is not necessarily the manifestation of either anarchic tendencies or a lack of faith in the Spirit. In fact, such criticism can reflect 'a secret longing' or 'injured love', especially in young people, for the realization of what the church is committed to be but, invariably, falls short of realizing.[53] It is worth recalling, therefore, the implications of the church's sacramental existence:

the recognition of the institutional Church as the 'fundamental sacrament' of the reign [of God] always requires a conversion—either because believers, too comfortably ensconced in the institution, forget

---

[51] Duquoc, *Provisional Churches*, 36.

[52] John Thornhill, *Sign and Promise: A Theology of the Church for a Changing World* (London: Collins, 1988), 2.

[53] Kasper, *Theology and Church*, 150.

that it is *only* a sacrament and overlook the distance between it and Christ or because their critical suspicions towards the institution result in their not seeing that it *is* indeed a sacrament. A too serene compliance with the Church is no less questionable than a resentment toward it.[54]

Approaching the institutional reality of the church in a way that does not err on one or other side of that divide is, unquestionably, no small challenge. It is, however, also a crucial one. If we overvalue the institution, there is a risk that we will lose sight of its need for conversion, of the dynamism of the Spirit that promotes that conversion, and of the eschatological orientation that leads the church beyond mere institutional security. In short, the danger is that we will attempt 'to capture Christ in our ideological nets or in the ruses of our desire'.[55] That tendency makes us vulnerable to various 'necrotic' or death-dealing temptations, such as assuming that our religious knowledge gives us control over God, that the sacraments will always do their 'job' without requiring a change of heart on our part, or that our good behaviour gives us leverage over God.[56]

Thus, while the existence of the church as a sacrament of the Spirit offers a means of encounter with the hope and possibility of God's Kingdom, it is also, paradoxically, a reminder of the gap between the fullness of the Kingdom and our present reality.[57] We cannot, therefore, be part of the church without being aware that we will not possess the Kingdom in this world.

Nonetheless, a chronic cynicism towards all things institutional can leave us clinging to the illusion that only an invisible, disembodied church would be truly worthwhile. Such an illusion does justice neither to the Incarnation and the reality of the sacramental presence of the Spirit, nor to the dynamics of humanity's social and historical existence. It also renders impossible a positive appropriation of the richness of a tradition, especially because that richness always comes clothed in the ambiguous reality of symbols.

---

[54] Chauvet, *Symbol and Sacrament*, 186. The emphasis is Chauvet's.
[55] Ibid. 173.
[56] Ibid. 174.
[57] Duquoc, *Provisional Churches*, 57–9.

The challenge, therefore, is to understand the church's institutions in a way that affirms their purpose while embracing the
need for their conversion. The need for conversion applies not
to 'institutions' as an abstract notion, but to the particular
people who have responsibility for the structures of the church.
Nor does this imply that 'they' are always the problem: even
institutions crewed entirely by saints would be ineffective if
'we' were not open to the possibility that the Spirit could work
through those saints in order to summon us to a more authentic
faith. Since the manifestation of the Spirit through the church
depends on every member of the church, so the conversion of
each member is vital.

To illustrate both the importance and the limits of the
church's institutional structure, we can examine more closely
the exercise of authority in the church, particularly the teaching
authority. Since authority is both the most prominent and most
controversial aspect of the church's structure, a thoroughgoing
appreciation of it requires an understanding not only of its
relationship to the Spirit and the faith of the community, but
also the fact that an impoverished exercise of it can create
obstacles to the positive appropriation of the church's tradition.
The remaining sections of the chapter will investigate all of
those dimensions

AUTHORITY AND COMMUNION

Whenever human beings are together, particularly when they
are trying to achieve a common purpose, 'authority' is inescapable. At its best, authority helps to maintain 'the conditions of
protection, security, direction, and orientation for a group'.[58] It
promotes respect for all the members of the group, while enabling them to negotiate challenges on the basis of a shared self-
understanding. At its worst, the exercise of authority is
self-serving and discriminatory; it divides the group and frus-
trates its common purpose. While the exercise of authority can
have a positive or negative impact, it is not possible to eliminate
the risks associated with it by abolishing all authority. Even if

---

[58] Brian McDermott, 'Authority, Leadership, and Theological Conversation', *Seminary News*, 32 (1994), 33–4.

there are no formal organs of authority, informal ones, which are often more problematic, emerge:

A lack of formal authority in a group also generates insidious forms of injustice and elitism. There really is no such thing as a structure-less group. If norms, rules, and procedures are not made formal and explicit, informal ones invariably emerge which are difficult to detect, criticize, or change. Authority in a group is like gravity. It just is.[59]

Since the church too is a group with a common purpose, 'authority' is a significant issue in its life. In the church, however, the evaluation of the role and exercise of authority takes place via criteria that are particular to the church's existence as a communion of faith centred on Jesus Christ. Indeed, 'authority' is one issue that members of the church can connect directly with the gospels' presentation of the life of Jesus. Thus, the gospels describe Jesus explicitly as a person of authority (Mark 1: 27; Luke 4: 32; John 5: 27)—a designation that witnesses to the fact that his words and actions evoked in other people the conviction that Jesus was inseparable from the possibility of freedom and hope. The gospels also contain a number of instances where Jesus rejects self-aggrandizing styles of authority as models for those who would be his disciples—'You know that the rulers of the Gentiles lord it over them, and their great ones are tyrants over them. It will not be so among you' (John 10: 25–6; see also Mark 9: 33–7).

By focusing on the church as 'a graced communion in common meanings', it is possible to develop an understanding of authority that both respects the gospels' injunctions and affirms the legitimate, and necessary role of ecclesial authority.[60] This starting-point also avoids the temptation to juxtapose authority in the church and the existence of the church as the communion of those who share the one Spirit, the one faith, and the one baptism (Eph. 4: 5). If the church is where the Spirit flourishes, then the legitimacy of authority in the church derives entirely from its dependence on the Spirit. Not only that: the emphasis on the communal reality of the church's faith

[59] Theresa Monroe, 'Reclaiming Competence', *Review for Religious*, 51 (1992), 447.

[60] David Tracy, 'Freedom, Authority, Responsibility', in Chamberlain and Howell (eds.), *Empowering Authority*, 46.

means that those who exercise explicit authority in the church can never have a monopoly of the Spirit, even if their authority expresses a particular gift of that Spirit. Thus, even the teaching authority exercised by bishops 'is not a super-criterion ruling over the Church and its common search for truth in lonely Olympian majesty'.[61]

The church, therefore, is not neatly divided between those who exercise authority and those who can do no more than receive, passively, what comes from those who rule over them. The Spirit's presence in all those who form the communion of faith means that authority in the church has multiple loci. To reinforce the truth of that principle, it is necessary to do no more than compare the following two passages from Vatican II:

The holy people of God has a share, too, in the prophetic role of Christ, when it renders him a living witness, especially through a life of faith and charity, and when it offers to God a sacrifice of praise... *The universal body of the faithful who have received the anointing of the holy one, cannot be mistaken in belief.* It displays this particular quality through a supernatural sense of the faith in the whole people when 'from the bishops to the last of the faithful laity', it expresses the consent of all in matters of faith and morals. Through this sense of faith which is aroused and sustained by the Spirit of truth, the people of God, under the guidance of the sacred magisterium to which it is faithfully obedient, receives no longer the words of human beings but truly the word of God.[62]

Among the principal tasks of bishops the preaching of the gospel is pre-eminent. For the bishops are the heralds of the faith who bring new disciples to Christ. *They are the authentic teachers, that is, teachers endowed with the authority of Christ, who preach to the people entrusted to them the faith to be believed and put into practice*; they illustrate this faith in the light of the holy Spirit, drawing out of the treasury of revelation things new and old, they make it bear fruit and they vigilantly ward off errors that are threatening their flock.[63]

What is clear from those passages is that, as a result of the universal presence of the Spirit, the identity and well-being of

---

[61] Kasper, *Introduction to Christian Faith*, 147.
[62] 'The Constitution on the Church', *LG* no. 12. The emphasis is mine.
[63] Ibid. *LG* no. 25. The emphasis is mine.

the church, its unity and faithful witness to Jesus Christ, depend on all of the baptized. What is equally clear is that the mechanisms of authority in the church exist to be of service to the unity and mission of the whole communion. A third factor that is obvious is the potential for disharmony if all the members of the church do not give priority to being attentive to the Spirit, who is the source of communion and the particular gifts and roles that nurture communion. When disharmony arises, it suggests a failure by at least some members of the church to remain open to the Spirit. A consequence of that failure is the loss of commitment to the universal responsibility for communion. There is, therefore, a constant need in the church for conversion to the catholic vision of the Spirit and the re-reception of the primacy of communion. That need is particularly urgent in the present situation of the Catholic church, where, as Chapter 1 illustrated, disharmony seems to be more evident than does its opposite.

While authentic ecclesial faith is inseparable from conversion to the primacy of communion, those who accept that primacy will inevitably be uneasy with any application of authority that seems to be unable to affirm or, perhaps even to accept, the presence of the Spirit in all believers. Similarly, conversion to the primacy of communion challenges the tendency to accept what the 'Catholic Common Ground Project' described as 'a highly individualistic view of the church', one that often resents authority as a restriction on freedom.[64] While that resentment might be an understandable reaction against particular experiences of authority or particular expressions of the church's institutional form, faith in Jesus Christ can never be a purely private matter:

When a believer says 'Amen' to Christ individually, a further dimension is always involved: an 'Amen' to the faith of the Christian community. The person who receives baptism must come to know the full implication of participating in the divine life within the Body of Christ. The believer's 'Amen' to Christ becomes yet more complete as that person receives all that the Church, in faithfulness to the Word of God, affirms to be the authentic content of divine revelation.[65]

[64] Bernardin and Lipscomb, *Catholic Common Ground Initiative*, 38.

[65] Anglican-Roman Catholic International Commission (ARCIC), 'The Gift of Authority', 1, *Origins*, 29 (27 May 1999), 17–29.

One consequence of the universal presence of the Spirit is that the church can never reflect either the neatness or lack of complexity that characterize structures where everything of importance originates at the top and works its way downwards. Indeed, without conversion to the fact that universal presence of the Spirit makes the church a variegated reality, those in authority are likely to act in ways that become an obstacle either to acceptance of ecclesial faith or to acknowledgement of the value of a structured communion. In regard to the articulation of faith in the contemporary Catholic church, those in authority do not always avoid those pitfalls:

Today in the Church we suffer, not from an excess of authority, but from a lack of genuine authority which is in a position to articulate the faith that is binding on all in such a way that all people of good will can see themselves represented in it and a consensus is created. Unfortunately authority has largely lost this mediating function because it has become a faction within the Church. This has brought it into a conflict of roles from which it has not yet found a way out.[66]

That situation makes urgent the need for further reflection on the implications of the church's existence as a communion of faith. Only within that framework is it possible to do justice to both the role and limits of authentic authority.

As with every other aspect of the church's life, then, authority is at the service of the communion: authentic authority promotes and maintains ecclesial communion.[67] Those who exercise authority in the church serve communion primarily through their responsibility for the emergence of a right relationship between the community of faith as it exists in the present and the content of faith prior to it.[68] Authority in the church, therefore, exercises a 'ministry of memory', which is intimately related to preserving the identity of *this* church as a communion of faith in the God of Jesus Christ.[69]

Conversely, the principal characteristic of dysfunctional authority in the church is that it leaves no room either for legit-

---

[66] Kasper, *Introduction to Christian Faith*, 148.

[67] Francis Sullivan, 'Authority in an Ecclesiology of Communion', *New Theology Review*, 10 (1997), 11.

[68] Kasper, *Introduction to Christian Faith*, 147.

[69] ARCIC, 'The Gift of Authority', 30.

imate diversity within the communion or for creative responses to particular historical circumstances. In short, the exercise of authority damages communion when it determines too narrowly what is reconcilable with the existence of the church as *this* communion. Inevitably, if sadly, that narrowness often prompts the individualism that can also imperil the communion of the church and its identity as *this* communion.

In order for authority in the church to function in a life-giving manner there are, clearly, numerous elements that need to be held in tension by all the members of the church: the fact that the church has a particular identity as a consequence of its faith in Christ and its existence as the sacrament of the Spirit; the existence of the church as a communion of faith; the need to 're-receive' the tradition of faith in new circumstances; the presence of the Spirit in every member of the church; the Spirit-generated responsibility of those in authority for the unity of the communion; the dynamism of the Spirit that draws the church onwards to the fullness of the Kingdom, rather than freezing it in any one time or culture. The complexity of each of those elements, to say nothing of the complex relationships between them, makes it impossible to formulate exceptionless norms to govern the exercise of authority in the church.

On the other hand, it is possible to exclude unequivocally ways of exercising authority that do not respect the freedom of believers, ways that deny, at least implicitly, the universal presence of the Spirit—'the feudal and absolutist forms of ecclesiastical life are not part of the gospel, nor are the forms of faith that correspond to these types of Church polity.'[70] This applies not just to matters of administration, but also, and more deeply, to the way in which the faith of the church is formulated and presented.

While the need to maintain the respective rights and roles of both the bishops and all the baptized might generate tension in the church, such tension can be creative, can ensure that the church does not become monolithic, which could ensue if there was only one channel for the Holy Spirit. A similar creative

---

[70] Avery Dulles, *The Survival of Dogma* (New York: Image Books, 1973), 26.

tension exists in another area of the church's institutional life: the relationship between the Pope and the church's other bishops, between central authority and local authorities. This issue, which has become increasingly important in the decades since Vatican II, will be the focus of the next section.

COLLEGIAL AND CENTRAL AUTHORITY

The various possible dynamics in the relationship between the Pope and the other bishops can convey different impressions of the church: either that it is a monolith with one all-powerful central government or that it is a communion, which is united but also capable of diverse expressions that do not damage its unity.

As Chapter 1 illustrated, the period between Vatican I and Vatican II witnessed the domination of a centralized understanding of the church. That development was partially the result of Vatican I's definition of papal infallibility, but it expressed also the continuing prominence in the church of a feudal model of society and authority. In addition, it reflected the conviction that only a strong central authority could protect the independence of the church from the machinations of various forms of secular authority that sought to control the church. In other words, the emphasis on papal monarchy was less the only theological model for authority in the church than a response to particular historical factors. Vatican II, on the other hand, developed an understanding of the relationship between various loci of authority in the church on the basis of an ecclesiology of communion.

Central to Vatican II's approach was its emphasis on the 'collegial' dimension of episcopal authority in the church. The defining characteristic of bishops, therefore, was their membership of the episcopal college.[71] Although reference to that college had not been prominent in the period after Vatican I, Vatican II highlighted its ancient roots:

---

[71] For an overview of Vatican II's theology of the episcopate see Hermann Pottmeyer, 'The Episcopate' in P. Phan (ed.), *The Gift of the Church: A Textbook on Ecclesiology* (Collegeville, Minn.: Michael Glazier, 2000), 337–53.

Just as, by the Lord's decree, St Peter and the other apostles constitute one apostolic college, so in a similar way the Roman Pontiff,
Peter's successor, and the bishops, successors of the apostles, are
joined together. The collegial character and nature of the episcopal
order is shown in the very ancient practice by which bishops ap-
pointed throughout the world maintained communion with each
other and the bishop of Rome in the bonds of unity, charity and
peace. . . . A person is constituted a member of the episcopal body by
virtue of sacramental consecration and by hierarchical communion
with the head and members of the college.[72]

In its description of the relationship between 'the head and
members' of that college, Vatican II produced a formulation
that both reinforced Vatican I's definition of papal prerogatives
and affirmed the rights and responsibilities of the episcopal
college:

the college or body of bishops does not have authority unless this
is understood in terms of union with the Roman pontiff, Peter's
successor, as its head, and the power of this primacy is maintained
intact over all, whether they be shepherds or faithful. For the Roman
pontiff has, by virtue of his office as vicar of Christ and shepherd of
the whole church, full, supreme and universal power over the whole
church, a power that he is always able to exercise freely. However,
the order of bishops, which succeeds the college of apostles in teaching authority and pastoral government, . . . is also the subject of supreme and full power over the universal church, provided it remains
united with its head, the Roman pontiff, and never without its head;
and this power can be exercised only with the consent of the Roman
pontiff.[73]

Although that formulation left no opening for a revival of
medieval conciliarism, which sought to use councils as a means
of bypassing the Pope, it was an affirmation of the world's
bishops as something other than the Pope's subalterns.[74] Vatican II envisaged the college as the means to reinforce the

---

[72] Vatican II, 'The Constitution on the Church', *LG* no. 22. William Henn,
*The Honor of My Brothers: A Brief History of the Relationship Between the
Pope and the Bishops* (New York: Herder & Herder, 2000) explores this
relationship in some detail.

[73] Vatican II, 'The Constitution on the Church', *LG* no. 22.

[74] For an overview of the theology and history of conciliarism see Michael
Fahey, 'Conciliarism', in McBrien (ed.), *HarperCollins Encyclopedia of Catholicism*, 341–2.

catholic dimension of the church, since 'individual bishops represent their own church, while all of them together with the pope represent the whole church in the bond of peace, love and unity'.[75] In this, the emphasis on the college of bishops complements Vatican II's focus on 'the local church':

This church of Christ is truly present in all the lawful local congregations of the faithful which, united to their shepherds, are themselves called churches in the new testament..... In these communities, although frequently small and poor, or dispersed, Christ is present by whose power the one, holy, catholic and apostolic church is gathered together.[76]

As in many other areas of its teaching, Vatican II's approach both to papal and episcopal authority and to the unity and catholicity of the church, which is the context in which to locate the relationship between the 'universal' and the 'local' church, maintained a stance that stressed 'both...and' rather than 'either...or'. In the forty years since the Council, however, the two elements that Vatican II held together have not always been equally significant in the life of the church.

Although it would be naïve to deny the danger that an excessive, even exclusive focus, on the importance of local churches and the individual bishop might damage 'the concept of the unity of the Church at the visible and institutional level', it is actually the dominance of the church's central authority that has been more evident in the period since Vatican II.[77] That dominance has frustrated those hungering for both the realization of the college of bishops as a cooperative venture between the Pope and the bishops and recognition of the particular contribution that local churches and national conferences of bishops might make to the life of the one church.[78] It is also a matter that has significant ecumenical implications, as

[75] Vatican II, 'The Constitution on the Church', *LG* no. 23.

[76] Ibid. *LG* no. 26.

[77] Congregation for the Doctrine of the Faith, 'Some Aspects of the Church as Communion', no. 8, *Catholic International*, 3 (1–30 Sept. 1992), 763.

[78] The most influential contemporary discussion of the issue of collegiality and the role of the papal curia is the lecture given at Campion Hall, Oxford in 1996 by John Quinn, the former Archbishop of San Francisco; see *Origins*, 26 (18 July 1996), 119–27.

the exercise of authority in the Roman Catholic church can become an obstacle to communion between the churches.[79]

Clearly, Vatican II bequeathed a complex gift to later ages through its use of 'both...and' in regard to the relationship between the papacy and the bishops, as well as between the 'universal' church and the 'local church'. Nonetheless, its approach highlights that any one-dimensional understanding that neglects either unity or catholicity can never reflect the authentic faith of the church. The need to hold in tension the legitimacy of more than one perspective means that the present era of the church's history, in which 'centralist tendencies have regained their strength', as a result of both globalization and 'modern possibilities of communication [that] have made contact with the "central office" much easier', cannot provide the norm for understanding those relationships.[80] What is necessary, therefore, is both a recovery of the tradition, which canonizes neither a simple focus on papal power nor the assertion of local autonomy, and an openness to the needs of the present, including the ecumenical imperative.[81]

The discussion of the vexed issue of central and local authority underscores that authority in the church is never merely a theoretical matter, but one that makes claims on the lives of believers. The next section of the chapter acknowledges that fact by exploring possibilities both for the creative exercise of authority in the church and the acceptance of that authority by the members of the communion.

---

[79] In his encyclical *Ut unum sint* (1995), Pope John Paul II invited other Christian churches to engage him in dialogue on the issue of papal authority.

[80] Walter Kasper, *Leadership in the Church: How Traditional Roles Can Serve the Christian Community Today*, tr. B. McNeil (New York: Herder & Herder, 2003), 161.

[81] These are the priorities emphasized by Walter Kasper in *Leadership in the Church*, 158–75. Recent years have spawned a considerable body of writing on the relationship between 'the centre' and 'the local', see, for example, Hermann Pottmeyer, *Towards a Papacy in Communion: Perspectives from Vatican Councils I & II*, tr. M. O'Connell (New York: Herder & Herder, 1998); Michael Buckley, *Papal Primacy and the Episcopate: Towards a Relational Understanding* (New York: Herder & Herder, 1998); Phyllis Zagano and Terrence Tilley (eds.), *The Exercise of the Primacy: Continuing the Dialogue* (New York: Herder & Herder, 1998).

LIVING WITH AUTHORITY

As John Henry Newman observed in the nineteenth century, it is likely that when those in authority simply demand acceptance of what they teach, such a demand 'in the educated classes will terminate in indifference, and in the poorer in superstition'.[82] In order to avoid that scenario, it is necessary that those in authority act in ways that encourage the members of the church to trust that submission to authority is reasonable—'Authority can be described as the quality of leadership which elicits and justifies the willingness of others to be led by it.'[83]

That understanding of authority does not imply that those who exercise it in the church must avoid all actions and pronouncements that are likely to be unpopular or never reject anything as incompatible with the faith of the church. Such 'authority' would be no less a distortion of that exercised by Jesus than would any form of dictatorship or self-aggrandizement. On the other hand, it would be facile to locate the strength and authenticity of the church's authorities in their willingness to say 'No' or their refusal to listen to those with points of view at odds with their own. Although their responsibility for fostering the unity of the church means that those in authority must retain the right to employ 'No', warning bells should sound if it is the first, the most frequently employed, or worst of all the only word in the vocabularies of those in authority.

Similarly, all disquiet with authority does not necessarily manifest an unwillingness to accept the implications of communal faith. In fact, the disquiet can express an inability to perceive the movement of the Spirit in particular acts of those in authority, either in their teaching or administration. On the other hand, the likelihood of acceptance of authority, especially in its function of teaching, increases when those who exercise it 'make its connection with the Gospel clear in institutional terms' and demonstrate 'in principle and practice' that such authority is at the service of the whole communion of faith.[84]

[82] John Henry Newman, *On Consulting the Faithful in Matter of Doctrine,* ed. J Coulson (London: Collins, 1986), 106. The original edition was published in 1859.

[83] Sullivan, 'Authority in an Ecclesiology of Communion', 18.

[84] Kasper, *Introduction to Christian Faith*, 147.

As Vatican II emphasized through its affirmation of the Spirit's presence in all the members of the church, those who exercise authority are not the sole carriers of the church's faith, even though they have a vital role in preserving the authentic faith of the communion. 'The faith of the church', then, is something other than either what the sum total of members of the church believes or the majority opinion among believers. At its richest, that faith suggests the Spirit alive in the church, evoking a willingness to appropriate 'the Tradition'. Particular beliefs are far from irrelevant to that faith, since they fill it out and provide direction for the living of it, but nor do they substitute for it:

it is the faith in the Church that actually exists in heads and hearts, and not properly official Church doctrine, that immediately and in itself is *the faith* that constitutes the Church...The faith of the average Christian is not just a pitiable sketch of the official faith. It is a salutary faith borne by God's self-communication. It is really the faith that God's grace wishes to bring forth and keep alive in the Church...Even when its objectification in words and concepts is very poor and deficient, it is still God's action in us, constituted by the self-communication of God in the Holy Spirit.[85]

While the relationship with the Spirit and acceptance of the church's doctrines are not in competition, it is impossible to appreciate the latter without an experience of the former. Doctrine can, of course, provide the vehicle for an experience of the Spirit, but is neither the only such vehicle nor the one that will invariably be most effective in the life of each member of the church. Nor does that argument imply a revolt against the community's faith or even against the role of the teaching authority. It does suggest, however, that the perception of a gap between the articulated faith of the church and the understanding, even acceptance, of its articulations by the members of the church—a gap that is, perhaps, more obvious today than in recent decades—ought not to induce panic or a looming sense that the faith of the church is on the verge of oblivion.

In order to appreciate why this is so, it is important to recall Vatican II's acknowledgement, in its document on ecumenism,

---

[85] Rahner, 'What the Church Officially Teaches', 169. The emphasis is Rahner's.

that dialogue between the divided Christian churches could benefit from recognition that the Catholic church accepts that there is a 'hierarchy' of truths in matters of doctrine.[86] Through that text, the Council affirmed that, in matters of doctrine, the search for reconciliation on topics that are central is more urgent than a focus on lesser issues, even if the latter still remain true. Similarly, it is likely that each member of the church will operate with a personal hierarchy of truths, one that expresses their particular reception of the Spirit. This can be so without implying, in any way, that it will involve rejection of what is central to the faith of the communion.[87]

Even though the content of a personal hierarchy of truths is unlikely to equate to the panoply of the church's doctrine, its existence is not necessarily at the expense either of the role and content of doctrine or of the teaching authority. It might be, however, the most appropriate response by individuals to the movement of the Spirit in their life. If that personal hierarchy of truths is indeed the work of the Spirit, then it has an orientation to the full articulation of the church's faith. Thus, even though an individual might not be able to appropriate at any given moment all the formulae of the church's faith, this is not tantamount to the expression of either a definitive rejection of those formulae or a definitive lack of interest in them.

In the context of contemporary pluralism, where it is less likely that all the members of the church will either understand or assent to everything that the church teaches, a greater engagement between the teaching authority and all the members of the church might help the latter to recognize the presence and activity of the Spirit in the former. Such engagement might also ensure that those who are not bishops feel neither that 'the faith of the church' is simply imposed on them nor that what they believe is irrelevant to that faith.

Authentic authority, then, promotes 'synodality', the common life of all the members of the church, who are called to live, work,

---

[86] 'The Decree on Ecumenism' (*Unitatis Redintegratio*), *UR* no. 11.

[87] For the notion of a personal hierarchy of truths, see Karl Rahner, 'Reflections on the Problems Involved in Devising a Short Formula of the Faith', *Theological Investigations*, 11, tr. D. Bourke (New York: Crossroad, 1982), 236.

and journey together in Christ.[88] The promotion of that synodality will require, at times, that those in authority make difficult
decisions, even that they stand against what is popular. That
fact makes more urgent the responsibility of those in authority
to highlight their dependence on the Spirit, especially as that
Spirit works through the rest of the communion. In practice,
however, as the anger directed at authorities in the church in the
wake of their response to clerical sexual abuse indicates, those
who exercise authority in the church do not always act in ways
that promote synodality or manifest acceptance of their own
accountability.

In the wake of *Humanae vitae*, it is possible that the members
of the church will simply reject any teaching or decision with
which they disagree. It is, however, also likely that there will be
a greater willingness to consider official teaching positively
when it appears to be more than an exercise in objective rationality or an impersonal edict. Above all, this requires that those
who teach are aware of the situation of those whom they are
addressing. Teachers in the church, therefore, ought not to
assume that every member of the church lives within a homo-
geneously Christian environment, and 'with a more or less
absolute respect for the authority of the Church's magisterium'.[89] That requirement is particularly urgent today when,
because the 'sacred canopy' no longer exists, even the reception
of what is specific to Christian identity takes place, as the next
chapter will showcase, within a pluralistic environment.[90]

In order both to serve the faith of the church and to facilitate
appropriation of the identity of *this* church, those who exercise
authority in the church must be able to show that their role 'is a
condition for and an enablement of freedom'.[91] This is possible
only when those who exercise authority are accessible as human
beings:

[88] ARCIC, 'The Gift of Authority', no. 34.

[89] Karl Rahner, 'What the Church Officially Teaches', 168.

[90] On the influence of the pluralistic environment on the reception of faith
see Francis Schüssler Fiorenza, 'Fundamental Theology, 135.

[91] Kasper, *Introduction to Christian Faith*, 10.

When the members of a community cannot truly know and love their shepherd, shepherding quickly becomes a subtle way of exercising power over others and begins to show authoritarian and dictatorial traits.[92]

At the opposite end of the scale from authoritarian attitudes is the embrace of accountability. 'Accountability', however, tends to be a neuralgic issue within the church. This is particularly so when it appears that accountability is presented as subversive of the hierarchical constitution of the church, which, as Vatican II reaffirmed, the tradition has always accepted as an expression of divine providence for the church.[93] Under those circumstances, any reference to accountability bears the stigma of being a ruse to 'democratize' the church and abolish hierarchy. Within the Catholic church, there is often a deep suspicion of the implications of democracy, particularly a fear that it would dilute the truth of God's self-communication by subjecting every aspect of the church's faith to a vote. To counter that fear, Edward Schillebeeckx argues that it is far from self-evident that democracy would obscure God's presence and freedom if 'imperial-authoritarian, feudal and later absolute monarchical government' in the church has not done so.[94]

Even more importantly, 'democracy' does not imply that every decision about the faith and action of the church would come via votes and ballot boxes. Indeed, it implies something that is already central to the church's constitution: that 'no function or court of appeal holds all the power'.[95] 'Democracy', then, is less like a recipe for anarchy in the church or the destruction of hierarchy, than a description of the communion of faith united under the one Spirit.

While the promotion of accountability and democracy could, of course, be the manifestation of an anti-hierarchical sentiment, it is unlikely to be always so. Conversely, a failure to

[92] Henri Nouwen, *In the Name of Jesus: Reflections on Christian Leadership*, (New York: Crossroad, 1989), 43–4.

[93] See 'The Constitution on the Church', *LG* no. 8.

[94] Edward Schillebeeckx, *Church: The Human Story of God*, tr. J. Bowden (New York: Crossroad, 1990), 218.

[95] Heinrich Fries, 'Is There a Magisterium of the Faithful?', in J. B. Metz and E. Schillebeeckx (eds.), *The Teaching Authority of Believers* (*Concilium*, no. 180) (Edinburgh: T. & T. Clark, 1985), 90.

develop procedures that highlight accountability—or, even worse, opposition to such a development—is more likely to engender suspicion of hierarchy than to enhance its status within the communion. Nor would the history of the church support any contention that hierarchy alone has been the well-spring of the Spirit or the sole explanation for the preservation of the church's faith. If individualism contributes to the impairment of the church's communion, so too does the practice of authority that obscures the Spirit's flourishing:

we are and have been in the grip of an authority structure with its fists tightly closed. What it seems many of us are demanding is the open palm model. What is more, this demand is not based on some perverse selfishness or egoism or some (as is often alleged) hostile bid for power; it is founded on an intrinsic belief that the true dignity of the person is only acknowledged in a system which does not enslave or dominate by intellectual, spiritual or physical force.[96]

In short, if the church's communal life is to reflect the presence of the Spirit in all those who form the church, there is not only a need for the ongoing conversion of all the members of the church, but also a need to grapple further with the possibility that 'hierarchy' and 'democracy' could both contribute to the life of the church—'to claim that the Church cannot be democratic because it is hierarchical is thus simply false reasoning and a magical ideological use of the word "hierarchy"'.[97]

One conclusion that emerges from each of the themes that this chapter has analysed is that a positive appropriation of the church's 'thisness', of its reliance on tradition as well as its institutional dimension and organs of authority, depends on being able to think about those features in connection with the presence of the Spirit. This, in turn, suggests that the identity of the church as *this* church is compatible with change and movement.

[96] Mary McAlese, 'Living with Authority', *Doctrine and Life*, 45 (1995), 598.

[97] Schillebeeckx, *Church*, 220. For a historical survey of 'democratic' movements in the church see Eugene Bianchi, 'A Democratic Church: Task for the Twenty-First Century', in Eugene Bianchi and Rosemary Radford Ruether (eds.), *A Democratic Catholic Church: The Reconstruction of Roman Catholicism* (New York: Crossroad, 1992), 34–51; see also Lakeland, *The Liberation of the Laity*, 207–15.

THE OPENNESS OF *THIS* CHURCH

Since the Spirit is at the heart of the church, it is crucial to understand the church 'relationally', rather than 'substantialistically'.[98] In other words, there is a need to focus on the church as a communion that is living and growing, rather than as a 'thing' whose every feature is immutable. This Spirit-generated capacity of the church to grow reinforces Vatican II's emphasis on the church's connection to the mystery of God.[99] That approach also provides a framework for considering whether the association between the Spirit and what is particular and permanent in the church, what it is that makes it *this* church, could have a parallel in a connection between the Spirit and change in the church.

A hint of an answer to that inquiry lies in Vatican II's stress on the church as a pilgrim in history, a pilgrim that looks for its completion only in the glory of heaven.[100] This echoes a point made earlier in this chapter: that a focus on 'the Tradition' stimulates an appreciation of the church's eschatological orientation. Although the Spirit's relationship to the church excludes the calling of a premature halt to the pilgrimage of faith, it does not imply that we can know without effort what constitutes an authentic response to the Spirit. This is so since, as the Acts of the Apostles illustrates powerfully, it is necessary to discern in the midst of a particular history and culture what is an appropriate, present-day expression of faithfulness to the Spirit.[101]

Indeed, the situation is even more complex, and certainly more paradoxical, since ensuring continuity might involve the need to promote change, but change that arises from what enables continuity—'[tradition] comprises a process of active remembering, a process that sustains continuity in the midst of change even as at the same time it generates changes out of that which gives continuity.'[102] The paradox, then, is that it can be

---

[98] Avery Dulles, *The Resilient Church: The Necessity and Limits of Adaptation* (Dublin: Gill & Macmillan, 1978), 33.

[99] As noted in Chapter 1, Vatican II chose 'The Mystery of the Church' as the title for the first chapter of its 'Constitution on the Church' (*LG* nos. 1–8).

[100] Ibid. *LG* no. 48.   [101] See, for example, Acts 13–15.

[102] Platten and Pattison, *Spirit and Tradition*, 59.

necessary to think about change in the context of what presents itself as unchangeable, including both doctrine and structures.[103]

The argument of this book is that the impetus for both continuity and change comes from the Holy Spirit. That specific role accords with the overall mission of the Spirit: to lead humanity to the fullness of life in God's Kingdom. Since the Spirit works through symbols, the questions and challenges to the church's traditions that arise from contemporary culture can be the vehicles of the Spirit. Those challenges, therefore, can be catalysts for the growth of that tradition, rather than its destruction.

Accordingly, the next chapter will explore further the contours of the present, with a particular focus on the issues they raise for the life of the church. The final chapter, then, will attempt to depict how the church might be both faithful to tradition and open to the sort of change that will enable it to respond creatively to present challenges. Such a church might be one that invites acceptance of the risk of ecclesial faith.

---

[103] See Karl Rahner, 'Basic Observations on the Subject of the Changeable and Unchangeable in the Church', *Theological Investigations*, 14, tr. D. Bourke (New York: Seabury, 1976), especially pp. 7–13.

5

The Existing Season

In her short story *Adams' Bride*, the Australian novelist Elizabeth Jolley depicts how an inability to live in the present
corrodes the spirit of a farmer. As Jolley portrays it, that
inability can become pathological: 'Wishing away the existing
season is more than a symptom, it is the complaint, the illness
itself.'[1] In the case of the farmer, the source of that illness is his
obsession with the next crop. Although members of the church
are not concerned with crops, they can, nevertheless, resemble
the farmer in a lack of ease with their present circumstances. In
the church, that tendency is likely to arise from one of two
sources.

The first is a sense that the institutional dimension of the
church has become an intransigent obstacle to any prospect that
the church could be 'an undreamed of possibility for love' or
represent the flourishing of the Spirit. The second is the conviction that the present moment of history, especially in Western cultures, is hostile not only to any notion of transcendence,
but also to 'organized religion', which the church typifies.
Although those two concerns are dissimilar, they both produce
a negative perception of the current experience of the church
and of its prospects: both imply that only decay and dissolution
await the church in the future. Neither perspective, therefore,
invites embrace of the risk of ecclesial faith.

Since the future is yet to arrive, it is not possible to know
whether those dark scenarios will actually eventuate. It is possible, however, to speak with some certainty about the present.
In regard to the impact of the institutional dimension of the
church, the previous chapter acknowledged the difficulties that
it can present, but argued also that only an active engagement

---

[1] Elizabeth Jolley, *Fellow Passengers: Collected Stories* (Ringwood, Vic.:
Penguin, 1997), 230.

between all the members of the church can prevent either the dominance of authoritarian attitudes or the loss of the particularity of the church's faith. While that is hardly a recipe that will dissolve all difficulties as if by magic, it does suggest that there are some grounds to hope that institutionalism will not totally stifle the Holy Spirit—a hope that the next chapter will amplify. The task for this chapter is to explore whether the emphases of contemporary society mean that there are only dismal prospects for ecclesial faith.

At the beginning of that inquiry it is important to keep in mind that human freedom, which suggests that in response to the same set of circumstances one person could lose faith while another gains it, means that we cannot definitively conclude that religious faith, even ecclesial faith, is not possible today.[2] Still, it would be disingenuous to act as if the dynamics of contemporary culture offered no significant contemporary obstacles to religious faith or to deny that many people regard God and the church, perhaps especially the latter, as having passed their 'use-by date'.

Nonetheless, wishing away the existing season could imply a denial of either the Holy Spirit's presence in this age or of the willingness of people today to respond to that Spirit. Since the Spirit's presence can take surprising forms, there is a need for some caution before declaring definitively that the Spirit could not be at work in the present-day world. Faith in the Spirit also requires openness to the possibility that the challenges arising from contemporary society might enrich, not simply endanger, ecclesial faith—'Even the Church cannot choose the situation in which she lives. It is given to her, and therefore it is good.'[3] This means that it is possible to understand present circumstances as a gift to the church, to see them as providing an invitation and opportunity to focus on what is central to the identity of *this* church.

An appreciation of the dynamism of the Spirit, the recognition that the Spirit promotes the continual renewal and fresh-

---

[2] See Leszek Kolakowski, *Modernity on Endless Trial* (Chicago: University of Chicago Press, 1990), 67.

[3] Karl Rahner, 'Christian Living Formerly and Today', *Theological Investigations*, 7, tr. D. Bourke (New York: Crossroad, 1977), 4.

ness of ecclesial faith and thereby challenges any tendency to ossification within the church, is inseparable from regarding ecclesial faith as a project. As noted in the previous chapter, an enduring characteristic of that project is the need for the communion of faith to 're-receive' the apostolic tradition. Since it is our evolving social situation that provides the context for the work of re-reception, Christians must remain aware of the elements of that social situation.

This chapter will examine some of the issues that not only express the flux of contemporary society, but that also influence the possibility of ecclesial faith, particularly in the context of Western societies. This will involve looking at challenges to the meaningfulness of faith in God, to the particular claims of Christian faith, and to various aspects of the church's life and practice. It will also involve highlighting the opportunities this situation presents for a renewal of faith, opportunities that suggest that the Spirit is not absent from contemporary society. In so doing, one of the aims is to nominate ways in which the response of the church to the present might express more creativity than was evident in the clash with the culture of the Enlightenment, which Chapter 1 detailed.

The final chapter of the book will attempt to sketch the contours of a church that is responsive to the present, faithful to the gift and challenge of its tradition, and open to the future without fear or illusion. Such a church would be one that promotes ecclesial faith as something conducive to human well-being, rather than inimical to it. The immediate requirement, however, is to gain some sense of the factors that lead to the description of the present era as 'postmodern'.

THE CHALLENGES OF THE POSTMODERN WORLD

Throughout this book, a particular focus has been on developing a sense of the church as more than a socio-political organization. Accordingly, the book has related the church to God's symbolic self-communication, which takes place in history and addresses humanity as embodied, rational, and social beings. It has also presented the church as a communion of faith united by the Spirit of God, a communion whose members commit themselves to live in the world as disciples of Jesus, a commitment indicative of the conviction that only the reign of God can provide ultimate fulfilment for humanity and the whole of creation. In addition, the book has sought to identify not only what might support and sustain the ongoing acts of self-surrender inseparable from the risk that is membership of the church, but also what might justify the claim that such an act of self-surrender is a reasonable exercise of human freedom.

Although the preceding chapters have acknowledged the challenging nature of faith in God, and the obstacles to appropriating a positive sense of the church, they have assumed that concepts such as 'truth' and 'meaning', both of which underpin all claims about God and the church, are themselves meaningful. In the shift from modernity to postmodernity, however, that assumption has come under critical scrutiny. The goal of this section is to explore why that has occurred and the implications both of that development and of other aspects of the prevailing postmodern spirit.

As Chapter 1 illustrated, the assertion of reason over faith underscored the work of the philosophers of the modern era. Their conviction was that reason, free of the constricting influence of faith and of the church, would deliver certainty and human progress. It is ironic, then, that postmodern theorists condemn modernity for giving birth to a wasteland of various limited perspectives based on class, race, or gender, all of which speak of anything but progress.[4] Even more devastating for the modernist vision is the postmodern rejection of the primacy of reason. In short, postmodernity has little sympathy for the Enlightenment's dream of a better world, a dream bolstered by the seeming triumph of human rationality and technological expertise in the Industrial Revolution. From a postmodern perspective, that dream was a dangerous illusion, one that resulted in two World Wars, the Great Depression, destructive socio-political ideologies, the widening gap between 'North' and 'South', environmental degradation, and various other experiences that compose a litany of frustrated hopes.

Consequently, postmodernism, which 'deconstructs' much that preceded it, tends to radiate pessimism. That quality,

---

[4] Thornhill, *Modernity*, p. viii.

which is in stark contrast to the ethos of modernity, means that the representative postmodern person:

wants a lot but expects little. The emotional range is narrow, between mild depression at one end and whimsical insouciance at the other. Postmodern heroes and heroines are safe, so far beyond that we could not possibly emulate them, avatars of power or success or money or sex—all without consequences. Postmodernity may be tragic, but its denizens are unable to recognize tragedy. The shows we watch, he movies we see, the music we hear, all are devoted to a counterfactual presentation of life as comic, sentimental, and comfortable. Reality doesn't sell.[5]

As significant as the pessimism of the postmodern age is its scepticism about the power of reason to know, to construct integrated systems, and to gain certainty. Thus, postmodernism promotes an awareness of what exceeds reason's power to control, of what remains 'different' and not subject to systematic analysis. There is, therefore, a deeper awareness of 'the other', that which is beyond our domination and requires respect.[6] In addition, a stress on bodiliness and on 'linguisticality', on language as not only a source of connection between us, but also as a source of personal identity—'speech makes intersubjectivity the matrix of personal subjectivity'—has replaced modernity's emphasis on disembodied rationality.[7] Indeed, the focus on language tends to replace one on truth. Language, then, marks the limits of reality: what we can say sets the boundaries of what we can think.[8]

The postmodern worldview not only rejects belief in the capacity of unfettered reason to deliver certainty and universal progress, it also calls into question whether there can even be certainty and truth. In place of truth as an absolute comes relative truth, competing perspectives, or various 'incommensurable language games'.[9] Consequently, unconditional assent

---

[5] Paul Lakeland, *Postmodernity: Christian Identity in a Fragmented Age* (Minneapolis, Minn.: Fortress, 1997), 8–9.

[6] Ibid. 30–1.

[7] Scanlon, 'The Postmodern Debate', 229–30.

[8] Lakeland, *Postmodernity*, 19.

[9] John Milbank, *Theology and Social Theory: Beyond Secular Reason* (Oxford: Blackwell, 1995), 279. The book was first published in 1990.

and commitment become meaningless since something we regard as true today is likely to be relativized tomorrow.

As a result, there is a pervading contemporary suspicion of 'metanarratives', worldviews that claim to be able to explain the whole of reality. Similarly, there is antipathy to 'totalising institutions' that seek universal control on the basis of the supposed supremacy of their metanarrative.[10] One consequence of such suspicion is an emphasis on pluralism and support for the particular, the regional, and the local over what claims to be universal.[11]

The stress on pluralism applies too in regard to religion. Thus, disengagement from Christianity need not be simply a response either to divisions within the Christian church or to the internal state of any particular church. At a deeper level, such disengagement can express the conviction that it is presumptuous for any one form of religion to claim either that it could be the locus of all truth or apply to all people and cultures—an issue with which a later section of the chapter will engage.[12]

Nonetheless, one of the paradoxes of the present era of Western civilization is that for all those whose rejection of metanarratives produces in them a passive resignation in the face of the mass of imponderables that shape contemporary life, there seem to be as many other people who make impassioned attempts to rise above the complexity by asserting unquestionable paths to truth. Characteristic of the present age, therefore, is a stark division between 'the scepticism of those who are tempted to disbelieve that our words can say anything and the intolerance of those who believe that their words say it all'.[13] The best exemplars of that intolerance are the numerous manifestations of religious fundamentalism.

The next two sections will profile, respectively, the fundamentalist phenomenon and what might seem to be the polar

---

[10] T. Howland Sanks, 'Postmodernism and the Church', *New Theology Review*, 11 (1998), 52.

[11] Ibid. 53.

[12] See John Farrelly, *Belief in God in Our Time: Foundational Theology* (Collegeville, Minn.: Liturgical Press, 1992), i. 19–20.

[13] Timothy Radcliffe, 'Rebuild Our Human Communities', *Priests and People*, 10 (1996), 470.

opposite of fundamentalism: New Age spiritualities. The point in so doing is to illustrate the variety of forms that the quest for certainty takes today in reaction against postmodern scepticism and nihilism.

FUNDAMENTALISM AND THE QUEST FOR CERTAINTY

Although 'fundamentalism' as an identifiable religious phenomenon has its origins in early twentieth-century American Protestantism, the term itself has enjoyed a second spring in recent decades. Today, 'fundamentalism' not only has currency within the Catholic church as well as Protestant ones, it is also in regular employ as a designation for certain adherents of most religions; indeed, it even has application to particular approaches in economics and the social sciences. Despite this burgeoning usage, even the non-religious applications of the term rely on its primary religious meaning: defending certain truths as God-given and, therefore, as beyond human manipulation, even investigation.[14] Just as the original fundamentalists were committed to defending what they regarded as true Christianity, especially its biblical foundations, against the ravages of liberal modernity, so today's fundamentalists, in all religions, draw lines in the sand against the ravages of postmodernity. More than anything else, contemporary fundamentalism is a frontal assault on the lack of certainty, as well as the lack of a means to certainty, that seems to abound in the postmodern era.

In the realm of fundamentalism, certainty is the key to identity. Not only is it possible to be certain, it is possible to be 'distinctly right, sublimely certain'.[15] For the fundamentalist, only connection to the transcendent or the divine can both guarantee identity and engender confidence that one's identity

---

[14] For a helpful overview of the origins and primary concerns of fundamentalism, such as defence of the inerrancy of Scripture and 'penal substitution' theories of redemption, see James Barr, 'Fundamentalism' in *The Encyclopedia of Christianity* (Grand Rapids/Leiden: Eerdmans/Brill, 2001), ii. 363–5. For a more extensive treatment, see Barr's *Fundamentalism*, 2nd edn. (London: SCM, 1984).

[15] Thomas O'Meara, *Fundamentalism: A Catholic Perspective* (Mahwah, NJ: Paulist, 1990), 52.

remains 'free from erosion, impenetrable, immune to substantial change, aloof from the vicissitudes of history and human reason'.[16] From the perspective of the fundamentalist, only those who can echo their particular version of pure faith can be a 'true believer'—'Catholic fundamentalists use "orthodox" to mean someone who thinks as they do.'[17]

Conversely, reliance on what is human leads only to uncertainty. As a result of the polarity between the human and the divine, which characterizes most forms of fundamentalism, it is necessary to resist all human interference with what comes from God. This applies most particularly to any text that is God's unalloyed word.[18] In regard to such texts, the fundamentalist mindset neither seeks nor allows 'any rational insight into the historical conditioning of its origin and its hermeneutical difference from the changed conditions of the present'.[19] While this attitude most typically applies to the way in which fundamentalists approach the Bible, it also has a particular extra-biblical form among Catholics:

> What an enthusiastically literal, if selective, reading of the Bible is to Protestant fundamentalism, the appeal to a few Vatican documents or to imaginary or imprecise papal stances, an appeal to an abstract and distant authority, is dominant Catholic fundamentalism.[20]

In Western societies, there is a tendency to equate 'fundamentalist' and 'conservative', but the linkage is not necessarily valid. The goal for fundamentalists is not defence of a social order originating in the past, but the implementation of what they regard, as a result of a particular reading of sacred texts, as God's vision for human existence. Indeed, the focus of fundamentalism is less likely to be on what comes from the past than on the future, when God's reign over all will be manifest. That future is one that God alone, not human reason or technology,

---

[16] Martin Marty and R. Scott Appleby, 'Conclusion: An Interim Report on a Hypothetical Family' in Martin Marty and R. Scott Appleby (eds.), *The Fundamentalism Project* (Chicago: University of Chicago Press, 1991), i. 817.

[17] O'Meara, *Fundamentalism*, 23.

[18] Jürgen Moltmann, 'Fundamentalism and Modernity', in H. Küng and J. Moltmann (eds.), *Fundamentalism as an Ecumenical Challenge* (*Concilium*, no. 1992/3) (London: SCM, 1992), 110–11.

[19] Ibid. 111.

[20] O'Meara, *Fundamentalism*, 26.

will bring about. More specifically, the future will be a reward for those who have been faithful to the demanding standards of God, as explicated in the unadulterated sacred texts.[21] In that emphasis, the fundamentalist urge is more a rejection of the present, especially of any tendency to idolize human achievement, than a glorification of the past.

The exclusive focus on what comes from God means that fundamentalists tend to be profoundly suspicious of the secular, to distance themselves from 'unbelievers', and to prize a 'contra-acculturative orientation': having a place in human society is without value, what counts is separating oneself from all that is not God's.[22] Fundamentalism, therefore, is less a refusal to face the modern world than a response to it, a response that rejects the world as it is. Despite the fact that popular portrayals of fundamentalism are likely to depict it as a return to the pre-Enlightenment world, fundamentalism is actually 'post-critical' rather than 'pre-critical'.[23] In other words, fundamentalism is not a refusal to use reason, but the rejection of reason as a means of negotiating a healthy response to the challenges of life. Although it sounds paradoxical, this means that it is valid to categorize contemporary fundamentalism as both a manifestation of postmodernism and an antagonist of it.

What is also crucial to note about fundamentalist Christianity is that its emphases are a critique of the many aspects of 'mainstream' Christianity. Thus, the stress on receiving God's word in Scripture without alteration or dilution suggests that the churches that have adopted modern methods of biblical interpretation, methods that owe much to the forms of literary criticism born out of the Enlightenment, have been responsible for reductionist approaches both to the Bible and, more broadly, to the place of God in the world. Similarly, while all types of religious fundamentalists reject, overwhelmingly, modern secular cultures and desire to replace them by 'the unitary religious state', the presence of those attitudes in Christian fundamentalists express a sense that many Christians, no

---

[21] Marty and Appleby, 'An Interim Report on a Hypothetical Family', 819.
[22] Ibid. 820.
[23] Cf. Moltmann, 'Fundamentalism and Modernity', 114.

less than the churches of which they are a part, have capitulated in the face of the secular challenge.[24]

In place of secularization and the privatization of faith, fundamentalist churches stress the need for political engagement by Christians committed to the defence of truth. Such engagement aims to ensure that no legislation, especially on issues of personal freedom and sexuality, embodies principles contrary to those of biblical truth, as the fundamentalist churches understand it.

As a religious response to postmodernism, fundamentalism offers hope and certainty where many features of mainstream churches seem only to deepen complexity, even confusion:

[Fundamentalism] meets the dilemma of the diminished prestige of the institution by constantly reassuring the believer that he or she has joined the most successful available religious option, as proved by miracles, physical and financial, and by evidence of ever-expanding numerical growth. It resolves the dilemma of Christianity's ambiguous and complex past by ignoring it completely, except where it can be communicated in rigorously controlled packets of information, an exercise to which the modern media lend themselves with unfortunate ease.[25]

Although it is crucial not to underestimate either the challenge to religious faith that postmodernity offers or the appeal of the fundamentalist response, it is difficult to reconcile the implications of the Incarnation, which marks God's commitment to the messy reality of human existence, with the one-dimensional fundamentalist portrayal of the relationship between God and human. Fundamentalism, then, is less an unconditional surrender to God's mystery, the hallmark of authentic faith, than the enlistment of God as support for particular ideological stances.

The various forms of fundamentalist Christianity might well be committed to a defence of God's truth, but they tend to approach that truth in a way that does not reflect the expansiveness of the creator God. Thus, it becomes difficult to distinguish fundamentalism from an absolutism that, ironically, controls God's manner of operating. In this it bears little

---

[24] Moltmann, 'Fundamentalism and Modernity', 112.

[25] Stephen Sykes, 'Faith', in Geoffrey Wainwright (ed.), *Keeping the Faith: Essays to Mark the Centenary of* 'Lux Mundi' (London: SPCK, 1989), 14.

relation to the fruitfulness of authentic Christian tradition. Indeed, it can even display features expressive of absolutism and idolatry:

the absolutist *incorrectly* supposes that the ways in which we have succeeded in making things to be *is* how they ultimately and appropriately are. The absolutist construes truth as reality *grasped*, as possession to be preserved against the ravages of time and change. The absolutist is an idolater.[26]

On the other hand, the particular expressions that bear the truth of 'the Tradition' in authentic Christianity, as explored in the previous chapter, promote change and growth as part of the journey to the fullness of life in God's reign. In order to highlight how different authentic Christian faith is from fundamentalist versions, a later section of this chapter will showcase the capacity of 'truth' to promote dialogue and reconciliation, rather than the separation of 'the orthodox' from the unfaithful, which is an outcome of fundamentalism. The immediate task, however, is to examine another form of postmodern religious response: the New Age spiritualities.

THE ALTERNATIVE CERTAINTIES OF THE NEW AGE

At first glance, it might seem difficult to accept that there could be any common ground between the fundamentalist stress on absolute transcendence and the various forms of 'New Age' spirituality, which tend to privilege the physical universe and human potential over any notion of transcendence. The two movements, however, share a distinctly postmodern suspicion of 'the insular Cartesian self' with its focus on individual rationality.[27] Where that suspicion leads fundamentalism towards an exclusive emphasis on an unalloyed connection to God, the New Age focus, like that of the Romantics, who opposed 'feeling' and the internal to what they regarded as the arid intellectualism of the Enlightenment, is on Nature

---

[26] Nicholas Lash, 'Criticism or Construction?: The Task of the Theologian', *New Blackfriars*, 63 (1982), 153. The emphasis is Lash's.
[27] David Toolan, 'Harmonic Convergence and All That: New Age Spirituality', *Cross Currents*, 46 (1996), 376.

and a diffuse 'spirituality', rather than on a personal God or 'institutional religion':

Many have rejected organized religion, because in their judgment it has failed to answer their needs, and for precisely this reason they have looked elsewhere to find 'spirituality'. Furthermore, at the heart of New Age is the belief that the time for particular religions is over, so to refer to [New Age] as a religion would run counter to its own self-understanding.[28]

As with fundamentalism, the primary New Age concern is not with the past, but what is to come: the harmony between peoples and between humanity and the whole cosmos. In this, 'New Agers' tend to be 'bullish millennialists' and 'the vanguard of a cultural reawakening that will lead, not just to the mending of society, but to its remaking' in the Age of Aquarius.[29] If fundamentalists incline towards disowning the world because it is at odds with God's vision and project, New Age spiritualities are equally at risk of avoiding engagement with the world as it is. Here, however, avoidance grows out of the 'innocent optimism and flightiness' of its practitioners, which can lead them merely to dream about a better world rather than to work for it.[30] Indeed, its critics hold that even the focus on reincarnation, prominent in much contemporary spirituality, can be a way of avoiding the challenge to work against present injustice.[31]

If fundamentalism appeals because of a desire for certainty, the attraction of the New Age vision is its focus on connection, harmony, and 'the Infinite'. It is also easy to appreciate the warmth of its appeal to those, especially young people, for whom the church can appear to be primarily a desiccated institution, one remote from people's real concerns and committed to a God who is even more distant.

---

[28] Pontifical Council for Culture and Pontifical Council for Interreligious Dialogue, *Jesus Christ the Bearer of the Water of Life: A Christian Reflection on the 'New Age'*, no. 2 (Strathfield, NSW: St Paul Publications, 2003), 17.

[29] Toolan, 'Harmonic Convergence', 371.

[30] Ibid. 377.

[31] David Millikan and Nevill Drury, *Christianity and the New Age* (Crows Nest, NSW: ABC Books, 1991), 97.

While those within the church might incline towards dismissing the New Age phenomenon as rampant naïveté, it is important not to ignore its implied critique of Christian faith, and especially of the church. Thus, for example, the contemporary interest in 'Celtic' or 'Gaia' spirituality can express a desire not only for a world unscarred by the ravages of industrialization and urbanization, but for access to God without the burden of the church.[32] Indeed, 'in many New Age contexts Church doctrine and practice are blamed for the failure of spirit, particularly in the Western world. It is presented as unimaginative, irrelevant, constricting, oppressive or pathological.'[33]

While both fundamentalism and New Age spiritualities might manifest a hunger for truth and meaning, neither offers a model for creative engagement with the postmodern world. The question, however, is whether the church can express itself in contemporary society in ways that not only present an alternative to postmodern nihilism, but also both a more authentic faith than fundamentalism and a richer and more challenging understanding of 'spirituality' than the various manifestations of the New Age. To do so successfully, the church must address both the challenge of radical scepticism and the sense that it is possible to find hope in the present only by embracing either an aggressive rejection of the human in favour of God or an idealized perception of the material world.

If it is to be possible for ecclesial faith to represent hope and genuine liberation in the present, there are two primary tasks for the church to negotiate: first, the church must be able to support its conviction that truth is not only possible, but that faith in the God of Jesus Christ, and in the communion that proclaims faith in him, provides access to that truth. It must also do this in a way that shows that while the commitment of faith is reasonable, it is not simply the application of an abstract rationality. Secondly, the church's presence in the world must manifest that faith in God, while it makes demands on how

[32] Loades, 'Word and Sacrament', 31–2. See also, Pontifical Council for Culture and Pontifical Council for Interreligious Dialogue, *Jesus Christ the Bearer of the Water of Life*, no. 1.4.

[33] Jack Finnegan, 'Christ or Aquarius?: A Christian Reflection on the New Age', *The Furrow*, 54 (2003), 344.

people live, is not at odds with a commitment to the pursuit of human well-being—an issue that will be the focus for a later section of the chapter. In other words, the church must show that it is able to respond to 'the often-silent cry in people's hearts, which leads them elsewhere if they are not satisfied by the Church'.[34]

The next two sections will take up the issues that orbit today around the church's approach to the possibility of faith and the likelihood that truth could be more than just relative. The first of these sections will begin by revisiting the church's response to modernity, especially the methods by which it sought in that context to establish the legitimacy of faith. The goal in so doing is both to locate the seeds of the current challenges facing the church and to establish possibilities for a creative response to those challenges.

THE SHAPE AND POSSIBILITY OF FAITH

In the wake of the Enlightenment, both the official teaching of the church and Catholic theology in general stressed that faith in God was neither irrational nor simply the product of reason. In order to make the case for the rationality of faith, the preferred method was to demonstrate that the claims of the church had a firm foundation in verifiable fact. Thus, for example, Vatican I argued that anyone who brought their reason to bear on the objective certainty of miracles, prophecies, and the holiness of the church would have to acknowledge that revelation was a fact:

in order that the submission of our faith should be in accordance with reason, it was God's will that there should be linked to the internal assistance of the holy Spirit outward indications of his revelation, that is to say divine acts, and first and foremost miracles and prophecies, which clearly indicating as they do the omnipotence and infinite knowledge of God, are the most certain signs of revelation and are suited to the understanding of all.[35]

---

[34] Pontifical Council for Culture and Pontifical Council for Interreligious Dialogue, *Jesus Christ the Bearer of the Water of Life*, no. 1.5.

[35] First Vatican Council (1870), 'Dogmatic Constitution on the Catholic Faith' (*Dei filius*), ch. 3.

The logic of this argument was that the foundation of faith in facts that any reasonable person would acknowledge—the inclusion of miracles in the category of 'facts' was because no other explanation could account for historical and verifiable events, such as cures—supported the conclusion that faith was reasonable; it was not simply a construct of the believer's personal horizon.[36] In addition, the argument suggested that an objectively certain ground for faith established that it was reasonable to accept the particular beliefs that built on that faith. That approach remained the favoured method of Catholic apologists until the middle of the twentieth century.[37]

Since it would be absurd to believe what was factually and demonstrably false, the strength of that apologetic technique lay in its attempt to highlight that the church's claims had a basis in reality. The danger of it, however, was that it reflected the spirit of the age in associating the truths of faith primarily with what was demonstrable.[38] Thus, in order to refute the Enlightenment's critique of faith as irrational, the apologetic argument ran the risk of confining faith within the limits of observable facts. A further consequence was that the method emphasized the ground of faith over the object or content of faith. This meant, for example, that in relation to the Resurrection of Jesus, there was a focus on the fact of the empty tomb, even though that fact does not disclose the meaning of the Resurrection or its implications for Christian faith.

In addition, the stress on the correspondence between fact and truth equated certainty with the least possible involvement of the human agent and human processes. By so doing, it omitted any connection between faith and our existence as part of a human community, whose history and tradition affect how we understand and appropriate what we believe to be true.[39] In its endeavour to amplify the credibility of faith, the apologetic method actually downplayed the religious dimen-

---

[36] Francis Schüssler Fiorenza, 'Fundamental Theology', 125–6.

[37] A good example of this form of apologetics is the first chapter—'Reason Speaks In Favour Of The Divine Institution Of The Church'—of the section on ecclesiology in Tanquerey, *A Manual of Dogmatic Theology*, 99–104. The book was published originally, in Latin, in 1914.

[38] Cf. Francis Schüssler Fiorenza, 'Fundamental Theology', 118.

[39] Ibid. 135.

sion of faith, which is always about what is more than simply a fact.[40]

There is, then, a need for an approach to faith that is more than a reflection of the concerns of modernity, but not simply an accommodation to the priorities of the postmodern world. This means that while it is important not to neglect the role of reason—'it is an illusion to think that faith tied to weak reasoning might be more penetrating; on the contrary, faith then runs the grave risk of withering into myth or superstition'[41]—it is also vital to highlight other elements that help to clarify the meaning and challenge of faith. More than anything else, there is a need to specify what is particular to the dynamics of religious faith.

It is not possible, therefore, to do justice to faith, or its claims to truth, without taking into account how participants themselves interpret their religious beliefs, symbols, and rituals.[42] Nor does such a focus imply that truth is merely relative to those who believe. It does imply, however, that even revealed truth is not 'an ontologically truncated immutable Word' that rises majestically above historical flux and renders superfluous the efforts of believers to interpret it.[43] This suggests that faith is always richer and more complex than the mere recognition of facts. Accordingly, a theology of faith must not diminish its subject by reducing it to neat categories that attempt to prove 'that the truth of faith resides elsewhere than in the act, the attitude, the gesture, the confession of faith as conscious adherence to the revealed Mystery of God.'[44]

If the truth of Christian faith that the church proclaims—the Tradition—is inseparable from the mystery of God revealed in Jesus Christ and made present in every age through the Spirit, who forms the church as a communion of believers, then the

---

[40] Francis Schüssler Fiorenza, *Foundational Theology*, 273–75.

[41] John Paul II, *Fides et Ratio* (Boston: Pauline Books, 1998), no. 48.

[42] Francis Schüssler Fiorenza, 'The Relation Between Fundamental and Systematic Theology', *Theological Quarterly*, 62 (1996–7), 153.

[43] Thomas Guarino, 'Postmodernity and Five Fundamental Theological Issues', *Theological Studies*, 57 (1996), 667–8.

[44] Joseph Doré, 'The Responsibility and Tasks of Theology in the Church and the World Today', *Theological Quarterly*, 62 (1996–7), 26.

truth is neither purely subjective nor merely objective. Since Christian truth is personal, it is possible to know it only by personal engagement; it is a truth that comes to us in a personal way and invites us into a communion of persons. Although reason facilitates its appropriation, it is a truth that discloses itself in relationship. This does not mean that it is less certain than what empirical science can demonstrate, but, as Chapter 2 argued, that it is an authentically human truth:

Human perfection, then, consists not simply in acquiring an abstract knowledge of the truth, but in a dynamic relationship of faithful self-giving with others. It is in this faithful self-giving that a person finds a fullness of certainty and security. At the same time, however, knowledge between persons is linked to truth: in the act of believing men and women entrust themselves to the truth which the other discloses to them.[45]

Even in the postmodern era, therefore, the emphasis of everyone in the church needs to be on more than defending the truth of Christianity as a set of ideas, as a 'metanarrative' that a person must accept without reserve or question. It is important, therefore, that members of the church recover the conviction that:

being Christian is not simply to be a person who subscribes to a set of beliefs or facts, though Christianity most certainly requires attention to what is true or false . . . Being Christian, engages imagination and emotion, energy and passion, not as an 'extra' to belief, but as integral, central to it. And we might inhabit our tradition with greater ease if we learned to give emotion and imagination greater weight as we try to find our way about in it. For if these dimensions of our lives are not engaged, can we effectively and seriously believe in any case?[46]

Clearly, establishing the truth of faith, and a shared commitment to that truth within the communion of the church, is a process that is both complex and demanding. It requires not just the engagement of all the members of the church, but the engagement of more than the intellect of those members. Since that faith has its focus on the mystery of God, it is also a lifelong project.

---

[45] John Paul II, *Fides et Ratio*, no. 32.
[46] Loades, 'Word and Sacrament', 30.

In the light of those challenges, it might seem that there could be little chance that anyone outside of the institutional boundaries of the church could accept that the church holds not simply a version of the truth, but *the* truth that is applicable to all people and all times. There might seem to be even less likelihood that the church's claims to truth would receive a positive reception in a pluralistic environment, where there are not only numerous other claims to the truth, but even a sense that all claims are as valid, or as meaningless, as one another. Those issues are the ones that frame the next section.

THE PARTICULARITY OF TRUTH

In order to avoid settling for unrestrained relativism or for a pluralism that makes it impossible even to imagine connections between individuals or between groups, it is necessary to grapple further with the issue of truth. More specifically, there is a need to consider whether it is possible that there might be 'the truth', which could challenge the perspectives offered both by 'your truth' and by 'my truth'.

The notion of 'the truth' suggests what 'for all possible times and places cannot be shown to fail to correspond to reality'.[47] If that is actually possible, it follows also that the truth must be true for everyone, not merely for those who accept it: 'Every truth—if it is really true—presents itself as a universal, even if it is not the whole truth. If something is true, then it must be true for all people at all times.'[48] This would mean that the truth could provide a resource that would not only enable all people to confront the entire range of human complexity, but would allow them to do so without evasion or resorting to what was less than the truth.[49]

Intimately connected to belief in 'the truth', then, is belief in the possibility of communion between human beings, a communion based on their shared acknowledgement of the truth. Nor does this mean that the truth must be monolithic, that it

---

[47] MacIntyre, *Whose Justice? Which Rationality?*, 363.

[48] John Paul II, *Fides et Ratio*, no. 27.

[49] Rowan Williams, 'Theological Integrity', *Cross Currents*, 45 (1995), 315–16.

precludes particular emphases or particular responses. What is irreconcilable with 'the truth', however, is the idea that contradictory perspectives could be equally valid or happily co-exist.

Since human beings are social beings, our varying understandings or traditions of truth do not exist in independent orbits, but encounter one another constantly. If we are aware of what we are experiencing and reflect on that experience, those encounters with 'the other', whose beliefs and ways of acting are different from ours, raise questions for us about the truth of our beliefs and ways of acting—'unbelief of people whom we respect imperils our convictions. Each faith therefore propagates itself by seeking to win converts. It must overcome or die.'[50] Our world, therefore, is not simply one with 'a multiplicity of perspectives among which we can move, but a multiplicity of antagonistic commitments, between which only conflict, rational or nonrational, is possible'.[51]

Since the ethos of 'live and let live' tends to dominate in Western societies, there can be a visceral reaction against the argument that different claims to the truth must, inevitably, come into conflict. As a result, there is a tendency to regard all traditions that lay claim to 'the truth' as being equally meaningless. While that response does not abolish the possibility of conflict between traditions, it does seal us into a nihilistic universe. Alternatively, we could simply assert the superiority of our metanarrative and demonize those who differ from us. Once again, such a response would not eliminate conflict; it would merely ensure that the conflict is 'nonrational'. A more creative option is to face the challenge of entering into dialogue with 'the other' in a common search for the truth.

To enable dialogue, we need to resist the temptation that lures us towards believing that we can defend the integrity of our tradition only by isolating it. As part of that temptation, it can appear that stubborn opposition to dialogue will attract those who are seeking the majesty of the truth and, ultimately, effect the unconditional surrender of those with lesser metanarratives. What is more likely, however, is that a refusal to engage in dialogue will produce only eccentricity and the decay

---

[50] Dulles, *The Craft of Theology*, 60.
[51] MacIntyre, *Whose Justice? Which Rationality?*, 368.

of a tradition. On the other hand, those committed to dialogue recognize that:

A tradition becomes mature just insofar as its adherents confront and find a rational way through or around those encounters with radically different and incompatible positions which pose the problems of incommensurability and untranslatability.[52]

What makes dialogue a daunting prospect is the likelihood that it might lead us to acknowledge that our tradition needs to change in order to express the truth more adequately. Similarly, the dependence of authentic dialogue, as distinct from efforts at dictation, on openness to what 'the other' offers, can also create anxiety. The implications of dialogue can be especially difficult for Christians to accept: How could 'the world', other religions, or non-believers express any truth that exceeds what is available to Christians, whose faith has its foundation in Jesus who is 'the way, the truth, and the life' (John 14: 6)? Not surprisingly, that question finds little sympathetic resonance in a pluralist culture.

There are, then, two issues that all Christians need to confront in regard to the matter of 'the truth': first, 'the scandal of particularity', the fact that Christian faith names Jesus Christ as having a unique, unsurpassable role in the relationship between God and humanity; secondly, whether the insistence on Christian uniqueness is compatible with dialogue and the situation of Christians as part of a pluralist society.

Christian faith is unashamedly particular. While it emphasizes the need to be aware of, and to beware of, the danger that we might obliterate God's Otherness by failing to distinguish between God and our understanding of God, it is wholeheartedly committed both to our God-given capacity to speak the truth about God and to the absolute connection between Jesus Christ and the truth about God.[53] Thus, the church dares to claim that, through Jesus Christ, finite human beings can know the infinite God. It dares to claim also, for example, that the liturgy provides a venue for encounter with God and that

---

[52] MacIntyre, *Whose Justice? Which Rationality?*, 327.
[53] See Dalferth, ' "I Determine What God Is!" ', 22.

doctrine about God can be true, that they do connect human beings to the mystery of God.

Those convictions, however, are at odds with the postmodern wisdom that either denies the truth claims of all religions or accepts an irreducible religious pluralism, which implies that all religions are equally true or false.[54] From that perspective, the only possible justification for any distinctions between religions does not arise on the basis of their claims to truth, but as a result of 'an ethical evaluation of the consequences of belief in each'.[55] Accordingly, the pluralist perspective privileges amongst religions only that 'which corresponds more to the dignity of the human being, and which better promotes this dignity'.[56] Furthermore, 'human dignity' has, in this context, no reference to anything that transcends the limits of history. It thus reflects the strong sense in contemporary Western cultures that life, flourishing, and driving back the frontiers of death and suffering are supreme values:

> To speak of aiming beyond life is to appear to undermine the supreme concern with the life of our humanitarian, 'civilised' world. It is to try to reverse the revolution . . . Hence, even believers are often induced to redefine their faith in such a way as not to challenge the primacy of life.[57]

Since the Christian concern with a transcendent God relativizes the value of 'the world', it is incompatible with, or even an affront to, an exclusive focus on that world. Of a different order, but just as offensive, is Christianity's insistence on the uniqueness of Jesus Christ in God's plan for the whole of humanity.[58] Further outraging postmodern sensibilities is the Catholic church's stress not only on the necessary role of

[54] For an overview of the thinking that underpins religious pluralism see Walter Kasper, 'Jesus Christ: God's Final Word', *Communio*, 28 (2001), 63–7.

[55] Daniel Leichty, *Theology in a Postliberal Perspective* (London: SCM, 1990), 86.

[56] Kasper, 'Jesus Christ', 66.

[57] Charles Taylor, 'A Catholic Modernity?', in James Heft (ed.), *A Catholic Modernity?* (New York: Oxford University Press, 1999), 24.

[58] The most recent restatement of the uniqueness of Jesus Christ is '*Dominus Iesus*: On the Unicity and Salvific Universality of Jesus Christ and the Church'; this was issued by the Congregation for the Doctrine of the Faith in August, 2000 (see *Origins*, 30 (14 Sept. 2000), 209–19).

the church in making present God's offer of life in Christ, but also on the fact that 'the unique church of Christ... subsists in the catholic church'.[59]

Such attitudes are not only out of step with the Zeitgeist, they can also invoke memories of the intolerance, even violence, that has sometimes characterized Christian, including Catholic, missionary efforts. While those concerns are significant, any demand that Christian faith abandon all claims to what is particular would be tantamount to demanding that it cease to exist. In other words, the faith of the church exists only because of what is particular to it. If there were a 'mystical-universal religion of an abstract idea of God', a religion without rites, laws, or officials, then it would indeed be either arrogant or obscurantist to insist on recognition for a particular tradition.[60] In fact, however, such a religion does not exist.

Since Christian faith is something other than a form of undifferentiated theism, since it exists only because of what is specific to it, a refusal to acknowledge its self-understanding can only distort its identity.[61] It is impossible, therefore, to remove the specifically 'Christian' in order to absorb that faith into a broader category, such as 'religion'. Dialogue between faiths, then, is possible only if Christians—and, indeed, every other party to the dialogue—are able to begin with what they mean when they say 'God'. Thus, dialogue depends on the existence of respect for the 'otherness' of each faith. If that condition seems to make it unlikely that there could ever be genuine dialogue, the challenge facing those wishing to engage in dialogue with 'Christians' is even more complex.

Despite the credal affirmation that there is only one church, and the Catholic claim that the one church 'subsists' in the Catholic church, the Christian church exists as a fragmented reality. This means that not only is undifferentiated theism a chimera, so too is generic Christianity.

---

[59] Vatican II, 'The Constitution on the Church', *LG* no. 8; this emphasis is reiterated in *Dominus Iesus*, nos. 16–17.

[60] Karl Rahner, 'Christianity's Absolute Claim', *Theological Investigations*, 21, tr. H. Riley (New York: Crossroad, 1988), 179–80.

[61] Cf. Schüssler Fiorenza, 'The Relation Between Fundamental and Systematic Theology', 155.

Nor is this line of argument an attempt to claim special status for Christianity or the Catholic tradition: if Christianity is particular, so too is every religion and every worldview. Christians, therefore, are not alone in claiming to be unique or to possess the truth. If the truth is indeed universal, then dialogue between competing claims is essential. While asserting what is particular is not necessarily arrogant, a refusal to test those claims in dialogue with other claims is more likely to be so.

It is, therefore, important to note that the particular claims of the Catholic church co-exist with its commitment to dialogue with other religions:

the church's proclamation of Jesus Christ, 'the way, the truth, and the life' (John 14: 6), today also makes use of the practice of interreligious dialogue. Such dialogue certainly does not replace, but rather accompanies the *missio ad gentes* directed towards that 'mystery of unity', from which 'it follows that all men and women who are saved share, though differently, in the same mystery of salvation in Jesus Christ through his Spirit.' Interreligious dialogue, which is part of the church's evangelizing mission, requires an attitude of understanding and a relationship of mutual knowledge and reciprocal enrichment in obedience to the truth and with respect for freedom.[62]

While it might seem absurd to suggest that there could be genuine dialogue with anyone who maintains a claim to absolute truth, the dialogue between the Christian churches, which has taken place in the generation since Vatican II, offers a helpful model of what can be possible. It is certainly true that these churches are more natural dialogue partners than Christianity and other faiths or the religious worldview and secularism, but it would be wrong to underestimate the damage that had been done by four centuries of division and mutual recrimination between the Christian churches. Although four decades of conversation have not obliterated that history or resolved every point of dispute, they have certainly opened possibilities that would have been unimaginable even as recently as the 1960s.

Although some members of the churches might regard such dialogue, and the consequent drawing-closer of the churches, as a watering-down of one or other of the Christian traditions,

[62] *Dominus Iesus*, no. 2.

such is not necessarily the case. A more accurate assessment would be that the dialogues have helped the churches to clarify their own faith, have cleared away centuries of flawed perceptions of one another, which a lack of contact had produced, and have challenged the churches to examine whether they might recognize each other's forms as complementary expressions of the one Christian faith.[63]

In all of this, the dialogues have required the conversion of those involved. That conversion has focused primarily on a willingness to give priority to 'the truth' over particular claims. This suggests, contrary perceptions notwithstanding, that the churches' claims to the truth are not snap-frozen or implacably resistant to the Spirit. To persist in that negative assessment of the Christian claim to truth, it would be necessary to ignore the fact that recent decades have witnessed, in the Catholic tradition as much as anywhere else, both a significant expansion in approaches to the Bible and a realignment of emphasis in Christology, which has stressed the need to recover a focus on the humanity of Jesus, rather than beginning with doctrine.[64] In other words, an insistence on 'truth' does not exclude the possibility of development in the church's faith. As the previous chapter stressed, the 'once-for-all' meaning of revelation in Jesus Christ promotes movement in the church, not fossilization.

Clearly, the dialogue between faiths and worldviews will not have the same dynamics as that between churches. Nonetheless, it too presumes that the participants will begin with a clear understanding of their own truth and an equally firm commitment to seek 'the truth'. Ironically, then, what can frustrate dialogue, and makes reconciliation unimaginable, is not that one or other party lays claim to the truth, but the refusal to accept that differences are real, that authentic catholicity is

---

[63] For an analysis of 'recognition' in the context of the relationship between churches see, Gerard Kelly, *Recognition: Advancing Ecumenical Thinking* (New York: Peter Lang, 1996), especially pp. 7–34.

[64] For a review of new methods of reading Scripture see 'The Interpretation of the Bible in the Church', a document published in 1993 by The Pontifical Biblical Commission, *Origins*, 23 (6 Jan. 1994), 497–524; for an overview of developments in Christology see Elizabeth Johnson, *Consider Jesus*.

different from homogeneity, or that a common search for the truth is possible.

The challenges to faith in contemporary culture all suggest that membership of the church will not long survive today if it is only a vestige from one's childhood. A merely formal attachment to the church is unlikely to withstand either postmodern scepticism or the implications of being part of a multifaith world, to say nothing of tensions within the church itself. Indeed, as we shall see in the next section, even when membership of the church is more than a formality and one's relationship to the God of Jesus Christ more than a relic, it can still be a struggle to know how to relate to contemporary culture, to know whether it is friend or foe.

THE GIFT AND CHALLENGE OF CONTEMPORARY CULTURE

Since many different aspects of contemporary culture do not communicate an awareness of the transcendent, it is not surprising that some Christians suggest that the culture is either radically incompatible with, or unsympathetic to, any such awareness. That attitude supports the conclusion that it is futile to seek a dialogue with 'the world'. Those who reject the value of dialogue tend to regard secular culture as being unable to offer anything that does not already exist, and in richer veins, within the wisdom of Christianity.[65] From that perspective, openness to the secular world, and even other faiths, achieves nothing other than the loss of the uniqueness and truth of Christian faith, a yielding of Christianity to paganism.[66]

---

[65] The most influential exposition of this approach is John Milbank's *Theology and Social Theory: Beyond Secular Reason* (Oxford: Blackwell, 1995). For critical assessments of Milbank's approach, see Gregory Baum, 'For and Against John Milbank', in *Essays in Critical Theology* (Kansas City, Miss.: Sheed & Ward, 1994), 52–66; David Herbert, 'Getting by in Babylon: MacIntyre, Milbank and a Christian Response to Religious Diversity in the Public Arena', *Studies in Christian Ethics*, 10 (1997), 61–81; and the various articles in *Philosophy and Theology*, 9 (1996), 419–59.

[66] For a challenging—especially challenging for being written by a non-Christian—example of the view that openness to secular culture and other religions dilutes Christian faith, see Ruiping Fan, 'The Memoirs of a Pagan Sojourning in the Ruins of Christianity', *Christian Bioethics*, 5 (1999), 232–7.

A more positive assessment of present-day culture insists on the possibility of 'a critical correlation' between the Christian tradition and contemporary worldviews.[67] Underpinning this approach is the conviction that the primary concerns of the Christian tradition are reconcilable with the manifestations of human longing and searching that are prevalent today. Accordingly, the commitment to correlation not only takes seriously today's questions, but also affirms the capacity of the Christian tradition to respond successfully to those questions.

While the effort at correlation has the virtue of approaching 'the world' as something other than the enemy of Christian faith, it is important to avoid assuming too casually that contemporary social and cultural processes coincide with the Christian message. Such a stance would do justice neither to modern thought nor to the content of Christian faith.[68] In other words, the emphasis on Christianity's claim to truth makes it unlikely that, for example, there would be 'sheer interpenetrative mutuality' between Christian theology and other disciplines.[69] That conclusion, however, ought not to excuse a refusal to engage with contemporary culture, a refusal that would risk portraying Christian faith as able to exist only in a self-enclosed world, perhaps even as opposed to rational discussion.

Although it is true that much in contemporary culture remains 'other' to the beliefs and emphases of the church, this does not prove that the culture is at war with the transcendent or even, more significantly, that it is utterly incapable of enriching Christian faith. In fact, the otherness of the culture can make us more sensitive to the Otherness of God. By so doing, it can remind us of what an earlier section of the chapter identified as the gap between God and our ideas about God. Consequently, an indiscriminate rejection of the culture or the refusal to consider the possibility of dialogue could lead us to reduce God to the dimensions of our closed systems. It is important to remember, therefore, that the Christian tradition's stress on the

---

[67] See David Tracy, 'The Uneasy Alliance Reconceived: Catholic Theological Method, Modernity, and Postmodernity', *Theological Studies*, 50 (1989), 548–70.

[68] Cf. Kasper, *An Introduction to Christian Faith,* 11–12.

[69] Guarino, 'Postmodernity and Five Fundamental Theological Issues', 685–6.

truth, which is an affirmation of the presence of God's Spirit in human history, is inseparable from a conviction of the 'not yet' nature of God's reign. There is, therefore, a need to remain open to the God whose capacity to lead us more deeply into an experience of the Kingdom can express itself through surprising sources.

In short, the church must continue to search for ways of acting in the world that suggest neither bloodless compliance with what is generally accepted nor an effort to dominate others and obliterate what does not seem to fit under the church's umbrella. This means that members of the church ought not to merge seamlessly into any aspects of society that either deny the possibility of the transcendent or seek humanity's fulfilment without reference to the transcendent:

Christians are obliged to resist the contemporary tendencies towards the privatization of faith, subjectivist mysticism, and the dissolution of religion into psycho-technical media of self-discovery. [Churches] must quite publicly take on the responsibility of living out of the perception of the divine reality, so as to make possible a free appropriation of the Christian faith that rests on insight and conviction, and not on persuasion, satisfaction of spiritual urges, or fulfilment of religious functions.[70]

Nonetheless, part of the difficulty confronting members of the church today is that so much of contemporary culture that is foreign to Christian faith seems to involve the rejection of that faith. The philosopher Charles Taylor, however, draws an important distinction here: it might well be that the object of such rejection is not Christian faith in itself, but the project of 'Christendom', which suggests the domination of the church over civil society.[71] Accordingly, Taylor argues that while the modern secular state has been able to grant universal human rights, rights that are independent of such issues as gender or religious allegiance, such a development would be more difficult to achieve in the world of Christendom, which would be less able to grant equality of rights to, for example, atheists, people of other religions, or homosexual people.[72]

---

[70] Dalferth, ' "I Determine What God Is!" ', 23.
[71] Taylor, 'A Catholic Modernity?', 16–17.   [72] Ibid.

While it is unlikely that many Christians would assert that
the God of Jesus Christ wants to deny people freedom in civil
society on the basis of their faith or sexuality, it is also true that
the history of explicitly 'Christian societies' does not provide a
stunning witness to the peace and justice that are the hallmarks
of God's Kingdom, a fact that the Catholic church has itself
acknowledged officially.[73] Although that fact does not require
the conclusion that Christian faith ought to have no role in the
public sphere or that members of the church ought to focus on
'the spiritual', understood narrowly, it does require that Christians remember that their faith is not a recipe for ordering the
State and its policies, especially not for controlling others—'the
gospel was always meant to stand out, unencumbered by
arms.'[74] It requires too that all members of the church continue
to wrestle with whether it could be true that aspects of contemporary society might point towards the embodiment of God's
love in ways that exceed what has been possible for the church
to embrace, even if such possibilities are actually part of the
church's constitution:

[the church] can and does benefit from the development of human life
in society, not in the sense that anything is lacking in the constitution
given it by Christ, but in order to gain a deeper appreciation of that
constitution and to express it in better terms and to adapt it more
successfully to the present day.[75]

At the very least it ought to be true that members of the
church neither persecute nor withhold compassionate service
from those whose beliefs or lifestyles they cannot endorse. In
other words, if members of the church cannot accept every
value and attitude in contemporary society, they can at least

---

[73] See the statement by the International Theological Commission,
'Memory and Reconciliation: The Church and the Faults of the Past', *Origins*,
29 (16 March 2000), 625–44. Of particular interest is 1.4, which argues that it
is always necessary to distinguish 'the responsibility or fault that can be
attributed to members of the church as believers from that which should be
referred to society during the centuries of "Christendom" or to power structures in which the temporal and spiritual were closely intertwined'.

[74] Taylor, 'A Catholic Modernity?', 18.

[75] Vatican II, 'The Pastoral Constitution on the Church in the World of
Today' (*Gaudium et spes*) GS no. 44.

seek to be more tolerant, a tolerance that does not necessarily imply indifference:

a religiously informed embrace of toleration is prone to a positive regard for all God's children in their differences and a positive concern for their well-being that prompts hopes for structural change in social relations towards greater justice and inclusivity.[76]

With that principle in mind, the next section will examine three particular examples of engagement between Christian faith and life in contemporary society. What those examples will illustrate is that trends in society can be a catalyst for the church to become aware of aspects of its mission that might have gone undeveloped; they can also provide an opportunity for the church to offer society a broader vision than one that would exclude openness to the transcendent.

THE CHURCH AND CONTEMPORARY CULTURE: THREE SNAPSHOTS

A caricature beloved of satirists is that of the conservative church-goer. The portrayal stresses the negative: members of the church are smug, intolerant, and unable to cope with any aspect of life that lacks the divine endorsement that comes by way of a text from the Bible, which seems to be full of passages promoting vengeance and destruction, or the approbation of clerics, who are archetypes of hypocrisy and ignorance. Underpinning the caricature is a sense that Christian faith not only has a negative impact on those who accept it, but that it acts as a brake on human progress, while itself contributing nothing worthwhile to society. Clearly, it is likely that clerical sexual abuse, as well as the response to it by authorities in the church, will reinforce those perceptions.

While the portrayal might be disturbing for those who do identify themselves as members of a church, it leaves no room to doubt that many people in our society do not perceive the church to be a source of good news. Many members of the church would, of course, dispute the legitimacy of the carica-

---

[76] Kathryn Tanner, 'The Religious Significance of Christian Engagement in the Culture Wars, *Theology Today*, 58 (2001), 39.

ture or argue that it is easier to ridicule Christian faith than to engage with the challenge that the church represents. Although those refutations might well be valid, the fact that there is a need for them highlights what seems to be an inescapable conclusion: that the church is marginal to contemporary culture.

This chapter has attempted to identify what underpins the alienation from the church that many people feel today. It has also traced some of its history, a history that has seen 'God' become an increasingly incomprehensible notion for many people. Inevitably, the loss of a central place for God has also made the position of the church in the modern world more tenuous. As a result of those developments, there is an urgent need for members of the church to consider not only how their faith differs from its portrayal in the caricature, but also how they relate as Christians to contemporary culture. This section will explore that relationship in the context of three key areas: the environment; science; and social and economic policies.

While the church has moved in recent years to embrace the need for environmental protection, the environmental movement itself is largely the product of those beyond the church. Most particularly, it is an aspect of the reaction against the 'entrancement' of Western society in the modern period by a vision of scientific progress.[77] That vision promised 'a millennium of earthly beatitude', but succeeded primarily in reducing the natural world to little more than raw material at the disposal of insatiable human demand.[78] Despite more than two centuries of unbridled exploitation of natural resources and relentless technological development, the hoped-for paradise did not eventuate. Instead, the deleterious impact of such an approach became more apparent: 'Decimating forests, damming rivers, draining wetlands, spreading copious amounts of toxic and long-lived materials, and destabilising the climate have all contributed to an unravelling of the Earth's complex ecological safety net.'[79] As a result, the last few decades have witnessed

[77] Thomas Berry, *The Dream of the Earth* (San Francisco: Sierra Club Books, 1988), 38–41.

[78] Ibid.

[79] Michael Renner, 'The Triple Health Challenge', in *Vital Signs: The Trends that are Shaping our Future* (Worldwatch Institute, London: Earthscan, 2001), 17.

an increasingly widespread, even if not yet universal, conversion to the need for strenuous environmental protection, as well as the imposition of limits on invasive economic and industrial policies and processes.[80]

The challenge for the church in this development is manifold. Most explicitly, there is a need to promote awareness among Christians that the cosmos is not 'religiously meaningless'.[81] Central to such awareness is the recognition that we cannot bypass the physical world, or our relationships with one another, for a more direct connection to God:

Even men and women without any particular religious conviction, but with an acute sense of their responsibility for the common good, recognize their obligation to contribute to the restoration of a healthy environment. All the more should men and women who believe in God the Creator, and who are thus convinced that there is a well-defined unity and order in the world, feel called to address the problem. Christians, in particular, realize that their responsibility within creation and their duty towards nature and the Creator are an essential part of their faith. As a result, they are conscious of a vast field of ecumenical and inter-religious cooperation opening up before them.[82]

In order to appropriate such a message, and to engage in the action that needs to flow from it, there must be a renewed sense of the connection between faith and life. There must also be an appreciation of the fact that the communal dimension of their faith challenges Christians to build relationships beyond their immediate group, to recognize the 'other', whether it is those whose beliefs differ from one's own or whether it is the physical world. While the church can thus endorse concern for the

[80] For a summary of the development of environmental awareness both in the wider society and in the church, see Stephen Scharper, 'The Ecological Crisis', in Baum (ed.), *The Twentieth Century*, 219–27.

[81] Zachary Hayes, 'God and Theology in an Age of Scientific Culture', *New Theology Review*, 8 (1995), 9. Theological reflection on ecological issues has increased significantly in recent years; see, for example, Sean McDonagh, *Greening the Christian Millennium* (Dublin: Dominican Press, 1999); Zachary Hayes, *The Gift of Being: A Theology of Creation* (Collegeville, Minn.: Liturgical Press, 2001); and Denis Edwards (ed.), *Earth Revealing—Earth Healing: Ecology and Christian Theology* (Collegeville, Minn.: Liturgical Press, 2001).

[82] John Paul II, 'Peace with God the Creator, Peace with All of Creation', Message for World Day of Peace (1 Jan. 1990), *Origins*, 19 (14 Dec. 1989), 468.

environment, and also add a dimension by highlighting the sacramentality of the environment, it is important not to lose sight of the fact that the initial impetus for increased environmental awareness has come from beyond the confines of the church. In other words, this is an instance where 'the world' has taught 'the church' to recover neglected aspects of its own tradition.

Just as the environmental movement can challenge the church to recover emphases that are part of its patrimony, so too can scientific developments. While a more creative interaction between the two has now become common, modern science and religious faith have had an uneasy relationship: the latter has tended to see the former as the archetype of unbridled rationality; while the former has tended to see the latter as the realm of superstition.

In recent decades, there has been a greater awareness of the human reality of science, of the fact that it is one way in which human beings seek to make sense of their world and that it is not independent of any presuppositions. Indeed, there is even recognition that, because scientific knowledge is personal knowledge, shifts in scientific understanding involve conversion experiences as much as they do empirical data.[83] That development has broken down the tendency to contrast science and faith. If science is more than the empirically verifiable, then the activity of theology, its endeavour to understand and evaluate the cognitive claims of religion, implies that faith is more than subjective preference, that it expresses a particular understanding of reality.[84] There are, therefore, grounds for dialogue between science and theology.

That dialogue can find its focus in a common commitment to human well-being. Since both science and theology attempt, albeit in their different ways, to render the universe and human beings as fully intelligible as possible, dialogue between them can only be beneficial to the whole human project.[85] While the faith of the church will always lead it to challenge any vision of this world as the sole end of humanity, the commitment of

---

[83] See Christopher Mooney, 'Theology and Science: A New Commitment to Dialogue', *Theological Studies*, 52 (1991), 295–6.
[84] Ibid. 301.   [85] Ibid. 318.

science to enriching human life through new ideas and processes means that the dialogue with science can remind
members of the church that 'we are not destined to be saved
from the world, but *in* this world'.[86]

Both the environmental movement and contemporary science illustrate well that not everything that originates from
outside of the church is either inconsequential to the concerns
of the church or an implacable threat to those concerns. Indeed,
a church that claims to be about the things of God ought not to
exclude any human activity from its interest; to do so would
mean that it could not express the universal vision of God.

Nonetheless, the church's focus on the reign of God means
that it is often in the position of challenging the priorities of
varying human activities. This does not reflect a fundamental
rejection of all things human, but the conviction that human
activity cannot legitimately set itself up in opposition to the
implications of God's reign. That focus means that the Christian community has, inevitably, a complex relationship with
various aspects of contemporary culture. A powerful illustration of that complexity is the church's response to contemporary economic and social policy.

At the heart of modernity's focus in economic matters was
the primacy of self-interest. From the time of Adam Smith,
self-interest and the pursuit of personal gain were equated
with economic rationality.[87] Accordingly, economic morality
became synonymous with what promoted self-interest, not
what challenged it. The advocates of that morality even
expected that the pursuit of self-interest by everyone would,
in some undefined manner, produce what was best for everyone.[88] That optimistic spirit underpinned the development of
capitalism in its modern form. While the experience of the
Great Depression damaged the rosy view of the market, it by
no means eliminated it; indeed, market capitalism has become

[86] Vincent Donovan, *The Church in the Midst of Creation* (Maryknoll, NY:
Orbis, 1989), 112. The emphasis is Donovan's.

[87] Adam Smith (1723–90) is one of the primary influences on the development of modern economics. His most important work, *An Inquiry into the
nature and causes of the Wealth of Nations*, was published in 1776.

[88] Donald Frey, 'The Good Samaritan as Bad Economist: Self-Interest in
Economics and Theology', *Cross Currents*, 46 (1996), 293.

even stronger in the last few decades. In its present incarnation, capitalism seeks to transcend national boundaries and controls—and, often, long-term planning—in pursuit of maximum profit within 'the global market'.

'Globalization' is now a major influence on socio-economic policy throughout the world. In many ways, it too is a manifestation of modernity since it stresses individual autonomy. Thus, it seeks both the end of regulation on entrepreneurs and the right of individual workers, rather than collective unions, to negotiate contracts. These measures are regarded as the means to prosperity, health care, and education for all.[89] While globalization is primarily an economic phenomenon, the surmounting of time and space by developments in information technology has enabled a greater sense of connection between people around the world, thus relativizing the role of nation-states. Paradoxically, the stress on the global has also produced a greater awareness of the local, as well as a greater opportunity for contact between groups or individuals with shared interests or concerns.[90]

So powerful a force is the globalized economy, that it influences even our understanding of personhood, which, when it is defined in terms that derive from the market, is about the capacity to produce and consume, about individualism, and about the relativizing of values. In the globalized market, virtue resides in innovation, efficiency, and technical rationality.[91] Innovation, however, does not always have a goal beyond itself, efficiency does not always equate to effectiveness, and technical rationality can be dehumanizing. While 'globalization' might imply the inclusion of everyone, it tends to be about the spread of particular aspects of Western culture throughout the world.[92]

Despite the rhetoric of globalization, the outcomes of financial deregulation and the push for global markets have not been to everyone's benefit. Not only have disparities of wealth,

---

[89] Robert Schreiter, *The New Catholicity: Theology Between the Global and the Local* (Maryknoll, NY: Orbis, 1997), 8.

[90] See T. Howland Sanks, 'Globalization and the Church's Social Mission', *Theological Studies*, 60 (1999), 630–2.

[91] Schreiter, *The New Catholicity*, 9.   [92] Ibid.

opportunity, and access to essential services continued, or even increased, but 'the hyperculture of consumption' has also had a deleterious effect on local cultures, economic systems, and values.[93] In addition, the volatility of the stock market from the late 1980s onwards and massive financial scandals and company collapses that have marked the first decade of the twenty-first century, all suggest that Adam Smith's faith in an invisible 'guiding hand', which would preserve order and balance in the market, has failed the test of reality.[94]

Since human well-being is central to the reign of God, the church cannot ignore those aspects of economic life that are damaging to that well-being. Nor is the church's criticism of economic and social policy a denial of the value of a global perspective or an attempt to manipulate or deny the autonomy of secular society. Indeed, while the church's claims to truth are often seen as incompatible with existence in a pluralist society, the very nature of such a society means that members of the church, as members of the church, have a right to seek to influence the direction of that society. What the church's criticism seeks to effect in economic matters, no less than in explicitly social issues, is both an awareness of the implications of particular policies and the recognition that there are alternatives.[95]

With its focus on the reign of God, the church has a sense of purpose for human life that exceeds a narrow concentration on the freedom of the market. At the same time, faith does not necessarily provide answers to particular economic or political problems.[96] That fact means that the voice of faith will not always be welcome in policy debates. Nonetheless, the withdrawal of people of faith from such debates would not only confirm the irrelevance of the church, it would also imply—falsely—that salvation and grace do not have, or need, some embodiment in space and time.[97]

---

[93] Ibid. 10.
[94] Frey, 'The Good Samaritan', 301–2.
[95] See Karl Rahner, 'The Function of the Church as a Critic of Society', *Theological Investigations*, 12, tr. D. Bourke (New York: Seabury, 1974), 234–5.
[96] Schreiter, *The New Catholicity*, 16.
[97] Rahner, 'The Function of the Church as a Critic of Society', 238.

In order for the church to speak prophetically to the world on social and economic matters, it is vital that a commitment to justice and compassion be characteristic of every aspect of the church's life. While the church has never lacked mechanisms for caring for those in need, it is particularly important today that those mechanisms reflect a focus on God's Kingdom. To do so, they need to be something other than agents of the State, a particular challenge in an age when the church's charitable works tend to rely significantly on government funding.[98]

It is vital to highlight here that neither criticism of social policy nor response to those in need is the exclusive prerogative of the church's hierarchy. Although there will be times when involvement by bishops in the name of the church is vital, the concern for justice in economic and social policy needs to be a priority for every member of the church.[99] This means, for example, that all members of the church, especially those in Western nations that tend to be the primary beneficiaries of cheap and easily available consumer goods, need to consider not only how they situate themselves in regard to a lifestyle that promotes consumption, but also whether they are aware of, and concerned for, those who are on the 'underside' of economic and social policies, those who are 'other' in terms of access to basic food and shelter. In addition, a flourishing community of faith is one in which caring for those in need is not something left to specialists, but is central to the activity of every member of the community:

the more this mentality of delegation and surrogacy spreads among normal members of congregations, the more the life of the average parish is reduced to worship, preaching and pious associations.[100]

A church whose members are closed to those who suffer is in danger of becoming not only banal, but a contradiction of itself, of having nothing to offer the world, and embracing forms of

[98] Hermann Steinkamp, '*Diakonia* in the Church of the Rich and the Church of the Poor: A Comparative Study in Empirical Ecclesiology', in Norbert Greinacher and Norbert Mette (eds.) *Diakonia: Church for Others* (*Concilium,* no. 198) (Edinburgh: T. & T. Clark, 1988), 67–8.

[99] Rahner, 'The Function of the Church as a Critic of Society', 242–4.

[100] Steinkamp, '*Diakonia* in the Church of the Rich and the Church of the Poor', 69.

piety that disconnect believers from life. As if that were not enough, the members of such a church would be at risk of validating the caricature outlined at the beginning of this section, a caricature that features those who acknowledge the legitimacy of no concerns other than their own. While there might always be a danger that the caricature will ring disturbingly true, this section has explored how Christian faith can facilitate creative engagement with a variety of aspects of contemporary culture. What remains for the final section of the chapter, then, is an attempt to provide an overview of how the members of the church might understand their place and mission in the present day.

THE CHURCH IN THE EXISTING SEASON

If modernity's vision focused on integrated systems that would ensure order and progress, the postmodern world is more familiar with the contradictory and the uneven. Thus, while the power of transnational or global corporations often exceeds the reach of nation-states, groups of activists with access to the Internet can make those same corporations quake by publicizing their personnel or environmental policies on Web pages that are accessible to all. Similarly, state-of-the-art communication systems, which already exceed the wildest dreams of an earlier generation of science-fiction writers, are vulnerable to invisible 'hackers' and creators of viruses. Most threateningly of all, the rise of terrorist groups, which transcend national boundaries and are signatories of no treaties, has shaken the grand vision of the twentieth century, which held that closer relationships between nations would be the key both to a more peaceful and just world and to the general sense of security in individual countries.

While Christian faith has a vision of universal peace and justice, it acknowledges God as the sole architect of such a possibility. Consequently, the church is both pessimistic about proposals to create heaven on earth and committed to working towards the realization of God's promise in Jesus Christ. Its pessimism extends to all visions for a world in which authenticity, individual as well as communal, comes without struggle, in which it is possible to meet the needs of all without sacrifice by anyone, and in which the future, especially the future that extends beyond death, does not generate some anxiety.

Nonetheless, in order that the church might be truly the symbol of the Spirit, the pessimism that can be proper to the members of the church must not become a justification for 'ceaseless grumbling' about either aspects of life within the church itself or about the society of which the church is a part.[101] Ecclesial faith, therefore, unlike what flows from much of fundamentalism and New Age spiritualities, ought not to approach the present, any present, as if it were the antithesis of God's work. The fact that Christian faith does not expect the emergence of the perfect world ought to allow members of the church to live with imperfection, within the perimeters of the church as well as beyond it, without thereby becoming insensitive to the impact of either mediocrity or injustice. It ought also to enable the members of the church to affirm whatever does speak of the hope and possibility that are symbols of the Kingdom, even if this emerges in the present from some unlikely sources.

While the circumstances of the present might cast more starkly into relief the difficulties that members of the church face, this book has stressed that Christian faith is most likely to suffer distortion when it seems to be obvious and free of all challenge:

Wherever Christianity becomes more at home, more easy to bear, wherever it becomes more liveable and ends up being for many the symbolic exaltation of what is going on anyway and of what determines the way of the world, there its messianic future is weak. Wherever it is difficult to bear, recalcitrant and thereby promises more danger than safety, more homelessness than security, there obviously it is closer to the reality of which Jesus spoke. Only if we remain faithful to the images of crisis will the images of promise remain faithful to us.[102]

This would mean that present circumstances do not make it more difficult to live authentically as a member of the church

---

[101] Karl Rahner, 'Christian Pessimism', *Theological Investigations*, 22, tr. J. Donceel (New York: Crossroad, 1991), 159.

[102] Metz, *A Passion for God*, 49.

than it was in any other period of history. Indeed, the challenges of today might support Christian faith and the authenticity of the Christian church by making it less likely that Christians could settle for a comfortable and respectable faith. Authentic Christian living in the present, then, requires what it always requires: a commitment to discipleship, to openness to the Spirit who enables the faithful following of Jesus Christ. Specifying what that might imply for the shape and dynamics of life within the contemporary church will be the concern of the next chapter.

6

The Overmuch and Unfamiliar

A popular bumper sticker insists 'If it ain't broke, don't fix it'. While the expression might be poor, the message is magisterial: it is an injunction against change for change's sake, an admonition against succumbing to a passion for novelty. Consistency, however, would require the adoption of a similarly uncompromising commitment to the repair of whatever is actually 'broke'. In order to display that consistency, this book, which began by surveying the brokenness of the contemporary church, needs now to explore possibilities for 'fixing' the church. Since that might seem a somewhat arrogant proposal, it is important to note that what follows is an attempt to apply the resources of earlier chapters to the present-day exigencies facing the church. Thus, this chapter is less a portrait of the ideal church than an endeavour to expound the implications of both faith in Jesus Christ and the gift of the Holy Spirit in order to seek alternatives to the mire that is 'the peril'.

Just as the previous chapter indicated how the church might manifest itself in the world today as something other than tired, timid, or tyrannical, this chapter will suggest what might indicate the flourishing of the Spirit within the contemporary church. In addition, it will attempt to do so without glossing over difficulties such as the divided state of the Catholic community and its fears about the future, and also without pretending that ecclesial faith is undemanding. At the heart of its argument is the conviction that the Spirit enables, rather than simply demands, a response to the challenges of the present-day. The Spirit, then, promotes dialogue, openness to 'the new', and the willingness to engage ourselves with questions to which there are no simple, or obvious, answers.

Throughout this chapter, the focus will be on creativity and imagination. That focus, however, is not an attempt to conjure a church that bears no relationship to the one that actually

exists at present. In fact, the chapter will buttress its approach
by emphasizing that 'tradition' is central to creativity and openness in the church, to movement and possibility. While this
openness will often imply the need for change, it can be true
that the embrace of 'risk' and of faithfulness to the Spirit, might
take the form of standing firm and resisting particular changes.
Such a stance, however, ought not to suggest mere intransigence
or the refusal to engage imaginatively with reality.

If a faithful response to the Spirit is something other than
stubbornness, it differs too from both a rejection of the historical grounding of Christian faith and the 'dumbing-down' of
that faith in the hope of courting popularity. Indeed, the first
section of the chapter will argue not only that the tradition of
faith provides the basis for development, but also that one mark
of authentic development is that it leads us more deeply into the
mystery of God by challenging whatever present-day expressions might distort or mask that mystery—'with the help of the
past [the church] liberates the future from the unconscious
limitations and illusions of the present.'[1] 'Creativity', therefore,
is less a synonym for reckless indifference to the received
formulae and customs of faith, than a way of mining their
potential in order to enrich the church's present and point the
way to the future:

> to be faithful to ourselves and to God, we must allow our analogies to
> break open and encircle us, to lead us in the dance from, into and out
> of ourselves towards the riotous plenty that is God. We must risk the
> overmuch, trust the unfamiliar. For only here, in this precarious place
> is love, and we will only know and taste it when we yield ourselves
> fully.[2]

This chapter, then, will explore some dimensions of an authentically Catholic reception of 'the riotous plenty that is
God'. It will examine particularly what such an appropriation
might mean for all those who form the church. Throughout the
chapter, therefore, the emphasis will be on the local church as

---

[1] Maurice Blondel, 'History and Dogma', 282. The original was published
in 1904.

[2] Ann O'Hara Graff, 'The Struggle to Name Women's Experience', in Ann
O'Hara Graff (ed.), *In the Embrace of God: Feminist Approaches to Theological
Anthropology* (Maryknoll, NY: Orbis, 1995), 85.

the primary venue for creative responses to the present, responses that must aim at the realization of the church as an inclusive and participatory communion that nurtures its relationship with other communions. In order to fulfil those objectives, the chapter will begin by reinforcing the potential for movement in 'tradition'; it will then focus on the implications of that potential for the church's structures and doctrines.

A CREATIVE—YET TRADITIONAL—CHURCH

As was indicated in Chapter 4, the association of 'tradition' with resistance, even violent opposition, to change tends to feature prominently in appraisals of the role that tradition plays in the church: 'when change is mooted [in the church] it seems invariably to occasion a level of anxiety and even trauma that is scarcely paralleled in the wider world.'[3] As a result, those who desire to embrace 'the overmuch and unfamiliar' might conclude that only the abandonment of any claims to authoritative tradition, including any role for doctrine or supposedly immutable structures, could facilitate movement in the church. On the other hand, this book, while acknowledging that aspects of the church's 'permanent constitution' loom large in analyses of what is 'broke' in the church, has highlighted the indispensable role that tradition plays in clarifying the identity and mission of the Christian community. The key question, then, is whether the fulfilment of that role requires opposition to movement in the church. In short: Does tradition make the church an irredeemably 'conservative' body?

In order to lay the basis for an answer to that query, it is necessary to clarify two underlying, and interrelated, issues: whether there can be a connection between tradition and movement; whether the central role of tradition means that the church is nothing more than a 'conservative' body that will necessarily be hostile to creativity.

The fact that much has already been made about the eschatological orientation of Christian faith, about the fullness of the Kingdom that is yet to come, certainly implies that an authentic presentation of Christian tradition must highlight its capacity

---

[3] Platten and Pattison, *Spirit and Tradition*, 43.

to promote movement. Without such an emphasis, there is a danger of failing to recognize that even those aspects of Christian faith that believers accept as irreducible elements both of God's self-revelation and humanity's response to God must be vehicles for 'the utter', which we will experience only in the fullness of God's reign.[4] The authenticity of the Christian tradition, then, does not reside in resistance to movement:

Christian truth is ... not an unvarying datum that is handed on from century to century in the form of a fixed deposit. It is rather a permanent coming that is exposed to the risk of history and the interpretative freedom of the Church under the impulse of the Spirit.[5]

While the emphasis on the 'permanent coming' highlights the eschatological orientation of tradition, it might be less than obvious how that sentiment can marry with the claim that there are aspects of the church's life—its doctrine, sacraments, and elements of its structure—that must be a permanent feature of its constitution. One way to address that concern is via an exploration of the purpose and dynamics of doctrine.

The value of doctrine is that it attempts to ensure that we are speaking of God, rather than of something mythological or something that concerns only the exercise of religious power.[6] In other words, doctrine highlights that Christian faith has content to which all believers can give assent, that it is something other than an ineffable, even private, feeling. In addition, doctrine supports the efforts of Christians to talk about their faith with those who inquire about it, rather than simply to impose it by force. While doctrine helps to distinguish faith from subjectivism, this ought not to imply that it renders faith impersonal. Indeed, doctrine is both the expression of the lived faith of the community and the product of a long history of refinement by that community, a refinement stimulated by the need to respond to new questions. Significantly, doctrine is also not the antithesis of change, especially if we understand 'change' as meaning something other than the coming into

---

[4] Heher, 'Why We Still Need Theologians', 70.

[5] Claude Geffré, *The Risk of Interpretation: On Being Faithful to the Christian Tradition in a Non-Christian Age*, tr. D. Smith (Mahwah: Paulist, 1987), 62.

[6] Williams, 'Theological Integrity', 323.

being of what bears no relationship to anything that had previously existed.

Thus, what continues in the church from age to age is not simply the same content, but reflection on the same texts and symbols, which have not only been handed down in the tradition, but also continue to make claims on believers.[7] While the texts remain normative, the understanding of them will always reflect the historical circumstances of their interpreters. The status of Scripture and doctrine in the church does presume an act of faith in the capacity of those aspects of the tradition to be effective in the present, but that act of faith does not commit believers merely to repetition of what has been significant in the past. Nor does it commit them to 'unimaginative immobilism' in regard to texts and traditions.[8] If, then, life in the church is impossible without faith, it is equally impossible without the exercise of imagination and the willingness to search for an understanding of faith that is appropriate for the present—'Tradition is thus the setting forth (not necessarily the mere *repetitio*) of the authentic meaning which is necessary if the *euaggelion tou Theou* is to be received in accordance with what God has really willed to offer humanity.'[9] In fact, a church without imagination, without openness to the possibility of movement, would be one without an appreciation of its own identity:

It would indeed be wrong to think of the church in passage as a concession to the post-modern age, a sacrifice on the altar of generalized relativity and of the evolution of Western culture. For the threat of social change on a planetary scale is not the reason that the church, too, has to change . . . The church needs to change simply because it is *itself* movement, taking to the road, journey. Founded in the midst of the Passover, a time of movement, the church 'is a place of passage'.[10]

Nor is the emphasis on creativity merely an endeavour to make life in the church appear more interesting in prospect than in fact. If the various aspects of the tradition that make the

---

[7] Guarino, 'Postmodernity and Five Fundamental Theological Issues', 687.

[8] Ibid. 672–3.

[9] Tillard, 'Faith, the Believer and the Church', 217.

[10] Graesslé, 'From Impasse to Passage', 26. The emphasis is Graesslé's.

church *this* church are truly expressive of the Spirit's presence, then they must invite us to grapple continually with the God who is always greater, the God who remains a mystery. That, in turn, must mean that they retain, always, the capacity to provide life and direction for the communion of faith. That fact provides a context that can help to clarify the 'conservative' nature of the church.

In its simplest and least polemical form in social and political thought, conservatism expresses a preference for what we know rather than for what we are yet to experience. The positive value in such conservatism is its capacity to recognize the worth of what is at hand:

To be conservative, then, is to prefer the familiar to the unknown, to prefer the tried to the untried, fact to mystery, the actual to the possible, the limited to the unbounded, the near to the distant, the sufficient to the superabundant, the convenient to the perfect, present laughter to utopian bliss.[11]

Conversely, those who are scornful of the past or who hunger insatiably after what does not yet exist might esteem nothing, or even be strangers to the experience of love and affection.[12] Genuine conservatives, then, are also likely to recognize that not all changes will be beneficial, that change can involve loss as well as gain. Its virtues not withstanding, there is also a negative potential in conservatism. The latter appears when its practitioners regard it as incompatible with any proposal for change. Viewed through such a lens, change seems to be an imposition or even a threat to identity: since identity must be defended at all costs, change must be resisted.

The blanket rejection of change, however, is likely to overstate the impact of such change. In fact, the history of social and political reform suggests that no change is ever so absolute that it abolishes everything that preceded it—'in any generation, even the most revolutionary, the arrangements which are enjoyed always far exceed those which are recognized to stand in need of attention ... the new is an insignificant

---

[11] Michael Oakeshott, 'On Being Conservative', in *Rationalism in Politics and Other Essays* (Indianapolis, Ind.: Liberty Press, 1991), 408. The essay was first published in 1956.
[12] Ibid. 409.

proportion of the whole.'[13] In addition, those who collapse authentic conservatism into a radical rejection of change dis-qualify themselves from being able to show that what they value has the capacity both to adapt to new circumstances and influence new ways of acting.

Although authentic conservatism in the church values what has been received from the past, it goes beyond the fundamen-tal desire for preservation that can prevail in the social and political arena. Since Christian faith affirms both the presence of the Spirit in what has been received via the apostolic trad-ition and its orientation to the future, conservatism in the church cannot be about simple preservation; there must also be the willingness to seek new possibilities that might grow out of what has been conserved. An example of this principle in action is Walter Kasper's argument that those who were labelled 'progressives' at Vatican II were actually 'the true "conservatives"'. This was so, argues Kasper, because they wanted to do more than preserve, especially if it was the case of preserving only those traditions—'with all their narrowness and encrustations'—that had been influential in the preceding two or three centuries.[14] In fact, the authentic conservatives wanted a renewal of the church based on the full richness of Scripture and the tradition. Thus, their commitment to preser-vation was also a commitment to change. Paradoxically, it was their faith in the tradition, and its orientation to future fullness, that fuelled their conviction that the church could speak to the contemporary world only if it changed.

This suggests that it is false to apply to the church the norms that govern the use of 'conservative' in the wider society, where the word functions often either as a rallying-cry, which gathers the guardians of 'the truth' in order that they might resist the ravages of 'liberals', or as a term of abuse, which is obvious when adjectives such as 'reactionary' accompany the invocation of 'conservative'. In the church, genuine conservatives ought to be people who situate suggestions for change within the larger

---

[13] Michael Oakeshott, 'Political Education', in *Rationalism in Politics and Other Essays*, 13. The essay was first published in 1951.

[14] Kasper, 'The Council's Vision', 481–2.

framework of the church's need to preserve its orientation to the fullness of God's reign:

It is strange that we Christians, who have to achieve the radical commitment of hope in which we venture upon that which is incalculable and uncontrollable in the absolute future, have incurred the suspicion both in the minds of others and in our own that so far as we are concerned the will to guard and preserve is the basic virtue of life. In reality, however, the sole 'tradition' which Christianity precisely as the people of God *on pilgrimage* has acquired on the way is the command to hope in the absolute promise and—in order that thereby this task may not remain at the level merely of a facile ideology of ideas—to set out anew from the social structures which have become petrified, old and empty.[15]

Paradoxically, then, it is the familiar in the church that is to give birth to 'the overmuch and unfamiliar'. The new, therefore, does not emerge only when we eliminate, totally and systematically, all that comes from the past. The paradoxical language of that conclusion will be unsurprising to those accustomed to the dialectic between death and Resurrection at the heart of Christianity. In fact, if the church is to be faithful to the revelation of God in Jesus Christ and the ongoing presence of the Spirit, the expectation in the church ought to be that the tradition will fuel creativity and movement.

In the Christian tradition, therefore, as in any tradition, there is a close connection between vitality and openness to change— 'Its principle is a principle of *continuity*: authority is diffused between past, present, and future; between the old, the new, and what is to come.'[16] Indeed, a tradition that can survive only by resisting all efforts at change is permanently endangered. Hence, Karl Rahner's assertion at the end of Vatican II, that the church's orientation towards the future, which the Council highlighted, was inseparable from its tradition:

God addresses to the Church the question whether it has the courage to undertake an apostolic offensive into the future and consequently the necessary courage to show itself to the world sincerely, in such a form that no one can have the impression that the Church only exists as a mere survival from earlier times because it has not yet had time to

---

[15] Rahner, 'On the Theology of Hope', 258–9. The emphasis is Rahner's.
[16] Oakeshott, 'Political Education', 61. The emphasis is Oakeshott's.

die. But even if it has the courage to change, time is needed and time must be taken ... For the Church cannot change into something or other at will, arbitrarily, but only into a new presence of its old reality, into the present and future of its past, of the Gospel, of the grace and truth of God.[17]

Although it might be easy to affirm the intent of Rahner's analysis, the difficulty for the church resides in determining what constitutes the 'new presence of its old reality'. The unfamiliar, then, might well arise out of the familiar, but it is likely that its birth will require prolonged, and often anguished, labour. The following section will explore the dialectic between the old and the new, especially as it applies to the relationship between the communion of the church and the structures that exist to serve, support, and guide that communion in its orientation to the fullness of God's reign.

AN INCULTURATED AND DISCERNING CHURCH

A principal obstacle to appropriating the dialectic between permanence and possibility in the church is that the familiar in the church seems, often, either to be set in concrete or to be actively hostile to change. Another difficulty is that the church as a whole either lacks, or applies inconsistently, clear processes that would make it possible to review the efficacy of its structures, to consider whether there could be more adequate avenues of communication within the church, to involve the communion of the faith at large in discernment of change, and to facilitate concerted action aimed at shifting the priorities of the church in directions more responsive to contemporary needs and to the mysterious movement of the Spirit. Clearly, the dearth of such processes is a stumbling block to the embrace of ecclesial faith, perhaps especially in contemporary Western societies. That deficiency, however, ought not to be beyond redemption.

Indeed, the fact that the Holy Spirit is central both to each aspect of the church's permanent constitution and to the life of

[17] Karl Rahner, 'The Changing Church', in *The Christian of the Future*, tr. W. O'Hara (London: Burns & Oates, 1967), 36. The article was first published in 1965.

every baptized person suggests that there needs to be in the church not only more resources at the disposal of efforts to promote communal discernment, but also a greater acceptance, even expectation, of the fact that such discernment could lead to the recognition of the unfamiliar as a vehicle for the Spirit. A necessary foundation for such a focus would be the promotion of the communal reality of the church. That emphasis, however, does not mean that there must be a choice between the communal dimension and the various structural elements in the church; it does not imply that the Catholic church must dissolve into congregationalism. Nonetheless, it does highlight the fact that, without a firm grounding in the spirituality of communion, the structures of the church are in danger of acting as 'mechanisms without a soul'.[18] A principal danger of such mechanisms is that they might regard opposition to change as fundamental to their purpose.

Since the life of the Spirit within the communion of faith can manifest itself in a variety of ways, it is not possible to determine in advance how reception of the Spirit might express itself within the communion of faith nor channel that reception according to administrative requirements. This suggests that we can do justice to the Spirit only if we allow for the emergence of the overmuch. In more strictly theological terms, it implies that faithful interpretation and development of the tradition will depend on prophetic action, rather than on mechanisms of control:

All communities need prophets, people who creatively shape the intractable here and now out of an affinity with the soul of a common tradition. In the long run, tradition is kept alive by authentic commentators, not by critics, and certainly not by task-masters, letter-worshippers, and hacks.[19]

In order to ensure faithfulness to the tradition and authentic development of it, more is needed than simply verbal continuity.[20] The prophetic charism is particularly necessary when it is

---

[18] The necessity of a spirituality of communion as an antidote to the possible emergence of 'mechanisms without a soul' is a central theme to Pope John Paul II's *Novo Millennio Ineunte*, see especially nos. 43 and 45.

[19] van Beeck, 'Divine Revelation', 221.

[20] See Tilley, *Inventing Catholic Tradition*, 34–5.

unclear how the tradition might respond creatively to the challenges that it faces at a given moment of history. In such circumstances, what is required, especially at the level of articulation, is 'imaginative conceptual innovation', which can take the tradition in new directions while being faithful to it.[21]

Although the prophetic charism resists easy definition, it is certainly true that only those who grasp the meaning of a tradition are capable of making suggestions for its authentic development. This indicates that creativity in the church will result from those who understand past expressions of faith through their dwelling within the community of faith. This relationship to the community's faith provides the basis for a 'connatural' sense of the things of God, out of which creativity grows.[22] It is this connatural understanding that facilitates 'an element of intuitive judgment', which recognizes that continuity might involve 'a kind of family likeness which may persist even when there is change in respect of each individual item involved'.[23]

In other words, translating a tradition from one milieu to another, like the translation of a language, is possible only for those whose understanding goes beyond the superficial, who can do more than transliterate it. Genuine translation is possible only for those who have learnt the tradition as 'a second first language'.[24] Conversely, those who assume blithely that they know what the tradition intends, especially that they know enough to be confident that it is incompatible either with change or continuity, are in danger of doing violence to it.

Discerning the right relationship between preservation and possibility is complex. This is so not simply because of the challenge of translating from one culture to another, but also because it involves the Spirit. Although the presence of the Spirit is always inseparable from historical experience, human beings do not have immediate access to either the presence or

---

[21] MacIntyre, *Whose Justice? Which Rationality?*, 362–3.

[22] See Avery Dulles, 'Tradition and Creativity: A Theological Approach', in Hagen (ed.), *The Quadrilog*, 319.

[23] See Maurice Wiles, *Working Papers in Doctrine* (London: SCM, 1976), 105–6.

[24] For the notion of a 'second first language' and its connection to the translation of both languages and traditions, see MacIntyre, *Whose Justice? Which Rationality?*, 374–5.

intentions of the Spirit, as the preceding chapters have emphasized. One consequence of this situation is that the faith of the church, whether it expresses itself in terms of the familiar or the unfamiliar, is always a response to the 'hiddenness' of the Spirit.[25] This does not mean that the church's faith lacks a firm foundation, but it does highlight that the community must live from faith. If we want absolute clarity and certainty, we can find them only in what has been authoritatively experienced and enacted in the past. Even what we receive now as the authoritative teaching of the past, however, was once clothed in the ambiguous presence of the Spirit.[26] In short, the church, in every age of its history, cannot abandon its pilgrim existence for a less risky way of living.

The fact that even those in authority cannot effortlessly 'read' the Spirit underscores the fact that the authentic exercise of authority in the church is possible only when that authority finds its place 'in a circle of faith in which believers aspire to faithfulness to the Spirit of God'.[27] It is, then, the connection of the Spirit to the communion of faith that ensures not only that 'possibility' continues to be applicable to life in the church, but also that the communion of the church remains something other than an undifferentiated collective or a dictatorship.

Although it is not valid for human beings to claim mastery over the movement of the Spirit, the fact that the Spirit is the self-communication of the God who has become incarnate in human history, rather than an impersonal principle, suggests that we must seek the Spirit in the particular situation in which we live, in what is both present and local. In other words, if God comes to meet us where we are, then not only *this* moment of history, but also *this* situation is where we are likely to encounter the Spirit. There is, therefore, a need to emphasize the indispensable role played by the local church in seeking to develop an authentic response to the Spirit:

[Local churches] constitute a horizon of understanding within which the faith tradition from the past is encountered and received. This reception, however, is a mutually critical one, in which the faith of the

---

[25] John Thiel, 'Responsibility to the Spirit: Authority in the Catholic Tradition', *New Theology Review*, 8 (1995), 64.
[26] Ibid.   [27] Ibid.

local church is shaped by the tradition from the past, and whereby the tradition of the past is reinvigorated and changed (or challenged) by the peculiarities of the local church culture.[28]

As Vatican II acknowledged, the local church, where 'the faithful are gathered together by the preaching of the gospel of Jesus Christ and the mystery of the Lord's supper is celebrated', is where the 'church of Christ is truly present'.[29] We ought to expect, then, that the local church would be the primary venue for the communion of faith to determine 'what of the realities coming from the past generation has to be perpetually kept and what has to be changed in order to permit the local church to find new ways appropriate to its own situation'.[30]

In the contemporary context, it seems that there is a strong sense in many local churches that the embrace of new possibilities, rather than simply a reaffirmation of particular traditions, is crucial to the future of the church:

Men and women today experience a real change in their self-understanding and sense a need to live authentically out of this changed self-understanding. The reason that they believe change is demanded by the times is not to toy with the Christian faith but precisely in order to be loyal to it in changed circumstances.[31]

Clearly, this emphasis on the local church and on its need to discern an appropriate expression of tradition in its present circumstances could fragment the unity of the church and of its tradition. That, however, is not an inevitable outcome. What is also possible is a meeting between the tradition and the culture of the local church:

Inculturation involves the incarnation of the one faith, expressed in categories of thought, symbols, liturgical practices, and ethical models which are newly formulated by a local people with fidelity both to the cultural heritage and to Christian revelation.[32]

---

[28] Paul Crowley, 'Catholicity, Inculturation, and Newman's *Sensus Fidelium*', *Heythrop Journal*, 33 (1992), 169–70.

[29] 'The Constitution on the Church', *LG* no. 26.

[30] Jean-Marie Tillard, 'Tradition, Reception', in Hagen (ed.), *The Quadrilog*, 336.

[31] John Burkhard, '*Sensus Fidei*: Theological Reflection since Vatican II, Part I: 1964–1984', *Heythrop Journal*, 34 (1993), 50.

[32] Kilmartin, 'Reception in History', 46.

While it could be possible to exercise authority in a way that seeks uniformity in the church, previous chapters have emphasized that efforts at authoritarian control express an impoverished—indeed, defective—theology of the church. In addition, they are never truly effective. Consequently, the only genuine antidote to anarchy in the church can be conversion to the truth, which, since it is indistinguishable from the Spirit, is an expression of the love that alone can create communion— 'Only the love that drives people to search for truth is genuine and lasting, and only the truth which is sought for out of love, and is realized in love, makes us free.'[33]

In addition, there are four criteria that can identify authentic openness to the Spirit in the context of the communion of faith seeking to discern an appropriate response to the present. These criteria can help us to determine whether communal discernment expresses 'a flair, a kind of spiritual sixth sense, an ecclesiastical instinct, a *sensus fidei*', which will ensure that it does not become an agent for the fragmenting of the church.[34]

First, there is the desire to be in continuity with the tradition, which implies a desire to nurture a genuinely ecclesial faith. Secondly, faithfulness to the Spirit, who is the source of the church's unity and catholicity, promotes acceptance of the need for the universal communion of local churches. This communion 'serves to prevent individual local churches from isolating themselves or identifying themselves with narrow cultural or national agendas'.[35] Thirdly, faithfulness to the Spirit at work in the church affirms the role of authority in the church, which seeks 'to ensure that the insights of the laity living out their faith, and the efforts of theologians to understand the faith anew, critically, convincingly, and systematically, are truly rooted in the Gospel and that the understanding of this Gospel today leads the faithful into the communion with God opened up by faith in that Gospel'.[36] Fourthly, genuine discernment is something other than the quest to secure a majority vote in order to change the church or to determine the structures and

---

[33] Kasper, *Theology and Church*, 146.

[34] Tillard, 'Tradition, Reception', 336.

[35] William McConville, 'Catholicity and Belonging: Challenges and Tensions', *New Theology Review*, 2 (1989), 6.

[36] Burkhard, '*Sensus Fidei*: Theological Reflection since Vatican II', 51.

actions of the church. In other words, authentic discernment is not equivalent to the determination of all actions according to the results of opinion polls, which might tell us no more than 'what a number of people of unknown religious practice and commitment think in response to questions frequently phrased to manipulate their response'.[37]

None of those features, however, invalidates the centrality of the local church or the fact that the Spirit received in our baptism summons us constantly to seek an appropriate translation of the tradition of faith into our *Sitz im Leben*. A church attentive to the Spirit, therefore, will be one that represents 'a society of explorers', rather than of 'map-readers'.[38] In the contemporary context, when society offers so many alternatives to Christian faith and the internal dynamics of the church do not reflect the settled pattern of previous generations, the need for such exploration is especially urgent.

Clearly, the advocacy of exploration suggests anything other than a church that sees itself as a fortress. If that situation calls for a universal commitment to be attentive to the Spirit, it generates also a particular need for courageous and creative forms of leadership. The contemporary church, then, needs leaders who can promote respect for, and engagement with, the tradition of faith, but who do so in ways that leave members of the church in no doubt that they are part of a communion, rather than 'a centralist and bureaucratically administered state seeking to decree from above more or less everything that is at all important'.[39] Such leaders will see themselves as having a responsibility for acting as midwives to the birth of 'the overmuch and unfamiliar'. The need for creativity in leadership includes also the exercise of the church's teaching authority. Here, the particular need is for the exercise of that role in a more pastoral spirit, a spirit that ensures the teaching authority is other than 'some ecclesial *Academie Francaise*, [that] seems to stand watchdog over the authenticity of the tradition conceived

---

[37] James Heft, '*Sensus Fidelium* and the Marian Dogmas', *One in Christ*, 28 (1992), 114.

[38] Richard, 'Reflections on Dissent and Reception', 14.

[39] Karl Rahner, 'Unity of the Church: Unity of Mankind', *Theological Investigations*, 20, tr. E. Quinn (New York: Crossroad, 1986), 171.

very statically as a body of truths, conformity to which constitutes orthodoxy and challenge, grounds for censure'.[40]

There must be room, therefore, for greater experimentation
in the church and for a greater openness to questions. While it
might seem that experimentation is the antithesis of tradition,
the willingness to experiment, to risk, can also express the
endeavour to be faithful to tradition in the unique circumstances of the present. A willingness to experiment can bear
testimony to the conviction that the continuity of tradition,
which the Spirit sustains and promotes, is not simply an abstract notion, but depends on particular expressions that
embody the tradition, expressions that are themselves subject
to change:

The changeable and unchangeable are not two entities simply existing
side by side as immediately empirically apprehensible each in its own
right. That which we immediately experience and make living contact
with is that which is in process of change, and it is the more immediate
to us and the more apprehensible of the two entities. It is precisely *in*
this . . . that this unchangeable factor has ever afresh to be believed in,
hoped in, and acted upon in a spirit of faithfulness as that which is the
more hidden of the two factors.[41]

There can be, then, no escape from the fact that the church
that lives by faith in the centrality of tradition will also be one
that is open to the value of change. Ultimately, the continuity of
tradition does not rest upon what we can verify empirically, but
'is an object of believing hope and of that faithfulness which
dares to commit itself on the basis of hope'.[42]

The need for experimentation also supports the focus on the
local church, since experimentation is most likely at the
local level. As has already been stressed, that focus need not
issue invariably in conflict between the local church and the
church at large. Indeed, it can actually be the case that what
begins at the local level can become the model for the whole
church. Thus, the church's history suggests that 'regional

---

[40] Lakeland, *Theology and Critical Theory*, 143.
[41] Rahner, 'Basic Observations on the Subject of Changeable and Unchangeable Factors in the Church', 7–8. The emphasis is Rahner's.
[42] Ibid. See also, Michael Fahey, 'Continuity in the Church Amid Structural Change', *Theological Studies*, 35 (1974), 415–40.

truth-claims', as even the gospels and the early Councils were originally, can become authoritative for the whole church.[43] This indicates that between the universal and local in the church there is 'a single web of belief in which catholicity and particular claims are mutually constitutive, mutually revisable, and expressive of the church's pluralism through time and culture'.[44]

The present moment of the church's history, then, needs the prophetic witness that manifests the creativity of the Spirit. That creativity can express itself in various forms of 'pro-Catholicism', which develop the tradition by 'promoting its creative potential and responding to an irresistible appeal which others may not yet recognize or appreciate'.[45] 'Pro-Catholicism' can also give voice to the 'historically voiceless and undervalued' groups that 'have been claiming the integrity of their own experience and offering it as a source of religious practice and theological insight for the whole church'.[46]

The possibility of such 'pro-Catholicism' reinforces the potential for development that is central to the church. To illustrate both that potential and the fact that all developments raise new questions for the church at large, thereby opening the prospect of further developments, the next section will focus on 'ministry'. As will be clear, this topic, which is a key category in the life of the contemporary church, highlights not only the impact of history on the church, but also that achieving the union of tradition and creativity is a challenging project.

AN UNFINISHED CHURCH

Vatican II emphasized that each member of the church shares Christ's identity as priest, prophet, and king.[47] Through that

---

[43] John Thiel, 'Pluralism in Theological Truth', in Claude Geffré and Werner Jeanrond (eds.), *Why Theology?* (*Concilium* no. 1994/6), (London: SCM, 1994), 67–8.

[44] Ibid.

[45] Robert Kinast, 'Vatican II Lives!: Foundation for the Future', *Church*, 13 (1995), 8.

[46] Ibid.

[47] See, for example, 'The Constitution on the Church', *LG* nos. 10–12.

designation, the Council sought a church enlivened by the gifts of all of the baptized, gifts that would contribute not only to the mission of the church, but also to the vitality of its communion:

Vatican II's whole conception of the People of God is shot through with the need for all the faithful to participate and commune in the prophetic, priestly and royal service of Christ, which is made manifest in active insertion into the various ecclesial services and in the charisms given for the common good.[48]

In practice, one response to the Council's vision of a more participatory church has been the greater engagement of 'the laity' in ministry.

Not only would it have been impossible before Vatican II to employ 'minister' in reference to anyone other than a cleric, it is also true that the Council itself did not use the term when speaking of 'the laity'. Nonetheless, the proliferation of 'ministers' in the contemporary church is not simply an outcome of the dramatic reduction in the numbers of ordained priests over the last forty years. It also expresses one direction taken by the church at large in its reception of Vatican II's teaching on the implications of baptism.[49] This development has enriched the church in many ways, but also raised new questions, and generated not a little concern, which, as will become clear below, emerged from a range of perspectives.

More than anything else, it is crucial that a focus on ministry not shade the importance of baptism as the key to living as a Christian.[50] Thus, while it seems valid to conclude that the contemporary prominence of 'ministry' highlights implications in the Council's understanding of both the communal existence of the church and the implications of baptism, it is also true that the Council was seeking more than the development of a cadre

---

[48] Leonardo Boff, 'The Uncompleted Vision of Vatican II: The Church—Hierarchy or People of God?', in Elisabeth Schüssler Fiorenza and Hermann Häring (eds.), *The Non-Ordination of Women and the Politics of Power* (*Concilium*, no. 1999/3), (London: SCM, 1999), 33.

[49] For an overview of the expressions and sources of the 'explosion' of ministry in the contemporary church see Thomas O'Meara, *Theology of Ministry*, rev. edn. (Mahwah, NJ: Paulist, 1999), 6–21.

[50] For a stirring challenge to the notion that being a minister is central to the life of the Christian, see John Collins, *Are All Christians Ministers?* (Newtown, NSW: E. J. Dwyer, 1992).

of ministers: in liturgy, mission, and the inner life of the church, Vatican II's goal was a fully participative community. In other words, it is important to ensure that 'ministry' remains at the service of the church's mission, since it is the latter that is the responsibility of every member of the communion. Any division in the church, therefore, between an elite group of active ministers, ordained or otherwise, and a mass of largely passive consumers can never be valid.[51]

If there is a danger that 'ministry' might become, even inadvertently, an instrument for dividing the church into active and passive members, the opposite danger is that every activity of every baptized person could come under the caption 'ministry'. As a result, that category would lose its specificity—'When everything is described as ministry, then the word loses definition and becomes meaningless, and nothing is distinguishably ministry.'[52] In many ways, such a development expresses a reaction against the perception that the ordained had aggregated to themselves all power, influence, and right to activity in the church. Identifying oneself as a 'minister' can, then, be a means of asserting something other than second-class citizenship in the church, asserting a right to share in the life of the church.

It is baptism, however, not ministry, that guarantees such a right. What must remain primary, therefore, is the realization of the church as a participatory communion that depends on the contribution of all its members. This would allow for a specific identity for 'ministry' as that which serves—not usurps, replaces, or renders unnecessary—the mission that all the baptized share. It would also emphasize that ministries are responses to the needs of the community. While authentic ministry can have its source only in the Holy Spirit, it is always more than the expression of personal charisms. Since the Spirit seeks the good of the communion, ministry in the name of the Spirit must also aid the discipleship of the whole community. This means that it must maintain a positive relationship to the

---

[51] For discussion of the danger of an elite group of laity see Teresa Pirola, 'Church Professionalism: When Does it Become "Lay Elitism"?', in Richard Lennan (ed.), *Refining the Church: Vision and Practice* (Alexandria, NSW: E. J. Dwyer, 1995), 71–87.

[52] Michael Lawler, *A Theology of Ministry* (Kansas City, Miss.: Sheed & Ward, 1990), 28.

church as a whole, including authorities in the church since they have a particular, Spirit-given, responsibility for the faith and unity of the community.[53]

While the relationship of ministry to the mission of all the members of the church is a primary issue, the expansion of ministry among those who are not ordained has also raised new questions about the meaning of ordained ministry. Indeed, as more and more people have become involved in 'ministry', one consequence has been the widespread perception that the ordained are simply 'other' ministers. As a result, it can be a challenge to appropriate Vatican II's teaching that the priesthood of the ordained differs 'in essence and not simply in degree' from that of every other baptized person.[54]

In response to this development, official documents have striven in recent years to underscore the differences between the baptized and the ordained. Indeed part of the strategy in those documents has been to distinguish 'ministry', which, 'properly understood' applies only to the ordained, from any *officia* that might be 'temporarily entrusted', as a result of a 'deputation by the church', to those who are not ordained.[55] In addition, there has been a refusal to endorse the appropriateness of applying certain titles—such as 'pastor', 'chaplain', 'coordinator', and 'moderator'—to the unordained on the grounds that such titles could 'confuse their role and that of the pastor, who is always a bishop or priest'.[56]

[53] For various views of what constitutes 'ministry' see ibid. 28; O'Meara, *Theology of Ministry*, rev. edn., 140–9; George Tavard, *A Theology for Ministry* (Wilmington, Del.: Michael Glazier, 1983), 80–3; of particular interest is the description of 'the lay ecclesial minister' by the National Catholic Conference of Catholic Bishops (USA), Subcommittee on Lay Ministry of the American bishops, 'Lay Ecclesial Ministry: State of the Questions', *Origins*, 29 (20 Jan. 2000), 500.

[54] 'The Constitution on the Church', *LG* no. 10.

[55] Congregation for the Clergy *et al.*, 'Instruction on Certain Questions Regarding the Collaboration of the Non-Ordained Faithful in the Sacred Ministry of Priests', *Origins*, 27 (27 Nov. 1997), 166. This document was published under the joint authorship of eight Vatican offices. For a valuable discussion of the document's presuppositions and arguments see Richard Gaillardetz, 'Shifting Meanings in the Lay–Clergy Distinction', *Irish Theological Quarterly*, 64 (1999), 115–39.

[56] 'Instruction on Certain Questions Regarding the Collaboration of the Non-Ordained Faithful in the Sacred Ministry of Priests', 166.

The primary concern of such documents is to defend in the present-day situation of the church the unique charism of the ordained ministry. In order to do so, the documents criticize 'certain practices', which are unnamed, but said to dominate in certain—again, unnamed—parts of the world, that might undermine, obscure, or even reject that charism.[57] While that concern is proper, the documents tend to provide little encouragement to further reflection on the meaning of baptism, the possibility of 'ministry' for the non-ordained as other than a response to an emergency or an exception, or the implications of church membership for witnessing to the gospel in the communion of the church, rather than simply 'in the world'. In other words, such documents are important as reminders to the whole church of the challenges inherent in its traditions, but less helpful as invitations to bring the tradition into a prophetic engagement with contemporary issues and questions.

Nor does such a criticism imply that there is no possibility that contemporary developments might distort vital traditions. On the other hand, it does suggest that it is possible both to affirm the uniqueness of ordained ministry and be open to greater collaboration and co-responsibility between the ordained and non-ordained.[58] It suggests too that contemporary developments in the life of the church, particularly in regard to ministry, will raise questions that the church has not had to face previously.[59] Consequently, it is not possible to determine a priori what responses might best embody the tradition of a pilgrim church—'the practice of pastoral ministry that led to engaging more and more lay people in parish minis-

---

[57] 'Instruction on Certain Questions Regarding the Collaboration of the Non-Ordained Faithful in the Sacred Ministry of Priests', 163.

[58] For examples of creative theologizing about the relations between ordained ministers and other members of the church see Gaillardetz, 'Shifting Meanings in the Lay–Clergy Distinction', 115–39; David Coffey, 'The Common and Ordained Priesthood', *Theological Studies*, 58 (1997), 209–36; Susan Wood, 'Priestly Identity: Sacrament of the Ecclesial Community', *Worship*, 69 (1995), 109–27; Kasper, *Leadership in the Church*, 45–75.

[59] For some of the questions about ministry confronting the church see Karl Rahner, 'Consecration in the Life and Reflection of the Church', *Theological Investigations*, 19, tr. E. Quinn (New York: Crossroad, 1983), especially 69–72.

try outstrips the theology and church policy regarding lay ministry.'[60] Hence, the 'unfinished' church.

Indeed, even the insistence on the essential difference between the ordained and non-ordained does not make instantly clear what are the appropriate forms of ministry and ways of living for the ordained in a situation characterized by features such as declining numbers, an ageing cohort, and the impact of clerical sexual abuse. Nor is that insistence sufficient to indicate a response to the fact that the Catholic church is becoming increasingly non-eucharistic as a result of the decreased number of ordained priests. There is, therefore, a need for the whole church, not simply the ordained, to engage in Spirit-filled discernment about such issues. It is not sufficient, therefore, either to reiterate the differences between clerics and everyone else in the church or simply to let time and inertia take their course:

we can back into the future, simply adjusting to changing circumstances on an ad hoc basis until we find ourselves with a new pattern of priesthood we did not directly choose and regret that we have inadvertently chosen. Or we can be more deliberate in shaping the roles of priests in the light of changing circumstances.[61]

While there might be many open questions about the future shape of ordained ministry in the Catholic church, what is certain is that a church seeking to realize itself as a communion of faith can have little place for clericalism. All members of the church, therefore, need to know that ordination does not provide a passport to exclusive influence, privilege, or the avoidance of accountability and co-responsibility with the rest of the baptized. Ordained ministers, then, need to forswear attitudes and presuppositions such as, 'gender-defined and shame-based rules of order' and the lack of respect for 'internal, personal authority', which are the hallmarks of 'the typical ecclesiastical official'.[62]

---

[60] This is the conclusion of a study of 'parish lay ministry' by the American National Pastoral Life Center, *Origins*, 29 (1 July 1999), 107.

[61] Oscar Lipscomb, 'Dialogue About and Within Priesthood', *Origins*, 28 (21 May 1998), 10.

[62] For a detailed list of 'typical unexamined presuppositions' common to 'the typical ecclesiastical official' see Schultenover, *A View From Rome*, 182–3.

In facing the contemporary challenges that orbit around 'ministry', the goal is to express the church as a communion of all the baptized, a church where the contribution of each member is vital. In other words, the church must continue the struggle to realize itself as a genuinely inclusive communion, one that does not leave any members at the margins. Today, there is a particular challenge in the Catholic church to overcome the marginality of women. Accordingly, the following section will focus on the role of women in the church. In doing so, it will also highlight how the emergence of debate concerning women in the church reflects the nexus between the church and the society of which it is a part. Finally, the section will note how the changed self-understanding of women in the church underscores the challenge for the church to become a communion in which participation, rather than passivity, is constitutive of identity.

AN INCLUSIVE CHURCH

In Western nations, the heightened awareness of the particularity of women's experience began late in the nineteenth century, but became a major influence on social policy and practice only in the second half of the twentieth century. The story of 'the women's movement' illustrates well a central aspect of postmodernity: the refusal to accept the 'totalizing' presumptions of any one perspective. If 'man' expresses the modern universal, then the recovery of women's experience has been an attempt to give prominence to the neglected 'other', to overcome the fact that an exclusive concentration on 'man' leads usually either to the denigration and infantilization of women or to the idealization of them.[63] The primary consequence, intended or not, of both denigration and idealization is that women cannot take an equal part in society; they remain spectators on the margins as men make the major decisions.

The first wave of feminist writing attempted to recover the value of women's experience by exposing the embedded systems of power, class, race, and gender interests that under-

---

[63] Elisabeth Schüssler Fiorenza, *Discipleship of Equals: A Critical Feminist Ekklesia-logy of Liberation* (New York: Crossroad, 1993), 57.

pinned an exclusive concentration on 'man'.[64] More recent developments in feminist literature, however, have highlighted the complexity of 'women's experience': too narrow a focus on white, middle-class, and well-educated women can lead to as much distortion about the truth of women as can the elevation of 'man' into an absolute.[65] The outcome of that awareness is the recognition that no single group of women can represent 'women's experience' comprehensively, just as the universal 'man' cannot express the truth about all human beings.

Even allowing for the diversity of women's experience, common themes are present in the literature that highlights women's perspectives. Accordingly, feminist studies have contributed to a heightened profile for issues such as bodiliness, community, and affectivity—'The emotional tenor of a response signifies meanings ... it is informative, not an opacity in the lens of a glass that must remain unsullied.'[66] These foci showcase feminism as another form of rebellion against the narrowness of modernity's emphasis on individual reason:

> Starting with *the body as common ground*, distinctiveness emerges, but it emerges second. It is a distinctiveness that doesn't separate persons, because we have recognized first our radical sameness and interconnection. The body as common ground invites a lifting up of every human body, not one body for this and another for that ... [67]

For the church, the recovery of a focus on women's experience has raised, to put it mildly, significant challenges. These challenges apply not simply to particular aspects of the church's life, but also to the very notion of ecclesial faith. Indeed, the fact that it is common practice to classify 'feminist theology' as a sub-set of 'liberation theology' reflects the fact that feminist ecclesiology, for example, identifies women as being victims of oppression and exclusion within the Christian community, just as they have been in the wider society. In other words, the feminist critique argues that the patriarchal values that have

---

[64] O'Hara Graff, 'The Struggle to Name Women's Experience', 71–2.
[65] Ibid. 73–7.   [66] Ibid. 80.
[67] Colleen Griffith, 'Human Bodiliness: Sameness as Starting Point', in Elizabeth Johnson (ed.), *The Church Women Want: Catholic Women in Dialogue* (New York: Crossroad, 2002), 66. The emphasis is Griffith's.

dominated society have also dominated the church, to the detriment of women.

Much of the feminist critique of the church centres on three issues: the institutional inequalities affecting women; theological anthropologies that have invoked divine sanction for the subordination of women to men; and the church's promotion of passive attitudes—meekness, humility, self-sacrifice, and self-denying love—that, understood in a certain way, 'can impede the development of self-assertion and autonomy by women'.[68] In short, much feminist writing has highlighted the failure of various aspects of religious structures and the paradigms of thought in the church to enhance the genuine humanity of women.[69] Taken together, those concerns culminate in questions about the capacity of the God of Judaeo-Christian tradition to be God for women, about whether Jesus functions as a saviour for women or as a tool of their further exclusion, and about the possibility that the church could provide a healthy environment for women.[70]

Although some feminist writing portrays the church as so flawed by patriarchy and sexism as to be incapable of enhancing women, it would be incorrect to claim that 'feminism' and 'the church' are irreconcilable—'The very concept of the Church as an exodus community from sin and evil, living in hope of redeemed humanity on a redeemed earth, implies the overcoming of patriarchy and its false sacralization as the *ecclesia* of patriarchy.'[71] Nonetheless, it remains true that 'alienation' is the category into which many women place their experience of the church. It is also important to recognize than it is less the case that feminism has produced that alienation, than that it has been a catalyst enabling women to identify and to express their dissatisfaction with many aspects of the church's life—'The comments of men, their ideas and their suggestions are often taken more seriously and are heard with more credibility than

---

[68] Elisabeth Schüssler Fiorenza, *Discipleship of Equals*, 58.

[69] Elizabeth Johnson, *She Who Is: The Mystery of God in a Feminist Theological Perspective* (New York: Crossroad, 1992), 25.

[70] Sandra Schneiders, *Beyond Patching: Faith and Feminism in the Catholic Church* (Mahwah, NJ: Paulist Press, 1991), 94.

[71] Rosemary Radford Reuther, *Women–Church* (San Francisco: Harper & Row, 1988), 64.

mine for no other reason than that I am a woman.'[72] In so doing, the feminist critique has highlighted distortions in the theology and practice of the church; this means that it has also highlighted the need for the ongoing conversion of all aspects of the church.

The challenge for the church at large, and perhaps especially for those who are in positions of leadership, is to appropriate the gift for the whole church in women's efforts to reclaim the value of their experience and the particularity of their faith. One aspect of that gift is the opportunity to reconsider the anthropology that underpins many aspects of the church's life. Where that anthropology has been accustomed to stress the differences between the sexes, even if it has done so at times in order to elevate women to a place of honour, feminist thought, as noted above, has helped to recover an emphasis on the primacy of our common humanity. That emphasis, which resonates with the contemporary quest to find common ground between churches, between faiths, and between humanity and all aspects of creation, is not an attempt to deny difference by homogenizing humanity, but showcases the commonality that precedes any distinctions.

More than anything else, the history of the last generation ensures not only that the voices of women will never again be silent in the church, but also that the emergence of 'the overmuch and unfamiliar' in the church is itself inseparable from the ongoing effort to redress the marginality of women in the church:

Women's claim to full membership in the human race and the church entails new forms of relationship between women and men encoded in structures, laws, and customs. The transformation involved is nothing short of seismic. And women themselves disagree about how best to negotiate the changes. . . . However if the glory of God is the human person fully alive . . . then the tensions of the present moment are filled with hope. For resisting women's subordination and struggling for full recognition of women's dignity is clearly the work of the Spirit. And She will not be quenched. From this point on there can be no

---

[72] Leodia Gooch, 'Who Are the Women in Diocesan Leadership?', *Origins*, 30 (29 March, 2001), 655.

future for the church which women have not had a pivotal hand in shaping.[73]

It might seem, however, that any 'new forms of relationship' within the Catholic church could be nothing more than cosmetic since women are excluded from ordination to the priesthood, an exclusion that Pope John Paul II not only reiterated in 1994, but also declared to be a 'definitive' teaching.[74] Certainly, the rejection of ordination as a possibility for women is a neuralgic issue for many Catholics. For those who view life primarily through the lens of the Western liberal tradition, that exclusion is both a violation of human rights and proof that the Catholic church is a medieval relic. Even for those Catholics who do not approach every aspect of the church from that perspective, but seek a positive relationship with the church's teaching office, it can still be difficult to appropriate the exclusion of women from ordained ministry or to understand why God would require a male-only priesthood.

The controversy surrounding the exclusion of women from priestly ordination brings under the one umbrella significant features of the church's present-day experience: the impact of social developments (in this case, the changed role and perception of women) on the community of faith; the difficulty in nurturing a communal faith when the truth of some of its aspects are at odds with the directions of the wider society; the relationship between authority in the church and the faith of all the baptized; the challenge of presenting the truth of a tradition in ways that are compelling today; the implications of ecumenical dialogue and the longing for a more perfect expression of Christian communion (in this case, the desire for greater communion must respond to the fact that some churches *do* ordain women to the priesthood, even to the episcopate). The complexity of those issues, and the diverse responses to them, suggests that in matters regarding the role of women in the church, unity in faith among Catholics is a project that demands patience and generosity.

[73] Elizabeth Johnson, 'Imaging God, Embodying Christ: Women as a Sign of the Times', in Johnson (ed.), *The Church Women Want*, 58.

[74] For the text of John Paul II's apostolic letter, *Ordinatio sacerdotalis*, see *Origins*, 24 (9 June 1994), 49–52.

Since that unity is essential to the well-being and witness of the church, its promotion needs to be a priority. One expression of that priority would be the willingness of bishops and others in authority to listen to and speak with women, to hear their concerns and disappointments, and to allow women to question them.[75] More than anything else, it is crucial that bishops convey by words and actions that women are not a second-class group in the church.

A similar dynamic must also apply in regard to those Catholics who are homosexual. Here too it is crucial that bishops in particular show themselves as able to listen and to treat homosexual people with respect, not just as fellow human beings, but also as fellow baptized people.[76] Such listening is not a covert way of undermining the church's teaching on homosexuality, any more than listening to women must imply rejection of the prohibition of women from becoming ordained ministers. The willingness to listen and to engage in dialogue, however, does manifest that bishops too are disciples of Christ, that they are committed to being sources of hope and compassion even in situations where they cannot assent to every longing or affirm every style of life.

Although it would be naïve to assume that such a dialogue would effortlessly overcome the sense of exclusion that women or homosexual Catholics might feel, genuine dialogue illustrates that ecclesial faith does not compel only silence and invisibility. When those who exercise authority in the church manifest creativity, compassion, and generosity, their actions

[75] One significant example of the endeavour of a local church to listen to the voice of women was the consultation launched by the Australian Catholic Bishops Conference after the publication of *Ordinatio sacerdotalis*, see M. Macdonald *et al.* (eds.) *Woman and Man One in Christ Jesus: Report on the Participation of Women in the Catholic Church in Australia* (Pymble, NSW: HarperCollins, 1999).

[76] For examples of ways of exercising a compassionate ministry to homosexual Catholics see Basil Hume, 'A Note on the Teaching of the Catholic Church Concerning Homosexual People', *Origins*, 24 (27 April. 1995), 765–9 and 'Always Our Children: A Pastoral Message to Parents of Homosexual Children and Suggestions for Pastoral Ministers', a document published by the Committee on Marriage and Family of the American Catholic Bishops Conference, in *Origins*, 27 (9 Oct. 1997), 285–91; see also Donal Godfrey, 'A Vision of Hope for Gay Catholics', *Chicago Studies*, 42 (2003), 177–87.

challenge all the members of the church to a deeper appropriation of the gift of communion. Indeed, that manifestation can even communicate the value of communion to those who would still want the resolution of particular issues to have an outcome different from what actually prevails.

Although the denial of ordination to women ought not to mean the exclusion of women from influence, even leadership, in the church, it will be possible for women to exercise leadership only if all the members of the church continue to value and seek the realization of the church as a genuinely participatory community. There is, therefore, a need to redress the fact that women in the church have suffered not only because the emphasis on the differences between women and men has tended to exclude the former from influence, even while exalting them as wives and mothers, but also because they were always on the wrong side of another gap: that separating the ordained and the non-ordained members of the church.[77] If such a gap affected non-ordained men—'there should be as much difference between the priest and any other upright man as there is between heaven and earth'—it affected women more, as for women there could be no prospect of ordination.[78]

Indeed, it is even possible that there might be less contention over the exclusion of women from ordained ministry if the everyday life of the church made it evident that the effectiveness of the church's mission, as well as the clarity of its faith, depends on all the baptized, not only the ordained. In other words, there might be fewer reasons to argue over who can be ordained—to say nothing of a greater readiness to accept the particular role of those who are ordained—if those who remain unordained did not have grounds to perceive themselves as dwelling on the margins of the church.[79]

---

[77] For the idea of the disadvantage of women as a result of being 'laity' see, Denise Desmarchelier, *Voices of Women: Women and the Australian Church* (Richmond, Vic.: Spectrum, 2000), 135.

[78] Pope Pius X, *Haerent animo* (8 Aug. 1908), in Odile Liebard (ed.), *Official Catholic Teaching: Clergy and Laity* (Wilmington, Del.: Consortium, 1978), 26.

[79] The final chapter, 'An Accountable Church' of Paul Lakeland's *The Liberation of the Laity*, 257–85, develops this point in detail.

The issues that relate to the relationship of women to the various manifestations of the church, like those affecting the broad area of 'ministry' in the church, are examples of questions that have not previously confronted the whole community of faith that is the church. Although it might not be possible to predict or to specify the movement of the Spirit in regard to those issues, faith in that Spirit generates certainty that the future for women in the church will be significantly different from what has been the case in the past.

In acknowledging and addressing new questions, there is a need to ensure the emergence of the church as a diverse community in which 'individual responsibility, risk, and courage for the public task are fostered through personal and liturgical prayer and through the authority of love and service'.[80] In order for the church to realize itself as 'an undreamed of possibility for love', a commitment to such a vision is crucial. The willingness to embrace such a vision, however, is itself a product of accepting that authentic ecclesial faith will always be challenging. The present-day dimensions of such a challenge will be the focus of the following section.

A CHALLENGING CHURCH

This book's theology of the church has stressed that the communion of faith exists, through the Holy Spirit, for the sake of an explicit, and shared, relationship to the God of Jesus Christ and, as a corollary of that relationship, for a particular way of interacting with the world. This means that the flourishing of the Spirit ought to be evident not only in the church's interaction with the wider society, but also in the promotion of an authentically catholic church. Such a church will not prize uniformity over the particular ways in which members of the communion respond to the Spirit.

Although it will always be true that divisions that rupture communion can never be an authentic expression of catholicity, it does not follow that all differences within the communion of the church manifest only an unwillingness to accept a shared

---

[80] Anne Carr, *Transforming Grace: Christian Tradition and Women's Experience* (New York: Continuum, 1996), 199.

faith. Indeed, unity in a genuinely catholic communion will always be 'unity-across-difference'—'the life of God itself, understood as trinitarian, is already a oneness of this kind. Human diversity is part of the way in which we are made in the image of God.'[81] This suggests that growth within the church must always result in 'an increase in the variety of devotions and spiritualities and liturgical forms and responses to Incarnation'.[82] Accordingly, it might well be that the struggles within the contemporary Catholic church for approbation of different styles of worship and forms of life are less indicative of a retreat from catholicity than expressions of the yearning for it.

The difficulty, of course, is that much within the messy reality that is today's Catholic church differs markedly from the neatness of previous eras. We must contend, therefore, with the possibility that the messiness might offer us a richer insight into the superabundance of the Kingdom than does neatness. That is not to imply that conflict and division will accompany the fullness of God's reign. Nonetheless, it does imply that even conflict can provide an opportunity for deeper reflection on the meaning of catholic faith and a fuller embrace of that faith. Indeed, as the Acts of the Apostles, particularly Acts 15, makes clear, it was only in the process of discussing issues that were polarizing the community that the first generation of Christians discerned what they believed to be the intent of the Spirit for the church, a discernment that not only led the church into a deeper appropriation of discipleship, but also challenged the predispositions of many in the church of Jerusalem. In the church, therefore, it can certainly be true that 'all unrest does not come from an evil source, every doubt is not destructive, not every fight is worse than a graveyard peace, not every little conflict is bad.'[83]

Paradoxically, then, it could be that any efforts to ignore or hide issues that cause tension in the communion of faith, to say nothing of the invocation of forms of oversight that crush divergent views as soon as they appear or insist on a narrow, even idiosyncratic, interpretation of 'orthodoxy', could place in

[81] Taylor, 'A Catholic Modernity?', 14–15.   [82] Ibid.
[83] Rahner, 'Christian Pessimism', 159.

jeopardy the movement of the Spirit. Such actions might also convey the conviction that change could not express an authentic response to the Spirit. Furthermore, the history of the church would confirm, unequivocally, that heavy-handed disciplinary efforts to prevent tensions or stifle perceived threats tend to succeed only in generating heightened tension or creating a climate of fear—the response to the Modernist crisis, which Chapter 1 examined, is a powerful example of such an outcome.

It is not, therefore, the absence of conflict that is vital to the well-being of the church, but the approach to that conflict by all parties. If we see conflict in the church as a battle between good and evil—with those who share our view arranged, invariably, on the side of the angels—then the object will always be to ensure that 'good' wins. If, however, conflict is something other than that apocalyptic clash, if it is the manifestation of attitudes and convictions that might be reconcilable, even while remaining different, then it offers all parties an opportunity, albeit a challenging one, to develop a deeper sense of the implications of catholicity.

It is worth noting here that the 'Catholic Common Ground Project', whose analysis of the current state of the Catholic church opened Chapter 1, stressed 'that no single group or viewpoint in the church has a complete monopoly on the truth'.[84] In addition, the document underlined that the well-being of the contemporary church depends on the willingness of all Catholics to approach one another in a renewed spirit of civility and generosity, and with a commitment to broad and serious consultation and dialogue.[85] Similarly, the 'Catholic Common Ground Project', in rejecting the notion that a part of the church might be 'a saving remnant' insisted that 'no group within the church should judge itself alone to be possessed of enlightenment or spurn the mass of Catholics, their leaders, or their institutions as unfaithful.'[86]

While the emphasis on openness and dialogue is honourable, there might be a fear that such discussions would produce only a bland or homogenized church, rather than a challenging, and

---

[84] Bernardin and Lipscomb, *Catholic Common Ground Initiative*, 42.
[85] Ibid. 34.   [86] Ibid. 43.

authentically catholic, one. On the other hand, the history of ecumenical dialogues in the last thirty years would indicate that such a fear is groundless. Theological dialogue, therefore, not only emphasizes the depth of the mystery of God, but also challenges both partiality and any tendency to substitute a one-dimensional approach for genuine catholicity:

> Theology will probe those aspects of religious practice which pull in the direction of ideological distortion, those things which presuppose that there is a mode of religious utterance wholly beyond the risks of conversation, a power beyond resistance, a perspective that leaves nothing out. It will challenge the fantasy that such things are available to human beings; but it will also challenge the notion that these are the terms in which *God* is to be imagined.[87]

Indeed, it might well be that ecclesial faith has limited appeal today because the presentation of it, perhaps especially at the local level, does not highlight sufficiently its intimate connection to both the ongoing journey into the mystery of God and the need to seek creative responses to contemporary dilemmas. In other words, any presentation of ecclesial faith that bleaches it of all that is demanding, including the need to be open to the possibility that the Spirit might be at work in those whose views differ from one's own, does an injustice to that faith. In order to ensure that they do not blunt the challenge of ecclesial faith, there are a number of attitudes that members of the church must adopt, and some that they must avoid.

First, the prevailing spirit in the church must be other than what Johann Baptist Metz describes as an 'aggressive backwardness'.[88] Such an attitude, which implies a belief in the supremacy of the past over the present, would convey the impression that members of the church believe their best days to be behind them. 'Backwardness' would also suggest a failure to appreciate the church's eschatological orientation. Whatever its motivation, any approach that divorces the church from the present is unlikely to have widespread appeal in a society that longs for the triumph of hope and a sense of possibility:

---

[87] Williams, 'Theological Integrity', 323. The emphasis is Williams'.
[88] Metz, *A Passion for God*, 53.

if the Church becomes the refuge of those who look for security and peace in some world of yesterday, then it should not be astonished when young people turn their back on it and look for the future to uplifting ideologies and redemptive utopias which promise to fill the vacuum which the church's pusillanimity has left there.[89]

Secondly, it is unlikely that the communion of faith would be able to express its identity as a communion dedicated to discipleship of Jesus Christ if it pursues an uncritical adoption of the prevailing social mores. The alternative, to draw again on Metz, is a spirit of 'creative noncontemporaneity', which prizes eschatological hope above the comfort that derives from merging seamlessly with the values of any particular moment of history.[90] The communion of faith, therefore, can model authentic human existence, which strives towards transcendence, only if it avoids 'a merciless confinement within the facticity of the existing order of things'.[91] This means that Christians, while affirming the world as the venue for an encounter with God, will also challenge those aspects of their culture that might obscure either the presence of God or humanity's orientation to God. Authentic ecclesial faith, then, requires that members of the church maintain the tension between the danger of fossilization and the embrace of values and ways of living that might suggest a denial of human transcendence.

The need to maintain that tension suggests that the primary concern of members of the church can never be simply 'to modernize' or 'to up-date' the church. The challenge, therefore, is less about discerning how to develop a church suited to the 'modern Catholic', a phrase that could imply that we are 'summing up and going beyond our less advantaged ancestors', than it is about seeking how to be authentically Catholic in the here and now.[92] In short, the urgent task is the articulation of what is conducive to genuine faith and discipleship in the present, rather than the pursuit of a church that can merge comfortably with what might be currently in vogue, ephemeral though it may be.

[89] Kasper, *An Introduction to Christian Faith*, 179.
[90] Metz, *A Passion for God*, 53.
[91] Kasper, *An Introduction to Christian Faith*, 15.
[92] Taylor, 'A Catholic Modernity?', 15.

Thirdly, members of the church must grapple with the fact that ecclesial faith will demand openness to the God who is always greater, the willingness to pursue authenticity, and to prize communion with others, as well as loving service of them. Those demands mean that we understand the church, and our place in it, only when we recognize it as something other than an association whose primary purpose is to provide for the needs of its members. The church, then, is not to be a religious consumer society, where somebody else is always responsible for meeting my needs. It is, however, as already noted above, a participatory communion that depends on the contribution of all. In a society where there is often an obsession with 'marketing' and consumer products, an emphasis on the challenge of ecclesial faith can be one expression of 'creative non-contemporaneity'.

Fourthly, healthy ecclesial faith requires openness to the questions that confront faith, both from within the church and beyond it. Such questions promote the need for theology.[93] In the toxic climate of division in the contemporary Catholic church, there can be a suspicion that theology promotes doubt, confusion, and truculent opposition to authority. While it would be disingenuous to claim that it is impossible to co-opt theology for a subversive purpose, theology's primary purpose is not ideological. Theology manifests the capacity of human beings to wrestle with the mystery of God. In fact, the willingness to address questions—to do theology—expresses the conviction that the members of the church are able 'to endure education, complexity ... and the irony that brings an end to innocence but the beginning of wisdom'.[94]

There is, then, a need for teachers and pastors within the church 'to provide an adequate passage towards greater complexity'.[95] Thus, for example, preachers need to encourage engagement between faith and contemporary questions. Conversely, preachers ought not to assume that any member of the church is above, or below, the need for nuance, insight, and a

---

[93] Doré, 'The Responsibility and Tasks of Theology', 215–16.
[94] Heher, 'Why We Still Need Theologians', 64.
[95] Ibid.

deeper understanding of faith. Nor ought they to assume that 'ordinary people' do not ask questions:

[preachers] fail to realize that in their own way, many ['ordinary people'] are making decisions about theological issues in an unsophisticated and commonsense manner—some staying with the church but with reservations, many others abandoning ship. Often, sad to say, this withdrawal is the result of a naïve grasp of the faith—sheer ignorance of what the more sophisticated theological stance of the tradition actually has been and is.[96]

Any refusal to engage with, or even to acknowledge, questions, can be a failure to accept that growth in human life comes primarily when we are open to what challenges the existing boundaries of our worldview, rather than when we are able either to fit more and more into a narrow space or to eliminate any challenges to our worldview. Indeed, we grow as human beings through experiences that are counter to our expectations, more than through those that confirm our expectations:

The truth of experience always contains an orientation to new experience.... The dialectic of experience has its own fulfilment not in definitive knowledge, but in that openness to experience that is encouraged by experience itself.... Real experience is that in which [we] become aware of [our] finiteness. In it are discovered the limits of the power and the self-knowledge of [our] planning. It proves to be an illusion that everything can be reversed, that there is always time for everything and that everything somehow returns.[97]

More explicitly, a refusal to open ourselves to questions could be a failure to appreciate that faith in the God of Jesus Christ neither grants us control over God nor eliminates the uncontrollable in any area of our lives. Faith, then, is inseparable from the invitation to surrender ourselves to God. The notion of a God who exceeds our grasp, a God whom we can know only when we abandon efforts to impose directions on how that God ought to be, will not be immediately attractive to those intent on imposing on life their own ideas about everything, including God. It remains true, however, that only the God whom we cannot control can be the God of Jesus Christ.

---

[96] Frances Young, *Can These Dry Bones Live?: An Introduction to Christian Theology* (Cleveland, Ohio: Pilgrim Press, 1993), 9.

[97] Gadamer, *Truth and Method*, 2nd edn., 319–20.

Consequently, the Christian spiritual tradition formulates our relationship to that God through terms such as 'self-emptying', 'dying to self', 'conversion', 'pilgrimage', and 'paschal mystery'. Although such terms have a daunting quality, all of them suggest faith in the God who offers us more than both the most treasured object we might possess and our own proposals to regulate life. In short, they invoke the central paradox of Christian life: that grief, sorrow, and death can be life-giving, in spite of everything that suggests they are absurd.[98] Thus, any construction of God and our relationship to God that does not couch them in such terms obscures not only the difference between God and the world, but also the dynamics of history and culture, which suggest that growth and struggle are not strangers to each other.[99]

It is important to emphasize here that embracing the pilgrimage to God does not express self-loathing or contempt for the physical world, which would imply that God had not made unconditional love available to us in history through Jesus. It does, however, recognize that nothing we have yet experienced in life can equal what God has promised us in the fullness of the Kingdom. To baulk, then, at the prospect of encounter with what might disturb our construct of how God's Spirit ought to work in the present moment of the church's history is to risk abandoning God for an idol. It can be, therefore, precisely in what seems to be too much for us that we are most likely to encounter God:

For Christians, perplexity in life is, in the final analysis, nothing but the concrete dawning of the sacred mystery that we call God. Our perplexity should ultimately not astonish us. Wherever we can, we should get rid of it, try to clear it up. But even if we fight it bravely and resolutely, we will not overcome it. It lingers, it overpowers individuals in their lives. The only question is whether we take it as the unveiling of the basic absurdity of life *or* as the concrete dawning of the Mystery that we accept as our saving, forgiving, fulfilling, and

---

[98] Josef Pieper, *In Tune With the World: A Theory of Festivity*, tr. R. and C. Winston (Chicago: Franciscan Herald Press, 1965), 21.

[99] On this point see Nicholas Lash, *Easter in Ordinary: Reflections on Human Experience and the Knowledge of God* (London: SCM, 1988), 290.

absolute future. This is ultimately the only alternative, from which we cannot run away.[100]

The impact of those qualities that manifest a church open to the Spirit will be most evident in the community's life of worship and its relationships to the rest of the world. Worship is crucial because it gives supreme value to something other than the worshipper. One consequence of that transcendental orientation is that the language of liturgy challenges the integrity of a community's language about God.[101] In other words, our language about God as the source of life can be authentic only if we are actually seeking to trust that God, a trust that liturgy enacts and strengthens. This, in turn, means that there is a need for the community to be a venue that not only helps its members to appreciate more deeply the implications of that trust, but also to enact it, both individually and communally. The authenticity of our liturgy—and also of our theology—expresses itself through our life in the world: in solidarity with others and in a commitment to service, sharing, and sacrifice.[102]

A church that is a communion of genuine freedom and hope will be one whose primary concern is not to guarantee its own survival or to secure positions of privilege in the world. Such a church, therefore, will be able to include the poor in its worship and resist the urge to wrest control of its future from God. In so doing, that community recognizes not only that utopian plans for the future usually have no place for the poor and powerless, but also that such plans are prone to turn the Cross of Jesus 'into a form of bourgeois well-being'.[103]

THE OVERMUCH AND UNFAMILIAR

One thing that will be clear from the issues that this chapter has explored is that the emergence of 'the overmuch and unfamiliar'

---

[100] Karl Rahner, 'Utopia and Reality: Christian Existence Caught Between the Ideal and the Real', *Theological Investigations*, 22, tr. J. Donceel (New York: Crossroad, 1991), 35. The emphasis is Rahner's.

[101] Williams, 'Theological Integrity', 317.

[102] These are some of the features that Pope Paul VI identifies as expressing Christian joy in the world; see *Gaudete in Domino* (Homebush, NSW: Saint Paul Publications, 1975), 12–14.

[103] Kasper, *Faith and the Future*, 60–1.

in the church is neither neat nor subject to our control. Indeed, it seems that only a church committed to endure complexity, 'unknowing', and even mess, can provide a venue for the deeper realization of its orientation to the fullness of God's Kingdom. While that conclusion might engender some frustration, it is difficult to imagine that anything other than the radically imponderable could result from the combination of the Holy Spirit and human freedom, which can express itself only in a particular context and at a particular moment of human history.

Nonetheless, this chapter has attempted to identify the considerations that might guide our efforts to determine when embrace of 'the overmuch and unfamiliar' can express both a faithful reception of our tradition and a creative response to our present circumstances. Even then, however, ecclesial faith remains inseparable from the pilgrimage to the fullness of God's reign.

Since that pilgrimage is not merely a personal one, but also a communal one, there is need for an understanding of what has shaped and inspired the community in its pilgrimage through history—'without a more effective socialization into the Church, the faithful may no longer be in a position to accept or interpret correctly the Scriptures, the narrative symbols, and the statements of faith that have come down from the past.'[104] This means, ironically, that for some members of the church an experience of 'the overmuch and unfamiliar' might involve coming to know more about the church's tradition of faith, especially in its challenge to individualism. On the other hand, there is also a need to ensure that 'new religious movements', which place a strong emphasis on belonging to a community, do not become a 'church within a church', a development that would divide the community, rather than model possibilities for the present.[105]

---

[104] Dulles, *The Craft of Theology*, 103.

[105] For some assessment of both the strengths and dangers implicit in 'new religious movements' see Jean-Paul Durand 'Catholic Movements and Communities of the Faithful Which Arose in the Twentieth Century: Some Challenges to Canon Law', and Luca Diotallevi, '"Catholicism by way of Sectarianism?" An Old Hypothesis for New Problems', in Alberto Melloni (ed.), *'Movements' in the Church* (*Concilium*, no. 2003/3) (London: SCM, 2003), 94–105 and 107–21, respectively.

In order to facilitate the appropriation of the tradition, the focus must remain on it as an invitation to communion with the Spirit and with other people of faith, rather than on the church as an instrument that organizes God—'the institution frees us from having to confront the void or the night, the suffering of profound desire, the intolerable pressure of a burning presence.'[106] The more, then, that every aspect of the church's life reflects the freedom and hope that come from God, the more likelihood there is that 'the overmuch and unfamiliar' of the church can be good news for society at large:

The Catholic Church, less as an institution than as a sacrament to the world, can feed the religiously hungry, the mystery-starved people who are the immigrants of this century, ready to make any pilgrimage to find a Golden Door. But the genuine sacramental pilgrimage brings not answers, but more profound questions. It delivers, however, a rich sense that, illogical or not, what we experience is what makes us human and transforms us spiritually.[107]

The conviction that the church exists to be a sacrament, to be the 'undreamed of possibility for love', prompts the desire for reform within the church and for more compassionate action in the world. That conviction expresses itself in the longing for a church that is open rather than closed, inclusive rather than narrow. Characteristic of such a church would be 'more truthfulness, freedom, humanity, by more broad-mindedness, tolerance, and magnanimity, more Christian self-confidence, supreme composure and courage to think and decide. Such a Church would not always be behind the times. It might be the avant-garde of a better humanity.'[108] Working towards the realization of those features is an aspect of the pilgrimage that is inseparable from being part of the church:

---

[106] For the dangers inherent in hiding behind the church's institutional expressions see Christian Duquoc, 'Postscript: The Institution and Diversion', in Christian Duquoc and Gustavo Gutierrez (eds.), *Mysticism and the Institutional Crisis* (*Concilium*, no. 1994/4) (London: SCM, 1994), 101–6.

[107] Eugene Kennedy, *Tomorrow's Catholics Yesterday's Church: The Two Cultures of American Catholicism* (New York: Harper & Row, 1988), 197.

[108] Hans Küng, *Reforming the Church Today: Keeping Hope Alive*, tr. P. Heinegg *et al.* (New York: Crossroad, 1990), 27.

We come from a beginning that we ourselves did not initiate. We plod along like pilgrims on a road whose end disappears in the incomprehensibility and freedom of God; we are stretched between heaven and earth, and we have neither the right nor the possibility of giving up either one. . . . Christian existence cannot forego any of these requirements. That constitutes its greatness, its radical difficulty, and its ultimate obviousness. . . . [109]

In the light of that challenge, the final task for this book is to draw some conclusions about the question implied in the book's title: to determine whether the church is indeed worth the risk.

[109] Rahner, 'Utopia and Reality', 32–3.

Epilogue

This book has argued that it is possible to develop a comprehensive understanding of the church only by situating it in relation to Jesus Christ and the Holy Spirit. More specifically, the book has identified the church as existing to be, through the Spirit, a symbol of the Kingdom or reign of God that Jesus initiated. Indeed, one of the central claims of this book has been that the church, through its existence as a communion of faith that expresses itself through such concrete realities as worship, doctrine, and institutions, ensures that 'the Kingdom' does not become merely an abstraction, a disembodied ideal that has no grounding in human experience and history. The church, then, gives 'the Kingdom' a face, a shape, that is accessible in the contemporary world.

If the church symbolizes the presence of the Spirit, who draws humanity into communion with God, then it is also the church that provides a means of encounter with the God who does not shy away from any aspect of human life, not even from failure, sickness, or death. The church does so not only through its liturgy, which both proclaims and celebrates the presence of God in all that is human, but also—indeed, more fundamentally—through its existence as a communion of people whose lives express all that it is to be human, including failure, suffering, and death, as well as generosity, compassion, and love. As a symbol of the Kingdom, therefore, the church is a reminder that humanity's journey into the fullness of life is not yet complete. In the present moment of human history, then, God's life-giving love reveals itself in the imperfect and incomplete.

Nonetheless, it is likely that a perfect church, since it would give the impression that a connection to God elevated believers above the messy realities of life, would be more appealing as a symbol of God's presence in human history than the church we encounter presently. Paradoxically, however, it would be difficult to appropriate such a church as a symbol of the God whose revelation in history has its high point in Jesus Christ, who associated with sinners and died on the cross as an outcast condemned for blasphemy.

The church's imperfections make clear the risk inseparable from ecclesial faith, but that risk can itself be a symbol of the greater risk that is inseparable from any involvement with God. The fact that God is inclined to write straight with crooked lines, rather than to conform to what conventional wisdom dictates is the way that God ought to act, can make God frustrating. It underscores, however, that our involvement with God will never ask of us less than the self-surrender of faith.

Risking the church, then, can be a symbol of risking God. As the book has emphasized, that claim is neither an attempt to license mediocrity, much less sinfulness, in the church nor to deny the gap between the church as symbol and the God whom it symbolizes.

Indeed, the focus of the book has been on the association between authentic ecclesial faith and the need for a deeper conversion by all believers to the Spirit, who alone can make the church a more transparent symbol of God's love. The commitment to allow the raising of questions, as well as embracing the need to be aware of the shape and challenges of present-day society, to be open to the presence of the Spirit in the lives of every member of the communion of faith, to search for appropriate contemporary expressions of the tradition of faith that leads from the apostles to the fullness of the Kingdom, and to recognize that no elite, ordained or otherwise, can ever substitute for the dependence of the church's mission on the contribution of all the baptized, are some of the ways in which conversion to the Spirit manifests itself in the church.

None of those actions is complete or sufficient in itself, but, taken together, they can create an environment that expresses the church as the communion of those who desire to realize 'an undreamed of possibility for love'. It is such a church that can convey the flourishing of the Spirit in the church, be good news, and be revelatory of God's reign. It is also such a church that is worth the risk.

BIBLIOGRAPHY

Documents of the Catholic church

Abbott, W. (ed.), *The Documents of Vatican II* (London: Geoffrey Chapman, 1967).

Carlen, C. (ed.), *The Papal Encyclicals 1740–1878* (Wilmington, NC: McGrath Publishing, 1981).

——(ed.), *The Papal Encyclicals 1878–1903* (Wilmington, NC: McGrath Publishing, 1981).

——(ed.), *The Papal Encyclicals 1903–39* (Wilmington, NC: McGrath Publishing, 1981).

Committee on Marriage and Family of the American Catholic Bishops Conference, 'Always Our Children: A Pastoral Message to Parents of Homosexual Children and Suggestions for Pastoral Ministers', *Origins*, 27 (9 Oct. 1997), 285–91.

Congregation for the Clergy *et al.*, 'Instruction on Certain Questions Regarding the Collaboration of the Non-Ordained Faithful in the Sacred Ministry of Priests', *Origins*, 27 (27 Nov. 1997), 397–410.

Congregation for the Doctrine of the Faith, 'Instruction on Certain Aspects of the Theology of Liberation' (Homebush, NSW: St Paul Publications, 1984).

——'Instruction on Christian Freedom and Liberation' (Homebush, NSW: St Paul Publications, 1986).

——'Some Aspects of the Church as Communion', *Catholic International*, 3 (1–30 Sept. 1992), 761–7.

——'*Dominus Iesus*: On the Unicity and Salvific Universality of Jesus Christ and the Church', *Origins*, 30 (14 Sept. 2000), 209–19.

International Theological Commission, 'Memory and Reconciliation: The Church and the Faults of the Past', *Origins*, 29 (16 March 2000), 625–44.

John Paul II, 'Peace with God the Creator, Peace with All of Creation', 1990 Message for World Day of Peace, *Origins*, 19 (14 Dec. 1989), 465–8.

——*Ordinatio Sacerdotalis, Origins*, 24 (9 June 1994), 49–52.

——*Ut Unum Sint* (Homebush, NSW: St Pauls Publications 1995).

——*Fides et Ratio* (Boston, Mass.: Pauline Books, 1998).

——*Novo Millennio Ineunte* (Strathfield, NSW: St Pauls Publications, 2001).

National Catholic Conference of Catholic Bishops (USA), Subcommittee on Lay Ministry, 'Lay Ecclesial Ministry: State of the Questions', *Origins*, 29 (20 Jan. 2000), 498–512.

Neuner, J. and Dupuis, J. (eds.), *The Christian Faith in the Doctrinal Documents of the Catholic Church* (London: Collins, 1986).

Paul VI, *Gaudete in Domino* (Homebush, NSW; St Paul Publications, 1975).

——*Evangelii Nuntiandi* (Homebush, NSW: St Paul Publications, 1975).

Pius X, *Haerent animo* (8 Aug. 1908) in O. Liebard (ed.), *Official Catholic Teaching: Clergy and Laity* (Wilmington, Del.: Consortium, 1978), 21–9.

The Pontifical Biblical Commission, 'The Interpretation of the Bible in the Church', *Origins*, 23 (6 Jan. 1994), 497–524.

Pontifical Council for Culture and Pontifical Council for Interreligious Dialogue, *Jesus Christ the Bearer of the Water of Life: A Christian Reflection on the 'New Age'* (Strathfield, NSW: St Pauls Publications, 2003).

Tanner, N. (ed.), *Decrees of the Ecumenical Councils*, 2 vols. (London/ Washington: Sheed & Ward/Georgetown University Press, 1990).

Walsh, M. and Davies, B. (eds.), *Proclaiming Peace and Justice: Papal Documents from* Rerum Novarum *through* Centesimus Annus, rev. edn. (Mystic, Conn.: Twenty-Third Publications, 1991).

Books

Alberigo, G. and Komonchak, J. (eds.), *History of Vatican II*, 4 vols. (Maryknoll, NY/Leuven: Orbis/Peeters, 1995–2003).

Barr, J., *Fundamentalism*, 2nd edn. (London: SCM, 1984).

Bernardin, J. and Lipscomb, O., *Catholic Common Ground Initiative: Foundational Documents* (New York: Crossroad Herder, 1997).

Berry, T., *The Dream of the Earth* (San Francisco: Sierra Club Books, 1988).

Boff, L., *Jesus Christ Liberator*, trans. P. Hughes (Maryknoll, NY: Orbis, 1979).

——*Church: Charism and Power*, trans. J. Diercksmeier (New York: Crossroad, 1990).

——and Boff, C., *Introducing Liberation Theology*, trans. P. Burns (Tunbridge Wells: Burns & Oates, 1987).

Braxton, E., *The Wisdom Community* (New York: Paulist, 1980).

Brown, D., *Tradition and Imagination: Revelation and Change* (Oxford: Oxford University Press, 1999).

Buckley, M., *Papal Primacy and the Episcopate: Towards a Relational Understanding* (New York: Herder & Herder, 1998).

Carr, A., *Transforming Grace: Christian Tradition and Women's Experience* (New York: Continuum, 1996).

Chamberlain, G. and Howell, P. (eds.), *Empowering Authority: The Charism of Episcopacy and Primacy in the Church Today* (Kansas City, Miss.: Sheed & Ward, 1990).

Chauvet, L-M., *Symbol and Sacrament: A Sacramental Reinterpretation of Christian Existence*, trans. P. Madigan and M. Beaumont (Collegeville, Minn.: Pueblo, 1995).

—— *The Sacraments: The Word of God at the Mercy of the Body* (Collegeville, Minn.: Pueblo, 2001).

Coffey, D. *Grace: The Gift of the Holy Spirit* (Manly, NSW: Catholic Institute of Sydney, 1979).

Collins, J., *Are All Christians Ministers?* (Newtown, NSW: E. J. Dwyer, 1992).

Comblin, J., *The Holy Spirit and Liberation*, trans. P. Burns (Maryknoll, NY: Orbis, 1989).

Congar, Y., *Tradition and the Life of the Church*, trans. A. N. Woodrow (London: Burns & Oates, 1964).

—— *I Believe in the Holy Spirit*, trans. D. Smith (New York/London: Seabury/Geoffrey Chapman, 1983), ii.

Daly, G., *Transcendence and Immanence: A Study in Catholic Modernism and Integralism* (Oxford: Clarendon Press, 1980).

Desmarchelier, D., *Voices of Women: Women and the Australian Church* (Richmond, Vic.: Spectrum, 2000).

Dix, G. (ed.), *The Treatise on the Apostolic Tradition* (London: SPCK, 1968).

Donovan, D., *Distinctively Catholic: An Exploration of Catholic Identity* (Mahwah, NJ: Paulist, 1997).

Donovan, V., *The Church in the Midst of Creation* (Maryknoll, NY: Orbis, 1989).

Doyle, D., *Communion Ecclesiology* (Maryknoll, NY: Orbis, 2000).

Dulles, A., *The Survival of Dogma* (New York: Image Books, 1973).

—— *Models of the Church* (New York: Image Books, 1978).

—— *The Resilient Church: The Necessity and Limits of Adaptation* (Dublin: Gill & Macmillan, 1978).

—— *The Catholicity of the Church* (Oxford: Clarendon Press, 1987).

—— *The Craft of Theology: From Symbol to System* (New York: Crossroad, 1992).

Duquoc, C., *Provisional Churches: An Essay in Ecumenical Ecclesiology*, trans. J. Bowden (London: SCM, 1986).

Edwards, D., *Jesus and the Cosmos* (Mahwah, NJ: Paulist, 1991).

Edwards, D. (ed.), *Earth Revealing–Earth Healing: Ecology and Christian Theology* (Collegeville, Minn.: Liturgical Press, 2001).

Farrelly, J., *Belief in God in Our Time: Foundational Theology* (Collegeville, Minn.: Liturgical Press, 1992), i.

Fries, H., *Suffering from the Church: Renewal or Restoration?*, trans. A. A. Swidler and L. Swidler (Collegeville, Minn.: Liturgical Press, 1995).

Fuellenbach, J., *The Kingdom of God: The Message of Jesus Today* (Maryknoll, NY: Orbis, 1997).

Gadamer, H-G., *Truth and Method*, 2nd edn. (London: Sheed & Ward, 1979).

Geffré, C., *The Risk of Interpretation: On Being Faithful to the Christian Tradition in a Non-Christian Age*, trans. D. Smith (Mahwah, NJ: Paulist, 1987).

Haight, R., *Dynamics of Theology* (Mahwah, NJ: Paulist, 1990).

——*Jesus Symbol of God* (Maryknoll, NY: Orbis, 1999).

Harrington, D., *The Church According to the New Testament: What the Wisdom and Witness of Early Christianity Teach Us Today* (Franklin, Wis.: Sheed & Ward, 2001).

Hayes, Z., *The Gift of Being: A Theology of Creation* (Collegeville, Minn.: Liturgical Press, 2001).

Henn, W., *The Honor of My Brothers: A Brief History of the Relationship Between the Pope and the Bishops* (New York: Herder & Herder, 2000).

Hitchcock, J., *Catholicism and Modernity: Confrontation or Capitulation?* (New York: Seabury, 1979).

Jay, E., *The Church: Its Changing Image through Twenty Centuries* (London: SPCK, 1977).

Johnson, E., *Consider Jesus: Waves of Renewal in Christology* (New York: Crossroad, 1992).

——*She Who Is: The Mystery of God in a Feminist Theological Perspective* (New York: Crossroad, 1992).

Johnson, M., *The Rites of Christian Initiation: Their Evolution and Interpretation* (Collegeville, Minn.: Pueblo, 1999).

Jinkins, M., *The Church Faces Death: Ecclesiology in a Post-Modern Context* (New York: Oxford University Press, 1999).

Kasper, W., *Jesus the Christ*, trans. V. Green (London/New York: Burns & Oates/Paulist, 1976).

——*An Introduction to Christian Faith*, trans. V. Green (London/New York: Burns & Oates/Paulist Press, 1980).

——*Faith and the Future*, trans. R. Nowell (New York: Crossroad, 1982).

——*Theology and Church*, trans. M. Kohl, (London: SCM, 1989).

—— *Leadership in the Church: How Traditional Roles Can Serve the Christian Community Today*, trans. B. McNeil (New York: Herder & Herder, 2003).

Kelly, G., *Recognition: Advancing Ecumenical Thinking* (New York: Peter Lang, 1996).

Kelly, T., *Seasons of the Heart* (Blackburn, Vic.: Dove, 1984).

Kennedy, E., *Tomorrow's Catholics Yesterday's Church: The Two Cultures of American Catholicism* (New York: Harper & Row, 1988).

Kolakowski, L., *Modernity on Endless Trial* (Chicago: University of Chicago Press, 1990).

Küng, H., *The Church*, trans. R. and R. Ockenden (New York: Image Books, 1976).

—— *Reforming the Church Today: Keeping Hope Alive*, trans. P. Heinegg *et al.* (New York: Crossroad, 1990).

Lakeland, P., *Theology and Critical Theory: The Discourse of the Church* (Nashville, Tenn.: Abingdon Press, 1990).

—— *Postmodernity: Christian Identity in a Fragmented Age* (Minneapolis, Minn.: Fortress, 1997).

—— *The Liberation of the Laity: In Search of an Accountable Church* (New York: Continuum, 2003).

Lash, N., *Easter in Ordinary: Reflections on Human Experience and the Knowledge of God* (London: SCM, 1988).

Latourelle, R. and Fisichella, R. (eds.), *Dictionary of Fundamental Theology* (New York: Herder & Herder, 2000).

Lawler, M., *A Theology of Ministry* (Kansas City, Miss.: Sheed & Ward, 1990).

Leichty, D., *Theology in a Postliberal Perspective* (London: SCM, 1990).

Ludwig, R. *Reconstructing Catholicism for a New Generation* (New York: Crossroad, 1995).

McCool, G., *Catholic Theology in the Nineteenth Century: The Quest for a Unitary Method* (New York: Seabury, 1977).

McBrien, R. (ed.), *The HarperCollins Encyclopedia of Catholicism* (San Francisco: HarperCollins, 1995).

McDonagh, S., *Greening the Christian Millennium* (Dublin: Dominican Press, 1999).

Macdonald, M. *et al.* (eds.), *Woman and Man One in Christ Jesus: Report on the Participation of Women in the Catholic Church in Australia* (Pymble, NSW: HarperCollins, 1999).

McEnroy, C., *Guests in Their Own House: The Women of Vatican II* (New York: Crossroad, 1996).

MacIntyre, A., *Whose Justice? Which Rationality?* (Notre Dame, Ind.: University of Notre Dame Press, 1988).

Macquarrie, J., *In Search of Humanity* (New York: Crossroad, 1983).
——*Jesus Christ in Modern Thought* (London/Philadelphia: SCM Press/Trinity Press International, 1990).
Markey, J., *Creating Communion: The Theology of the Constitutions of the Church* (Hyde Park, NY: City Press, 2003).
Metz, J. B., *Faith in History and Society: Towards a Practical Fundamental Theology*, trans. D. Smith (New York: Seabury, 1980).
——*A Passion for God: The Mystical-Political Dimension of Christianity*, trans. J. M. Ashley (Mahwah, NJ: Paulist, 1998).
Milbank, J., *Theology and Social Theory: Beyond Secular Reason* (Oxford: Blackwell, 1995).
Millikan, D. and Drury, N., *Christianity and the New Age* (Crows Nest, NSW: ABC Books, 1991).
Neuner, J. and Dupuis, J. (eds.), *The Christian Faith in the Doctrinal Documents of the Catholic Church* (London: Collins, 1986).
Newman, J. H., *On Consulting the Faithful in Matter of Doctrine*, ed. J. Coulson (London: Collins, 1986).
Nouwen, H., *In the Name of Jesus: Reflections on Christian Leadership* (New York: Crossroad, 1989).
Oakeshott, M., *Rationalism in Politics and Other Essays* (Indianapolis, Ind.: Liberty Press, 1991).
O'Brien, E. (ed.), *Theology in Transition: A Bibliographical Evaluation of the 'Decisive Decade', 1954–1964* (New York: Herder & Herder, 1965).
O'Donnell, J., *The Mystery of the Triune God* (London: Sheed & Ward, 1988).
O'Malley, J. W., *Trent and All That: Renaming Catholicism in the Early Modern Era* (Cambridge, Mass.: Harvard University Press, 2000).
O'Meara, T., *Fundamentalism: A Catholic Perspective* (Mahwah, NJ: Paulist, 1990).
——*Theology of Ministry*, rev. edn. (Mahwah, NJ: Paulist, 1999).
Osborne, K., *Christian Sacraments in a Postmodern World: A Theology for the Third Millennium* (Mahwah, NJ: Paulist Press, 1999).
Pailin, D., *The Anthropological Character of Theology* (Cambridge: Cambridge University Press, 1990).
Pieper, J., *In Tune With the World: A Theory of Festivity*, trans. R. and C. Winston (Chicago: Franciscan Herald Press, 1965).
Platten, S. and Pattison, G., *Spirit and Tradition: An Essay on Change* (Norwich: Canterbury Press, 1996).
Pottmeyer, H., *Towards a Papacy in Communion: Perspectives from Vatican Councils I & II*, trans. M. O'Connell (New York: Herder & Herder, 1998).

Radford Reuther, R., *Women–Church* (San Francisco: Harper & Row, 1988).

Rahner, K., *Inspiration in the Bible*, trans. H. Henkey (New York: Herder & Herder, 1964).

—— *Foundations of Christian Faith: An Introduction to the Idea of Christianity*, trans. W. Dych (New York: Seabury, 1978).

—— *The Love of Jesus and the Love of Neighbour*, trans. R. Barr (Middlegreen, Slough: St Paul Publications, 1983).

—— *I Remember*, trans. J. Bowden (London: SCM Press, 1984).

—— *Faith in a Wintry Season: Conversations and Interviews with Karl Rahner in the Last Years of his Life*, ed. H. Egan (New York: Crossroad, 1990).

Reardon, B., *Liberal Protestantism* (London: Adam & Charles Black, 1968).

Schillebeeckx, E., *Church: The Human Story of God*, trans. J. Bowden (New York: Crossroad, 1980).

—— *Jesus: An Experiment in Christology*, trans. H. Hoskins (New York: Crossroad, 1981).

—— *Interim Report on the Books 'Jesus' and 'Christ'*, trans. J. Bowden (New York: Crossroad, 1982).

Schneiders, S., *Beyond Patching: Faith and Feminism in the Catholic Church* (Mahwah, NJ: Paulist Press, 1991).

Schreiter, R., *The New Catholicity: Theology Between the Global and the Local* (Maryknoll, NY: Orbis, 1997).

Schultenover, D., *A View from Rome: On the Eve of the Modernist Crisis* (New York: Fordham University Press, 1993).

Schüssler Fiorenza, E., *Discipleship of Equals: A Critical Feminist Ekklesia-logy of Liberation* (New York: Crossroad, 1993).

Schüssler Fiorenza, F., *Foundational Theology* (New York: Crossroad, 1984).

Segundo, J. L., *The Community Called Church*, trans. J. Drury (Maryknoll, NY: Orbis, 1973).

—— *The Historical Jesus of the Synoptics*, trans. J. Drury (Melbourne: Dove Publications, 1985).

Sullivan, F., *The Church We Believe In: One, Holy, Catholic and Apostolic* (Dublin: Gill & Macmillan, 1988).

—— *Creative Fidelity: Weighing and Interpreting Documents of the Magisterium* (Mahwah, NJ: Paulist, 1996).

Tanquerey, A., *A Manual of Dogmatic Theology*, trans. J. Brynes, (New York: Desclee, 1959).

Tavard, G., *A Theology for Ministry* (Wilmington, Del.: Michael Glazier, 1983), 80–3.

Thompson, W., *The Jesus Debate: A Survey and Synthesis* (Mahwah, NJ: Paulist, 1985).

Thornhill, J., *Sign and Promise: A Theology of the Church for a Changing World* (London: Collins, 1988).

——*Modernity: Christianity's Estranged Child Reconstructed* (Grand Rapids, Mich.: Eerdmans, 2000).

Tillard, J-M., *Flesh of the Church, Flesh of Christ: At the Sources of the Ecclesiology of Communion*, trans. M. Beaumont (Collegeville, Minn.: Pueblo, 2001).

Tilley, T. W., *Inventing Catholic Tradition* (Maryknoll, NY: Orbis, 2000).

Tracy, D., *The Analogical Imagination: Christian Theology and the Culture of Pluralism* (London: SCM, 1981), 104.

Tyrrell, G., *Medievalism: A Reply to Cardinal Mercier* (Allen, Tex.: Christian Classics, 1994).

Vorgrimler, H., *Commentary on the Documents of Vatican II*, 5 vols. (London/New York: Burns & Oates/Herder, 1967–9).

——*Understanding Karl Rahner: An Introduction to his Life and Thought*, trans. J. Bowden (New York: Crossroad, 1986).

Wiles, M., *Working Papers in Doctrine* (London: SCM, 1976).

——*Faith and the Mystery of God* (London: SCM, 1982).

Witherington, B., *The Jesus Quest: The Third Search for the Jew of Nazareth* (Downers Grove, Ill.: Inter Varsity Press, 1995).

Young, F., *Can These Dry Bones Live?: An Introduction to Christian Theology* (Cleveland, Ohio.: Pilgrim Press, 1993).

Zagano, P. and Tilley, T. (eds.), *The Exercise of the Primacy: Continuing the Dialogue* (New York: Herder & Herder, 1998).

Articles

American National Pastoral Life Center, 'Study of Parish Lay Ministry', *Origins*, 29 (1 July 1999), 101–7.

Anglican–Roman Catholic International Commission (ARCIC), 'The Gift of Authority', *Origins*, 29 (27 May 1999), 17–29.

Barr, J., 'Fundamentalism', in *The Encyclopedia of Christianity* (Grand Rapids/Leiden: Eerdmans/Brill, 2001), ii. 363–5.

Barron, R., 'Beyond Beige Catholicism', *Church*, 16 (2000), 5–10

Baum, G., 'For and Against John Milbank', in *Essays in Critical Theology* (Kansas City, Miss.: Sheed & Ward, 1994), 52–76

Bianchi, E., 'A Democratic Church: Task for the Twenty-First Century', in E. Bianchi and R. Radford Ruether (eds.), *A Democratic*

Catholic Church: The Reconstruction of Roman Catholicism (New York: Crossroad, 1992), 34–51.

Blondel, M., 'History and Dogma', in *'The Letter on Apologetics' and 'History and Dogma'*, trans. A. Dru and I. Trethowan (London: Harvill Press, 1964), 264–87

Boff, L., 'The Uncompleted Vision of Vatican II: The Church— Hierarchy or People of God?', in E. Schüssler Fiorenza and H. Häring (eds.), *The Non-Ordination of Women and the Politics of Power* (*Concilium*, no. 1999/3) (London: SCM, 1999), 31–9.

Burkhard, J., '*Sensus Fidei*: Theological Reflection since Vatican II, Part I: 1964–1984', *Heythrop Journal*, 34 (1993), 41–59.

Byrne, B., 'Scripture and Vatican II: A Very Incomplete Journey', *Compass*, 37 (2003), 3–9.

Byrne, J., 'Theology and Christian Faith', in C. Geffré and W. Jeanrond (eds.), *Why Theology?* (*Concilium*, no. 1994/6) (London: SCM, 1994), 3–12.

Coffey, D., 'The Common and Ordained Priesthood', *Theological Studies*, 58 (1997), 209–36.

Collins, R., 'Did Jesus Found the Church? Which Church?', *Louvain Studies*, 21 (1996), 356–65.

Congar, Y., 'Moving Towards a Pilgrim Church', in A. Stacpoole (ed.), *Vatican II Revisited By Those Who Were There* (Minneapolis, Minn.: Winston Press, 1986), 129–52.

Cooke, B., 'Jesus of Nazareth, Norm for the Church', *CTSA Proceedings*, 49 (1994), 24–35.

Cordeiro, J., 'The Liturgical Constitution, *Sacrosanctum Concilium*', in A. Stacpoole (ed.), *Vatican II Revisited By Those Who Were There* (Minneapolis, Minn.: Winston Press, 1986), 187–94.

Crowley, P., 'Catholicity, Inculturation, and Newman's *Sensus Fidelium*', *Heythrop Journal*, 33 (1992), 161–74.

Dalferth, I., ' "I Determine What God Is!": Theology in the Age of "Cafeteria Religion" ', *Theology Today*, 57 (2000), 5–23.

Diekmann, G., 'The Constitution on the Sacred Liturgy' in J. Miller (ed.), *Vatican II: An Interfaith Appraisal* (Notre Dame, Ind./New York: University of Notre Dame Press/Association Press, 1966), 17–30.

Diotallevi, L., ' "Catholicism by way of Sectarianism?" An Old Hypothesis for New Problems', in A. Melloni (ed.), *'Movements' in the Church* (*Concilium*, no. 2003/3) (London: SCM, 2003), 107–21.

Doré, J., 'The Responsibility and Tasks of Theology in the Church and the World Today', *Irish Theological Quarterly*, 62 (1996–7), 213–27.

Dulles, A., 'The Ecclesial Dimension of Faith', *Communio*, 22 (1995), 418–32.

—— 'Tradition and Creativity: A Theological Approach', in K. Hagen (ed.), *The Quadrilog: Tradition and the Future of Ecumenism* (Collegeville, Minn.: Michael Glazier, 1994), 312–27.

—— 'Vatican II: The Myth and the Reality', *America*, 188 (24 Feb. 2003), 7–11.

Duquoc, C., 'Postscript: The Institution and Diversion', in C. Duquoc and G. Gutierrez (ed.), *Mysticism and the Institutional Crisis* (*Concilium*, no. 1994/4) (London: SCM, 1994), 101–6.

Durand, J.-P., 'Catholic Movements and Communities of the Faithful which arose in the Twentieth Century: Some Challenges to Canon Law', in A. Melloni (ed.), *'Movements' in the Church* (*Concilium*, no. 2003/3) (London: SCM, 2003), 94–105.

Elizondo, V., 'Emergence of the World Church and the Irruption of the Poor', in G. Baum (ed.), *The Twentieth Century: A Theological Overview* (Maryknoll, NY: Orbis, 1999), 104–17.

Fahey, M., 'Continuity in the Church Amid Structural Change', *Theological Studies*, 35 (1974), 415–40.

The Faith and Order Commission of the World Council of Churches, 'The Unity of the Church as *Koinonia*: Gift and Calling' (Canberra, 1991), in G. Gassmann (ed.), *Documentary History of Faith and Order: 1963–1993* (Geneva: WCC Publications, 1993), 3–5.

Fan, R., 'The Memoirs of a Pagan Sojourning in the Ruins of Christianity', *Christian Bioethics*, 5 (1999), 232–7.

Finnegan, J., 'Christ or Aquarius?: A Christian Reflection on the New Age', *The Furrow*, 54 (2003), 341–6.

Frey, D., 'The Good Samaritan as Bad Economist: Self-Interest in Economics and Theology', *Cross Currents*, 46 (1996), 293–302.

Fries, H., 'Is There a Magisterium of the Faithful?', in J. B. Metz and E. Schillebeeckx (eds.), *The Teaching Authority of Believers* (*Concilium*, no. 180) (Edinburgh: T. & T. Clark, 1985), 82–91.

Gaillardetz, R., 'Shifting Meanings in the Lay–Clergy Distinction', *Irish Theological Quarterly*, 64 (1999), 115–39.

Godfrey, D., 'A Vision of Hope for Gay Catholics', *Chicago Studies*, 42 (2003), 177–87.

Gooch, L., 'Who Are the Women in Diocesan Leadership?', *Origins*, 30 (29 March 2001), 653–6.

Graesslé, I., 'From Impasse to Passage: Reflections on the Church', *Ecumenical Review*, 53 (2001), 25–35.

Griffith, C., 'Human Bodiliness: Sameness as Starting Point', in E. Johnson (ed.), *The Church Women Want: Catholic Women in Dialogue* (New York: Crossroad, 2002), 60–7.

Guarino, T., 'Postmodernity and Five Fundamental Theological Issues', *Theological Studies*, 57 (1996), 654–89.

Haight, R., 'Appropriating Jesus Today', *Irish Theological Quarterly*, 59 (1993), 241–63.

—— 'Systematic Ecclesiology', *Science et Esprit*, 45 (1993), 253–81.

—— 'The Structures of the Church', *Journal of Ecumenical Studies*, 30 (1993), 403–14.

—— 'Ecclesiology From Below: Genesis of the Church', *Theology Digest*, 48 (2001), 319–28.

Hayes, Z., 'God and Theology in an Age of Scientific Culture', *New Theology Review*, 8 (1995), 5–18.

Heft, J., '*Sensus Fidelium* and the Marian Dogmas', *One in Christ*, 28 (1992), 106–25.

Heher, M., 'Why We Still Need Theologians', in D. Kendall and S. Davis (eds.), *The Convergence of Theology* (Mahwah, NJ: Paulist, 2001), 55–71.

Herbert, D., 'Getting by in Babylon: MacIntyre, Milbank and a Christian Response to Religious Diversity in the Public Arena', *Studies in Christian Ethics*, 10 (1997), 61–81.

Himes, M., 'Church Institutions: A Theological Note', *New Theology Review*, 14 (2001), 6–15.

Hitchcock, J., 'Version One: A Continuum in the Great Tradition', *Commonweal*, 128 (9 March 2001), 16–19.

Hume, B., 'A Note on the Teaching of the Catholic Church Concerning Homosexual People', *Origins*, 24 (27 April 1995), 765–9.

Johnson, E., 'Imaging God, Embodying Christ: Women as a Sign of the Times', in E. Johnson (ed.), *The Church Women Want: Catholic Women in Dialogue* (New York: Crossroad, 2002), 45–59.

Kasper, W., 'The Council's Vision for a Renewal of the Church', *Communio*, 17 (1990), 474–93.

—— 'The Church as Communion', *New Blackfriars*, 74 (1993), 232–44.

—— 'Jesus Christ: God's Final Word', *Communio*, 28 (2001), 61–71.

Kilmartin, E., 'Reception in History: A Theological Phenomenon and Its Significance', *Journal of Ecumenical Studies*, 21 (1984), 34–54.

Kinast, R., 'Vatican II Lives!: Foundation for the Future', *Church*, 13 (1995), 5–9.

Komonchak, J., 'Returning from Exile: Catholic Theology in the 1930s', in G. Baum (ed.), *The Twentieth Century: A Theological Overview* (Maryknoll, NY: Orbis, 1999), 35–48.

—— 'The Significance of Vatican II for Ecclesiology', in P. Phan (ed.), *The Gift of the Church: A Textbook on Ecclesiology* (Collegeville, Minn.: Michael Glazier, 2000), 68–92.

Komonchak, J., 'Is Christ Divided? Dealing with Diversity and Disagreement', *Origins*, 33 (17 July 2003), 140–7.

Lash, N., 'Criticism or Construction?: The Task of the Theologian', *New Blackfriars*, 63 (1982), 148–59.

—— 'Son of God: Reflections on a Metaphor', in E. Schillebeeckx and J. B. Metz (eds.), *Jesus, Son of God?* (*Concilium*, 153) (Edinburgh: T. & T. Clark, 1982), 11–16.

Lennan, R., 'The Eucharist: Sacrament of the Church', in M. Press (ed.), *The Eucharist: Faith and Worship* (Strathfield, NSW: St Pauls Publications, 2001), 27–41.

Lipscomb, O., 'Dialogue About and Within Priesthood', *Origins*, 28 (21 May 1998), 8–12.

Loades, A., 'Word and Sacrament: Recovering Integrity', in N. Brown and R. Gascoigne (eds.), *Faith in the Public Forum* (Adelaide: ATF, 1998), 28–46.

McAlese, M., 'Living with Authority', *Doctrine and Life*, 45 (1995), 596–602.

McConville, W., 'Catholicity and Belonging: Challenges and Tensions', *New Theology Review*, 2 (1989), 5–19.

McCord, H. R., 'Participation by Laity in Church Life and Mission', *Chicago Studies*, 39 (2000), 47–58.

McDermott, B., 'Authority, Leadership, and Theological Conversation', *Seminary News*, 32 (1994), 28–41.

McEvoy, J., 'Narrative or History?—A False Dilemma: The Theological Significance of the Historical Jesus', *Pacifica*, 14 (2001), 262–80.

Marty, M. and Appleby, R. S., 'Conclusion: An Interim Report on a Hypothetical Family', in M. Marty and R. S. Appleby (eds.), *The Fundamentalism Project* (Chicago: University of Chicago Press, 1991), i. 819–34.

Marzheuser, R., 'A Revised Theology of Catholicity: Toward Better Communication with Those Who Talk Differently Than We Do about the Church', *New Theology Review*, 8 (1995), 48–55.

—— 'The Holy Spirit in the Church: A Truly Catholic *Communio*', *New Theology Review*, 11 (1998), 60–6.

—— 'A New Generation is on the Rise in Seminaries', *Seminary Journal*, 5 (1999), 21–31.

Moltmann, J., 'Fundamentalism and Modernity', in H. Küng and J. Moltmann (eds.), *Fundamentalism as an Ecumenical Challenge* (*Concilium*, no. 1992/3) (London: SCM, 1992), 109–15.

Monroe, T., 'Reclaiming Competence', *Review for Religious*, 51 (1992), 432–52.

Mooney, C., 'Theology and Science: A New Commitment to Dialogue', *Theological Studies*, 52 (1991), 298–329.

Moore, G., 'Fording the Impasse: Beyond the "Reform of the Reform" of the Liturgy', *Compass*, 37 (2003), 9–15.

O'Hara Graff, A., 'The Struggle to Name Women's Experience', in A. O'Hara Graff (ed.), *In the Embrace of God: Feminist Approaches to Theological Anthropology* (Maryknoll, NY: Orbis, 1995), 71–89.

O'Malley, J., 'Reform, Historical Consciousness and Vatican II's *Aggiornamento*', *Theological Studies*, 32 (1971), 573–601.

—— 'Developments, Reforms, and Two Great Reformations: Towards an Historical Assessment of Vatican II', *Theological Studies*, 44 (1983), 373–406.

—— 'Vatican II: Historical Perspectives on its Uniqueness', in L. Richard, D. Harrington, and J. O'Malley (eds.), *Vatican II: The Unfinished Agenda—A Look to the Future* (New York: Paulist, 1987), 22–32.

—— 'Version Two: A Break from the Past', *Commonweal*, 128 (9 March 2001), 17–22.

—— 'The Style of Vatican II', *America*, 188 (24 Feb. 2003), 12–15.

Pirola, T., 'Church Professionalism: When Does it Become "Lay Elitism"?', in R. Lennan (ed.), *Refining the Church: Vision and Practice* (Alexandria, NSW: E. J. Dwyer, 1995), 71–87.

Pottmeyer, H., 'The Episcopate', in P. Phan (ed.), *The Gift of the Church: A Textbook on Ecclesiology* (Collegeville, Minn.: Michael Glazier, 2000), 337–53.

Power, D., 'The Holy Spirit, Scripture, Tradition, and Interpretation', in G. Wainwright (ed.), *Keeping the Faith: Essays to Mark the Centenary of* 'Lux Mundi' (London: SPCK, 1989), 152–78.

Quinn, J., 'Lecture at Campion Hall, Oxford', *Origins*, 26 (18 July 1996), 119–27.

Radcliffe, T., 'Rebuild Our Human Communities', *Priests and People*, 10 (1996), 468–74.

Rahner, K., 'On the Significance in Redemptive History of the Individual Member of the Church', *Mission and Grace*, trans. C. Hastings (London: Sheed & Ward, 1963), 114–71.

—— 'The Individual in the Church', *Nature and Grace*, trans. D. Wharton (London: Sheed & Ward, 1963), 51–83.

—— 'The Changing Church', in *The Christian of the Future*, trans. W. O'Hara (London: Burns & Oates, 1967), 9–38.

—— 'The Function of the Church as a Critic of Society', *Theological Investigations*, 12, trans. D. Bourke (New York: Seabury, 1974), 229–49.

Rahner, K., 'Basic Observations on the Subject of the Changeable and Unchangeable in the Church', *Theological Investigations*, 14, trans. D. Bourke (New York: Seabury, 1976), 3–23.

—— 'What is a Sacrament?', *Theological Investigations*, 14, trans. D. Bourke (London: Darton, Longman and Todd, 1976), 135–48.

—— 'Christian Living Formerly and Today', *Theological Investigations*, 7, trans. D. Bourke (New York: Crossroad, 1977), 3–24.

—— 'The New Image of the Church', *Theological Investigations*, 10, trans. D. Bourke (New York: Seabury, 1977), 3–29.

—— 'On the Theology of Hope', *Theological Investigations*, 10, trans. D. Bourke (New York: Seabury, 1977), 242–59.

—— 'Immanent and Transcendent Consummation of the World', *Theological Investigations*, 10, trans. D. Bourke (New York: Seabury, 1977), 273–89.

—— 'On the Theological Problems Entailed in a "Pastoral Constitution"', *Theological Investigations*', 10, trans. D. Bourke (New York: Seabury, 1977), 293–317.

—— 'The Development of Dogma', *Theological Investigations*', 1, trans. C. Ernst (New York: Crossroad, 1982), 39–77.

—— 'The Prospects for Dogmatic Theology', *Theological Investigations*, 1, trans. C. Ernst (New York: Crossroad, 1982), 1–18.

—— 'The Theology of the Symbol', *Theological Investigations*, 4, trans. K. Smyth (New York: Crossroad, 1982), 221–52.

—— 'The Sinful Church in the Decrees of Vatican II', *Theological Investigations*, 6, trans. K-H. and B. Kruger (New York: Crossroad, 1982), 270–94.

—— 'Reflections on the Problems Involved in Devising a Short Formula of the Faith', *Theological Investigations*, 11, trans. D. Bourke (New York: Crossroad, 1982), 230–44.

—— 'Theology in the New Testament', *Theological Investigations*, 5, trans. K-H. Kruger (New York: Crossroad, 1983), 23–41.

—— 'Consecration in the Life and Reflection of the Church', *Theological Investigations*, 19, trans. E. Quinn (New York: Crossroad, 1983), 57–72.

—— 'Courage for an Ecclesial Christianity', *Theological Investigations*, 20, trans. E. Quinn (New York: Crossroad, 1986), 3–12.

—— 'Unity of the Church Unity of Mankind', *Theological Investigations*, 20, trans. E. Quinn (New York: Crossroad, 1986), 154–72

—— 'Basic Theological Interpretation of the Second Vatican Council', *Theological Investigations*, 20, trans. E. Quinn (New York: Crossroad, 1986), 77–89.

—— 'Natural Science and Reasonable Faith', *Theological Investigations*, 21, trans. H. Riley (New York: Crossroad, 1988), 16–41.

—— 'Christianity's Absolute Claim', *Theological Investigations*, 21, trans. H. Riley (New York: Crossroad, 1988), 171–84.

—— 'Utopia and Reality: Christian Existence Caught Between the Ideal and the Real', *Theological Investigations*, 22, trans. J. Donceel (New York: Crossroad, 1991), 26–37.

—— 'Christian Pessimism', *Theological Investigations*, 22, trans. J. Donceel (New York: Crossroad, 1991), 155–62.

—— 'What the Church Officially Teaches and What the People Actually Believe', *Theological Investigations*, 22, trans. J. Donceel (New York: Crossroad, 1991), 165–75.

—— 'Baptism and the Renewal of Baptism', *Theological Investigations*, 23, trans. J. Donceel and H. Riley (New York: Crossroad, 1992), 195–204.

Ratzinger, J., 'Revelation and Tradition', in K. Rahner and J. Ratzinger, *Revelation and Tradition*, trans. W. J. O'Hara (New York: Herder & Herder, 1962), 26–49.

Rausch, T., 'The Ecclesiology of Communion', *Chicago Studies*, 36 (1997), 282–98.

Richard, L., 'Reflections on Dissent and Reception', in P. Hegy (ed.), *The Church in the Nineties: Its Legacy, Its Future* (Collegeville, Minn.: Liturgical Press, 1993), 6–14.

Rush, O., 'The Offices of Christ: *Lumen Gentium* and the People's Sense of Faith', *Pacifica* (2003), 137–52.

Sanks, T. H., 'The Church: Context for Theology', in T. H. Sanks and L. O'Donovan (eds.), *Faithful Witness: Foundations of Theology for Today's Church* (New York: Crossroad, 1989), 99–116.

—— 'Postmodernism and the Church', *New Theology Review*, 11 (1998), 51–9.

—— 'Globalization and the Church's Social Mission', *Theological Studies*, 60 (1999), 625–51.

Scanlon, M., 'The Postmodern Debate', in G. Baum (ed.), *The Twentieth Century: A Theological Overview* (Maryknoll, NY: Orbis, 1999), 228–37.

Scharper, S., 'The Ecological Crisis', in G. Baum (ed.), *The Twentieth Century: A Theological Overview* (Maryknoll, NY: Orbis, 1999), 219–27.

Schüssler Fiorenza, F., 'Thy Kingdom Come', *Church*, 10 (1994), 5–9.

—— 'The Jesus of Piety and the Historical Jesus', *CTSA Proceedings*, 49 (1994), 90–9.

—— 'Fundamental Theology and Its Principal Concerns Today: Towards a Non-Foundational Foundational Theology', *Irish Theological Quarterly*, 62 (1996–7), 118–39.

Schüssler Fiorenza, F., 'The Relation Between Fundamental and Systematic Theology', *Irish Theological Quarterly*, 62 (1996–7), 140–59.

Steinkamp, H., '*Diakonia* in the Church of the Rich and the Church of the Poor: A Comparative Study in Empirical Ecclesiology', in N. Greinacher and N. Mette (eds.), *Diakonia: Church for Others* (*Concilium*, no. 198) (Edinburgh: T. & T. Clark, 1988), 65–75.

Sullivan, F., 'Authority in an Ecclesiology of Communion', *New Theology Review*, 10 (1997), 18–30.

Sweet, W., 'The Future of Tradition', *Science et Esprit*, 54 (2002), 299–312.

Sykes, S., 'Faith', in G. Wainwright (ed.), *Keeping the Faith: Essays to Mark the Centenary of* 'Lux Mundi' (London: SPCK, 1989), 11–34.

Taylor, C., 'A Catholic Modernity?', in J. Heft (ed.), *A Catholic Modernity?* (New York: Oxford University Press, 1999), 13–37.

Thiel, J., 'Pluralism in Theological Truth', in C. Geffré and W. Jeanrond (eds.), *Why Theology?* (*Concilium* no. 1994/6) (London: SCM, 1994), 57–69.

—— 'Responsibility to the Spirit: Authority in the Catholic Tradition', *New Theology Review*, 8 (1995), 53–68.

Tillard, J-M., 'Faith, the Believer and the Church', *One in Christ*, 30 (1994), 216–28.

—— 'Tradition, Reception', in K. Hagen (ed.), *The Quadrilog: Tradition and the Future of Ecumenism* (Collegeville, Minn.: Michael Glazier, 1994), 328–43.

Toolan, D., 'Harmonic Convergence and All That: New Age Spirituality', *Cross Currents*, 46 (1996), 369–78.

Tracy, D., 'The Uneasy Alliance Reconceived: Catholic Theological Method, Modernity, and Postmodernity', *Theological Studies*, 50 (1989), 548–70.

Tanner, K., 'The Religious Significance of Christian Engagement in the Culture Wars, *Theology Today*, 58 (2001), 29–43.

van Beeck, F. J., 'Divine Revelation: Intervention or Self-Communication', *Theological Studies*, 52 (1991), 199–226.

Vogel, A., 'Tradition: The Contingency Factor', in K. Hagen (ed.), *The Quadrilog: Tradition and the Future of Ecumenism* (Collegeville, Minn.: Liturgical Press, 1994), 255–69.

Weakland, R., 'Introduction', in P. Hegy (ed.), *The Church in the Nineties: Its Legacy, Its Future* (Collegeville, Minn.: Liturgical Press, 1993), pp. xvii–xxviii.

Whalen, D., 'The Emergence of the Contemporary Traditionalist', *Review for Religious*, 61 (2002), 585–93.

Williams, R., 'Theological Integrity', *Cross Currents*, 45 (1995), 312–25.

Wood, S., 'Priestly Identity: Sacrament of the Ecclesial Community', *Worship*, 69 (1995), 109–27.

—— 'The Church as Communion', in P. Phan (ed.), *The Gift of the Church: A Textbook on Ecclesiology* (Collegeville, Minn.: Michael Glazier, 2000), 159–76.

Wright, J., 'The Meaning and Structure of Catholic Faith', *Theological Studies*, 39 (1978), 701–18.

—— 'Theology, Philosophy, and the Natural Sciences', *Theological Studies*, 52 (1991), 651–68.

INDEX